Navigating the Narrow Path to Life:

Daily Reflections from a

Fellow Traveler

DONNA NOBLE

WestBow
PRESS
A DIVISION OF THOMAS NELSON

WestBow Press books may be ordered through booksellers or by contacting:

WestBow Press
A Division of Thomas Nelson
1663 Liberty Drive
Bloomington, IN 47403
www.westbowpress.com
1 (866) 928-1240

ISBN: 978-1-4908-2040-8 (sc)
ISBN:978-1-4908-2042-2 (hc)
ISBN: 978-1-4908-2041-5 (e)

Printed in the United States of America.
Library of Congress Control Number: 2013923126
WestBow Press rev. date: 10/7/2014

Dedication

This book is dedicated
to the Love of my Life,
the only Faithful and True:
my Lord and Savior,
Jesus Christ.

Contents

Introduction

I've often wondered throughout my life why it is that when I simply live from one moment to the next I find myself living a 'better life' – one that is more prone to doing what I deem 'right.' On the other hand, when I make a conscious decision to try to live a certain way, do certain things, I fail miserably. It's like a rebellion within me. I always had a plan for everything; then I got married. But that's another story.

Devotion doesn't come naturally to most people. It takes a lot of effort, especially when you can't physically see, touch, or hear from the one you're devoted to. And if God or Jesus is the one you're striving to be close to, you must learn to draw near to them frequently. This book is filled with verses from Scripture that have spoken to me in my reading. They are not the most-often quoted (or misquoted) passages from the Holy Bible, but they have proved to be moving and instructive for me.

I started reading the Bible with a more focused approach in 2003. At that time, I prayed for the Lord to teach me his truth and share his wisdom with me. He was faithful to lead me to many of the answers that I was seeking, and He will do the same for you if you are serious about wanting to know him. Just remember that He does have a sense of humor. If you don't tell Him how you'd like to receive a specific gift, He'll take you down the hard path that will insure that you won't miss it or forget it.

I didn't write this book to make anyone feel good, but rather to make people think. There is a lot of politically and socially incorrect material, given the current state of the world. Unfortunately, my purpose in serving the kingdom tends to be poking people in the eye, pointing out shortcomings, and offering real-life options for correcting bad behaviors. God doesn't love anyone less because they sin, but He does desire that we try to put those things that are offensive to Him out of our lives. And just remember: there isn't any problem that is too big (or small) for God to fix; He's simply waiting for us to ask.

God loves his children deeply and wishes that we would seek Him more often in a quiet setting that fosters one-on-one communication. I know it can be tough in these days of busy-ness to find time to stop and be at peace, but I can't stress strongly enough how critical it is, every day, to find time to be alone with God and his word. I spend time every night before sleep reviewing my day, asking forgiveness, and allowing God to speak to me through the reading of scripture. It's a system that works for me. Maybe it can work for you, as well.

I have also shared some prayers that I find are helpful to me as I try to support those around me in their struggles to keep the faith. They are short and simple. Jesus said that the Pharisees prayed with many words for their own glory, so these have few words – simply the words that are needed. I have put them in the front so that they are easy to find.

For reference, a list of the Scriptures used can be found in the Appendices: the first list is by the calendar day on which they appear, and the second is alphabetical by the books of the Bible. Citations are generally from the New American Bible[1], yet when greater clarity was needed, the New International Version[2] was used.

My faith choice is Catholic, although I wasn't born that way. When I asked God to teach me his truth and feed my spirit, He led me to the Catholic Church. I like the fact that there are things and events that are still held as sacred there, given that I found little or nothing was sacred in many of the churches that I attended in the past. I don't personally recommend one church brand over another; every person must seek that source which feeds them best. Perhaps these reflections will help you ask the questions that need asking in your life, start you on the path you were meant to travel, and enable you to walk boldly to the throne room of God and request admittance.

May God richly bless you on your journey.

September 11, 2013

Helpful Prayers

For Salvation

Lord Jesus, I believe that you are the Son of God and that you came to rescue me from my sinfulness. I believe that you died on the cross to reconcile me to the Lord, our God, forever. Come into my heart, and be my guide to holiness. Strengthen me to say 'Yes' to you in all things, to make your will my will. And I pray this in your holy name, Jesus. Amen.

To Find my Purpose in Life

Lord Jesus, help me find the purpose for which you created me. Show me the path you have planned for me. Help me to understand and use the gifts you have given me to fulfill that purpose. Amen.

In Thanksgiving

Thank you, Lord Jesus, for rescuing me from myself. Thank you for all your blessings, especially the ones that I am unaware of. Thank you for sharing your Spirit with me, teaching me what I need to know, and leading me where I need to go. Thank you for providing for all my needs. I trust you to always be with me, to be a light in the dark times, and to ensure my salvation. Amen.

For Forgiveness

Lord Jesus, I failed you today. I sinned against your covenant and failed to do the good deeds I should have. Please forgive me this day and remind me next time to do that right thing. Thank you for your mercy, Lord. Amen.

For Release from Unclean Spirits

Lord Jesus, please bind the unclean spirits that torment me and send them to the place of darkness to await your day of judgment. Set me free to be the child you created me to be. I beg your mercy and pray in your name, Lord Jesus. Amen.

For Wisdom

Lord God, grant me your wisdom. Guide my actions and words. Help me to make good decisions that serve others and bring you glory. Amen.

For Special Graces

Lord God, grant me the grace to make it through this trial. I need your strength, guidance, and counsel to make it through the tough times. Thank you for sustaining me. Amen.

For Guidance or Counsel

Lord Jesus, please show me the road I should choose. Guide me through this time that challenges me. Help me to make wise decisions and follow your leading. Amen.

For the Sick

Lord Jesus, please have mercy on ... (insert name here.) Align his/her body with your Word and grant them healing. Give ... the grace to accept your will, even if that means that you choose not to heal him/her. Amen.

For the Dying

Lord God, have mercy on ... Please do not make him/her suffer unnecessarily, and grant safe and peaceful passage to your side. Amen.

For the Recently Deceased and Those Left Behind

Lord, please grant the spirit of our friend safe passage to your side. Grant him/her peace and rest. And please grant peace and comfort to the friends and family that he/she has left behind. Amen.

For Providence and Need

Lord God, I am desperate. Please have mercy on me. My faith is in you, and I trust you to provide what I need. Amen.

For the Unsaved

Lord Jesus, please have mercy on ... and bring him/her to a saving knowledge of you. Show yourself to them in such a manner that he/she cannot help but believe in you. Amen.

For Our Nation

Lord God, open the hearts and minds of the people of America so that we may see ourselves as you see us. Create in us a desire to serve one another instead of serving only ourselves. Amen.

For Our Leaders

Lord Jesus, please be the force that guides the leaders of our nation. Turn their hearts toward those whom they serve and not toward their own interests and desires. Amen.

For a National Revival

Lord Jesus, we need you in more hearts in our nation: too many have left your service and fallen to the wayside. Bring them and their children back to the path to righteousness and to the kingdom – for your glory and their salvation. Amen.

The Simplest Prayer

Lord, help me!

January

January 1

"No one can serve two masters. He will either hate one and
love the other, or be devoted to one and despise the other.
You cannot serve God and mammon." Matthew 6:24

Once again we come to the beginning of a fresh calendar year, a day
when many people start something new in their lives. Some people start
too many new things at once and set themselves up for failure. It's much
easier to make a single change here and there and get used to each one
rather than adding or subtracting many things or practices at one time.
At least that's been my experience. But then I see things differently than
most people. For me, every day is Christmas. And every day is Easter.

I like to celebrate my salvation every day by choosing to remember
that Jesus stepped down from heaven to become a man and show me
the Father in a form that I can understand. He lived, breathed, ate,
and drank like me; went to weddings and dinner parties, and taught,
healed, and reprimanded many. He showed me the way to the Father
and to eternity in heaven. He died one of the most horrific deaths that
human beings have created, and was resurrected by God Almighty. I
believe this to be true.

Today is a good day to ask yourself some questions: What do I believe?
Whom do I serve? How can I better serve the world and leave it a
better place than I found it? If you already have these answers down
pat, maybe you don't need this book. But if you, like me, are always
looking for ways to improve your own little world and the larger one as
well, keep reading.

Today's quote is from Jesus, and its deeper meaning lies at the core of many of the problems in our society today. Both inside and outside the Church, the accumulation of wealth and stuff is too often the focus of many people. *Mammon* is a Hebrew word meaning 'wealth' or 'property', and this is Jesus' warning that it is mutually exclusive to serve God and our self. We can only be truly devoted to one person, thing, or practice, and if my focus is on taking care of me, then I'm not serving God. As an example, I've heard people say, "I don't have enough money to tithe. I barely have enough to live on." Their problem is not a lack of money; it's a lack of faith. If you would trust God to provide for you, he'd bless you with more than enough. Allow Him to show you how He works: you can't out-give God. (See Malachi 3:10 and Luke 6:38.)

Many problems in America today lie at the feet of its people. Greed and corruption are rampant in our country, and the greatest area of service is the service of the self. We've become a nation of narcissists.

So today is the beginning of a brand new year. What are your resolutions for this one? Do you want to lose weight? Quit smoking or drinking? Be a better servant? Take the focus off of yourself, turn it over to God, and pray every day for Him to show you how to get where He wants you to go. You might be surprised at how much easier keeping those other resolutions can be.

Lord Jesus: Teach me how to focus on you instead of me.

January 2

Teach me, LORD, your way that I may walk in your truth,
single-hearted and revering your name. Psalm 86:11

There are many 'truths' in this day and age, but only one that matters: God's truth. Every day there are literally thousands of distractions that try to get our attention: people, billboards, commercials, distracted drivers, and the voice in our own head. There is so much noise in the world it's a wonder we can ever find a place to be in silence. And there are those who don't want to be in silence, for then they can hear the voice of their conscience – the voice of the Lord telling them to get their act together. But changing and growing and focusing on God is what we must do if we want to be better servants.

Several years ago I prayed for the Lord to teach me His truth. He sent me to the books of Isaiah, Jeremiah, Daniel, Revelation and the Gospels. The truth is this: the Lord is merciful to those who believe and trust in Him, but He will judge those who believe yet don't put their belief into action. Those who don't believe in Him or don't believe they need Him will find themselves kneeling before Him just before He throws them into the fires of hell. Those who don't fear His power here on earth will see it manifested to their horror on the last day.

Believing in God and choosing not to serve Him is a huge mistake. He wants to be Lord of our lives, our purpose for living. Yes, we have other responsibilities to attend to such as family and work, but it's when we give those responsibilities over to His management that our lives see more achievements: the sun seems brighter, problems are less troublesome, and the weeds in the yard don't seem nearly as heinous as they used to. It's an attitude adjustment of the most positive kind.

Jesus said the path to heaven is narrow and few people find it. That isn't very encouraging. If I trust in myself to find it, I will surely fail. I don't want to take that chance. I pray daily for God's truth and wisdom to be shown to me, along with the path that I am to take. I can't figure it out on my own, and I don't trust myself to see the good that I should do. Only in listening to God do I believe that I have a chance to stand before Him and be told, "Well done, good and faithful servant." It truly *is* a fearful thing to fall into the hands of the Living God.

Lord Jesus: Allow me to understand you and your truth so that I can be devoted to your will.

January 3

Therefore, let us celebrate the feast, not with the old yeast,
the yeast of malice and wickedness, but with the unleavened
bread of sincerity and truth. 1 Corinthians 5:8

I hear people say that they can't wait for the time when Jesus will wait on us at the great banquet. It will be a time of peace, cleanliness, and righteousness; no pain, no sorrow, or negativity. Sounds ideal, doesn't it? Why can't we start that banquet right here and now? You don't have to wait for God to wipe out the negatives and only allow positives; you can start living that life today. All it takes is a change of heart and mind – a conscious decision to be positive every moment.

I prefer to not be around negative people or ones who whine and moan about every little thing. It doesn't solve the problem, it just puts people off. I like to be positive and upbeat as much as I can – it makes me feel better, and the day goes by faster and more smoothly. It doesn't make everything go right, it just helps me to keep perspective and put a positive spin on the trials. Many are the days when I could be overwhelmed, but I refuse to give in to that frustration. I take one thing at a time until it all gets done. And if it doesn't all get done today, there's always tomorrow. And if tomorrow doesn't come for me, it didn't matter anyway.

Lord Jesus: Remind me to be positive all day long.

January 4

This is the LORD's message to Zerubbabel: Not by an army,
nor by might, but by my spirit, says the LORD of hosts.
Zechariah 4:6

As humans, we think we're pretty tough. We think that with the right number of troops and a strategic plan, there is no battle that can't be won. Anyone who thinks this has forgotten the battles of the Israelites when they came to the Promised Land. The Bible relates stories where the Lord slew thousands without the Hebrews ever lifting a finger. There is nothing stronger than the works of the Lord. As an example, look at the universe – God created everything in it, and He can un-create it any time He chooses. The holy Spirit is the One who carries out the works of the Lord. He knows all, hears all, and understands all. He is everywhere and in all things. When God wants something done, He sends His Spirit.

When the Israelites left captivity in Babylon and went home to rebuild Jerusalem, the neighboring settlements didn't want them to have restoration. They did everything they could to stop them from rebuilding the city, the walls, and the temple. But the Lord put a stop to them. No Hebrew army needed. The Lord wanted the city and temple rebuilt, and He saw that the work got done. (See the book of Nehemiah.)

Sometimes we try to make things happen that aren't in the Lord's plan, and those ideas will ultimately fail. Alternatively, when the Lord offers you an open door and you don't walk through it, He finds someone else who will. Many have been the opportunities that I have missed because of my own lack of vision and trust – not in him, but in myself. When I did listen and act, He always made things work out better than I could ever have imagined. Such are the lessons we learn in our walk with the Lord: His Spirit always makes a way and makes the day.

Lord Jesus: Grant me the grace to trust the works of the holy Spirit.

January 5
Bear your share of hardship along with me like a
good soldier of Christ Jesus. 2 Timothy 2:3

I'm sure you've heard the saying that people come alongside us for reason, a season or a lifetime. Sometimes that reason is to help bear a burden of suffering for someone; other times it can be that someone needs to hear the word.

Speaking up for God isn't always easy – many people don't want to be told that they're a sinner. They don't want to change their life. They like having their head stuck in the proverbial sand. They don't want to have to face the thought of giving up their fun and their greed, their self-satisfying lifestyle, or their worldly pleasures for a life of drudgery. That's how many people see a life in Christ and the Church – it's all about what they can't have rather than what they can have. And the people that bring the message are nearly always ridiculed for their efforts.

Christians are seen as weak, hypocrites, and dependent on idealism: many are. Others just try to do the best they can every minute of every day, asking forgiveness when necessary and praying for grace and mercy. Many moments of the Christian life are very gratifying and pleasant, and they're also legal and moral most of the time. Jesus didn't promise us happiness: He promised trials and tribulations and told us to take up our own cross for him, just as He took up His cross for each one of us.

You'll know if you're really living the 'right' life because the trials and hardships will become greater as Satan tries to shoot you down and discredit your testimony. If you're not having hardship as a Christian, you're not doing it right.

Lord Jesus: Give me the strength to keep going despite the hard times.

January 6
"Woe to the rebellious children," says the LORD, "who carry out plans that are not mine, who weave webs that are not inspired by me, adding sin upon sin." Isaiah 30:1

Anybody remember King Saul? He was the first human king of the Israelites. God did not want the people to have a human king, but they wanted to be like the nations around them; so the Lord chose Saul from the tribe of Benjamin and had the prophet Samuel anoint him as king. But Saul did not follow the Lord in all that he was ordered to do. Saul took it upon himself to offer a sacrifice because Samuel didn't appear 'on time' while they were waiting to go to war with the Philistines. As a result of Saul's disobedience, the Lord removed His anointing from him and gave it instead to David, son of Jesse. (1 Samuel 13:13, 14)

How about the Israelites hiring the Egyptians to help fight off the Babylonians who had come to destroy Jerusalem? They didn't seek the counsel of the Lord, but took it upon themselves to hire protection. The Lord tried to tell them that they were wasting their time, but they wouldn't listen to anything He told them. (See the book of Jeremiah.)

All too often we make plans for ourselves and never once ask the Lord about His plan for us. I believe that everyone has a plan set out for them before they are born. Some people find their way to that plan quickly and easily while others traipse off the path designed for them, try to make it on their own, and then wonder why nothing ever seems to work out. Hear the voice of experience: life is so much easier when you put the Lord and His plan in the lead when moving forward. You can live your life on purpose when you let the Lord lead the way. The key is prayer. You have to learn to listen for and hear the voice of the holy Spirit. How many times have you wondered what to do, heard a little voice, immediately dismissed it as craziness, and regretted it later? If I had a quarter for every time I've said, "I wish I'd have listened to that little voice!" I'd be able to retire quite comfortably. And still to this day I find myself occasionally making that statement.

Lord Jesus: Make known to me your plans for my life.

January 7
"Blessed are they who hunger and thirst for righteousness,
for they will be satisfied." Matthew 5:6

At the very core of every human being is a need that only the Blessed Trinity can fill. No matter what else you may try to fill it with, you will never be satisfied until you place them there.

Two events changed my life and set me on the path to seeking eternal life with Christ and God. The first happened during an event called holy hour during a Christ Renews His Parish weekend. We were praying for a group of men who were in attendance, the lights were dim, and music was playing softly in the background. I had my eyes closed. Suddenly, Jesus appeared in my mind. He walked up to me, took my face in His hands, and kissed me with great passion. I thought I had conjured it on my own, and so I shook my head and opened my eyes. Same room, same music, same group. I closed my eyes and the vision continued. He put His arm around my shoulders, and we walked away. I heard no voice. My heart told me that He wanted me to continue to walk with Him from now on.

Some months later, I dreamed that I was in heaven. I was surrounded by heavy black velvet drapes like you would find on a stage, but it wasn't dark. I was working my way toward a light when an angel stopped me and said that I could go no further: I wasn't yet clean, and I could not see the Lord God. I asked if I might at least place my hand in His glory – the Shekinah glory. I was permitted. The feeling of joy and weightlessness is indescribable. I flew away and then woke up.

Now, at the end of my days before I sleep, I sometimes close my eyes and go to heaven and see Jesus, God, the holy Spirit and Our Lady. (She's a tiny little lady, by the way.) Sometimes Jesus and I dance. It's always a waltz, even though I have no idea how to do it here. These visions allow me to continue to strive for the righteousness that will keep me on the path to His side. Having spent so much time here being separated from

Him and 'teased' by His affections, I can only hope to remain faithful and be fulfilled at the end of my earthly days.

Lord Jesus: Create in me a hunger for you and your righteousness.

January 8

But if you and your descendants ever withdraw from me, fail to keep my commandments and statutes which I set before you, and proceed to venerate and worship strange gods, I will cut off Israel from the land I gave them and repudiate the temple I have consecrated to my honor. 1Kings 9:6, 7

God warned the people through Moses that He would withdraw His blessings if they ever turned away from him. Here in the book of Kings He repeats that warning through Solomon. As the only nation besides Israel to be built on the premises of God, America was made subject to the same promises that God delivered to the Israelites when He brought them out of bondage in Egypt: follow me, and I will bless you; turn away from me, and I will curse you. Repudiate means to disown.

America has been the leader of the world since its freedom from England was established in the 1700's. It grew to be the greatest nation ever to have existed until the Christians became complacent and allowed one woman to eradicate prayer from the schools. Since that day, America has been on a downhill slide. Crime and graft are rampant; morals are rarely taught to children – in school or at home; the sanctity of marriage as ordained by God has been all but erased. And what do people worship today? Cell phones, video games, television, social media sites, sports and sport figures, celebrities, and themselves. Jesus said, "Where your treasure is, there your heart will be also." (Luke 12:34)

God has been shaking this nation since September 11, 2001, but the people aren't listening. Not even the people in the Church. It still surprises me that so many 'Christians' are walking around with their head in the clouds thinking that there is hope for this nation – that somehow we will pull out of the this economic mess we're in. I don't believe that is possible. (I would love to be proved wrong!)

I give you the city of Sodom as an example: God told Abraham that if ten righteous people could be found in the city, He would spare it. (Genesis 18:32) But ten could not be found. What was their sin? Homosexuality. The numbers of gays and lesbians in this country is very high today. Don't misunderstand my intention: I do not condemn anyone who is homosexual – judgment is God's job, not mine, and I have many homosexual friends. Just because someone sins different than me, doesn't make either one of us better than the other. All I'm saying is that He didn't like it then, and God doesn't change.

Alternatively, He made no such bargain for the city of Jerusalem when He gave them over to the Babylonians; the good people died along with the evil ones. When sin becomes so rampant that no reparation can be made, God has to act to eliminate sin. When Isaiah prophesied against Jerusalem 300 years before the fall, he delivered the following message from God: Woe to those who call evil good and good evil, who put darkness for light and light for darkness, who put bitter for sweet and sweet for bitter. (Isaiah 5:20)

The Church is slowly being deprived of its freedoms. In Colorado it is now unlawful to say anything against homosexuality, which makes the Bible illegal. How long will it be before they begin to force this legislation on the Church? And why doesn't it work in reverse? The Constitution of the United States of America grants me freedom of speech and religion, so why is it that they can speak against my life of faith, but I can't speak against what I see as their sinfulness? There is only one explanation: we are experiencing the beginning of the birth pangs that Jesus warned us about in His Olivet sermon. (Matthew 24 and Luke 21)

Lord Jesus: Create in me a penitent heart.

January 9

And do not grieve the holy Spirit of God, with which you
were sealed for the day of redemption. All bitterness,
fury, anger, shouting, and reviling must be removed from
you, along with all malice. Ephesians 4:30, 31

Someday I hope to grow up into the mature Christian that Jesus wants me to be. Until then, I fight battles within myself. Of the list above, I struggle with anger the most, usually over drivers who regularly run red lights or pull out in front of me so that I have to slam on my brakes to avoid hitting them.

In the Christian world, the quote is, "You reap what you sow." In other circles it's the premise of karma: what you pump into the universe returns to you. If you want to keep getting hostility and anger toward you, keep giving it out. If you focus on harsh and negative feelings and positions, you will always find yourself in harsh and negative conditions. You have to let go of the negative and look for the positive – always. Just remember that Christians are called to love. It was Jesus' only command: "As I have loved you, so you also should love one another." (John 11:34b) Follow the word of the Lord and grow into your faith. Anger and hostility are for immature people. Become an adult in the Christian world and let go of your negativity. It poisons the mind.

Lord Jesus: Help me to let go of all hostility and anger; teach me to love like you do.

January 10

"Pardon me, my lord," Gideon replied, "but how can I
save Israel? My clan is the weakest in Manasseh, and
I am the least in my family." Judges 6:15 (NIV)

God loves a great underdog story. There are many of them in the Bible. For instance, Gideon was hiding in a cave beating out the wheat to keep it away from the Midianites who kept stealing their harvest. The angel of the Lord came and told him that he was 'the one' to lead the assault against their enemies. His response was the same as Moses: "Who am I?" I think it's the response of almost everyone (except Isaiah) who gets that call.

Gideon was likely the youngest in the family, hence his calling himself the 'least.' In those days, the youngest would not likely inherit anything. Only the first born male would be the heir in most Jewish families; no splitting up of the estate. The youngest got little besides disrespect most of the time. It's like Jesus' saying about a prophet without honor in his home town and amongst his own family. But God provided the plan and a handful of timid men, and Gideon and his band prevailed.

Why does He seem to want the weak and the insecure to be the leaders of His ventures? Maybe because we take orders better, we're more agreeable to opportunities. Don't misunderstand me. I'm not a follower when it comes to most people and their bossy attitudes, and I typically find that I'm the one that ends up leading some group for this or that. I have leadership abilities; I simply don't have a type A personality that desires to be out front all of the time. It's not my most comfortable scenario, but it's one that I'm frequently called to. Someone has to do it, and I like the return on investment in the works of God.

I don't know who started the saying, "God doesn't call the equipped, He equips the called," but I do agree with it most of the time. Some of the things He has asked me to do I could not have accomplished without His intervention. He sends the right people, places, and things just when they're needed. Alternatively, there have been times when I knew without doubt that the experiences of my past uniquely qualified me to do a particular job for Him. And while I don't necessarily like many of those past experiences, I wouldn't change them now. They have made me the person that I am today, and I like that person very much. I like to love and forgive people for being human, since I am too. And I would hope that they would offer me that same grace.

God chooses to use people that have a heart like His – the ones who will do the job the way He wants it done – the ones who will agree to His plan because they know that He knows all things, and that ability makes Him exceedingly qualified to make the plan. It took me a long time and a lot of mistakes to get to that point of understanding. And I still have to remind myself constantly that He knows so much better than me what needs done and the best way to do it.

Gideon put out a fleece and asked the Lord for two special signs that He was serious about using him, and God agreed to his requests. I've never had much luck with signs and ultimatums for God – He just doesn't work that way with me. But I do know that he has a specific plan for each of us. And when we think we know so much about what would be good for us that we slip away from that plan, I bet He just shakes His head.

Lord Jesus: Create in me a willing heart to become an instrument of your plan.

January 11

If there is any encouragement in Christ, any solace in love, any participation in the Spirit, any compassion and mercy, complete my joy by being of the same mind, with the same love, united in heart, thinking one thing. Philippians 2:1, 2

I'm certain that Paul (and Jesus) is sorely disappointed in the Church of today. There are so many denominations and splinter groups that it is hard for Christians to present a united front. And more often than not, we're fighting amongst ourselves over piddly details that are only important in our minds but not in the big picture.

When churches work together it's called ecumenism. I think it's time that the leadership of all of the groups in America get together and start working on a plan for a mass revival for our nation. Hard times have passed in recent years – harder times are coming. The fiscal policies of our government will eventually cause a complete collapse of the American monetary system. All of the savings that our people have accumulated will be of no value. It is time to work together and build a plan to take care of the American people, because you can bet that our government won't do it.

Several churches in our area have started gardens and aquaponic setups to feed their people and then sell the rest to raise funds for their organizations. Alliances need to be developed amongst our people, from every denomination, to help build an infrastructure that will care for us and our neighbors when things turn sour. And if you can start a garden at your place, you may be ahead of your neighbors in helping to feed those around you who are less fortunate. Have a public offering in mind as you build and grow, for if you think it is only yours, you will be hurt and disappointed when someone who is hungry steals from your plot.

Lord Jesus: Give me wisdom to think for the future of my neighbors and myself.

January 12

The wicked plot against the just and grind their teeth at them;
but the LORD laughs at them, knowing their day is coming.
Psalm 37:12, 13

I love this verse. I love that the Lord laughs. I'm sad that it has to be this way, though. I'm sad that people are so cold and unloving that they can't feel God's love. Mother Teresa said that Jesus and God *thirst* for our love[3], and yet the repayment that they get from some is hatred. The unjust are plotting wickedness against the children of God because of their hatred of Him and therefore us. The times are evil, but as the darkness grows darker, the light must grow brighter. I believe that the Lord will protect most of His children from the variety of unjust things that will come into the world in the years to come. The wicked will grow stronger and more vocal, but the children of God will band together and support one another. And as we come together, the Lord will laugh with joy, for His children will have finally learned how to work together. There will be no denominations and no race, only the love *of* God, the love *for* God, and love for our neighbors. Oh that it could be this way today.

Lord Jesus: I hope to make you laugh with joy today.

January 13

When they had finished breakfast, Jesus said to Simon
Peter, "Simon, son of John, do you love me more than
these?" He said to him, "Yes, Lord, you know that I love
you." He said to him, "Feed my lambs." John 21:15

One responsibility for those who love Jesus is to look after the children who are sent to us. We are to teach them His words, His ways, and His principles. We are to teach love and kindness, faithfulness and purity, prayer and commitment. Everyone desires to be filled in their inmost being. If we are not taught at an early age how to fill that void with Jesus, we will fill it with something else to cover the pain and loneliness: alcohol, drugs, or sex, perhaps.

There is no job more important or gratifying than being able to say to Jesus, "I love you," by fulfilling this ordinance given to Peter: Feed my lambs. These lambs will grow to one day feed other lambs. And so the chain repeats itself. It's how the Church has continued to grow for nearly 2000 years. And remember: the devil isn't after you – he's after your children. So, what are you feeding your lambs?

Lord Jesus: I do love you. Send me the ones you would have me to teach.

January 14

The men of Israel have thrown away what is good;
the enemy shall pursue them. Hosea 8:3

In this day and age it's hard to know what is 'good.' Sometimes I think that circumstances dictate that determination, and then I remember that when the rich young man called Jesus 'good teacher', Jesus said, 'Only God is good.'

So what is good? Paul gives us a list in Galatians: love, joy, peace, patience, kindness, generosity, faithfulness, gentleness and self-control. Alternatively, he also lists things that aren't good: immorality, impurity, licentiousness, idolatry, sorcery, hatred, rivalry, jealousy, outbursts of fury, selfishness, dissensions, factions, envy, drunkenness, orgies and the like. Which list do you fit into most of the time?

Hosea's story is a sad one. He had no good news to proclaim to the Israelites. They had backslid themselves into pagan idolatry and sexual promiscuity to the point that God had to step in and destroy the nation in order to get their attention. I can't help but wonder how long it will be until He finds it necessary to do the same to us. He's already allowed the enemy to have a victory on our soil on 9-11. That was the first wakeup call. The second happened seven years later with financial collapse of 2008. Seven: the number of God. I'm looking for something to happen in 2015. Are you ready?

Lord Jesus: Teach me to love good and turn from evil.

January 15

As we did not appease the LORD, our God, by turning back
from our wickedness and recognizing his constancy, so the
LORD kept watch over the calamity and brought it upon us.
You, O LORD, our God, are just in all that you have done,
for we did not listen to your voice. Daniel 9:13b, 14

I'm old enough to remember the character Geraldine from **The Flip Wilson Show.** The reason she gave for doing the ornery things she did was, "The devil made me do it." In essence, she was refusing to accept responsibility for her actions. Many people refuse to acknowledge that the devil is around and seeking the ruin of souls. They think if they ignore Him, He can't have an impact on their life. All they are really doing is ignoring the fact that He is the one who brings temptations to them. It's easier (in my mind) to know who brings trials to me. The Bible says God tempts no one (James 1:13), so when trials do come, they aren't from Him. He does, however, allow Satan to tempt us in order for us to grow and learn to lean on His (the Lord's) strength to overcome.

So back to Geraldine: the devil makes no one do anything. All he does is present a situation that brings us into contact with the thing(s) that he knows we have a weakness for (alcohol, loneliness, spider solitaire, pornography) and lets our own lack of self-control take over. He will do whatever he can to keep us feeling guilty about our behavior and away from God. Don't give him space or time in your head. Acknowledge that he brings things, but he is the loser in the end. The Bible says, "Those who are victorious will inherit all this (the kingdom of heaven), and I will be their God and they will be my children" (Revelation 21:7). The only way that Satan can defeat God is to steal His children; the faithful children of God will prevail. Will you be victorious?

Lord Jesus: I am weak; lead me to victory!

January 16

"Take the staff and assemble the community, you and your brother Aaron, and in their presence order the rock to yield its waters." ... Then, raising his hand, Moses struck the rock twice with his staff, and water gushed out in abundance for the community and their livestock to drink. Numbers 20:8a, 11

Maybe you know this story. The Israelites grumbled all the way to the Promised Land. They really didn't know God, nor did they trust Him to provide for their food and water needs as they crossed the desert. In this passage, God told Moses to assemble the community and speak to the rock. God would then open the rock and water would come forth for the people and their livestock. But the people were a serious bunch of complainers. They were constantly trying to go back to Egypt where they would have reliable sources of food and water (as well as slavery). So, as usual, the people showed up complaining, and Moses got angry. He struck the rock with his staff instead of speaking to it. God was faithful, nonetheless, and the water came out. But Moses lost his chance to go into the Promised Land because of his temper and his disobedience.

Who are you in this story? One of the Israelites that didn't trust God to provide something out of nothing? Constantly complaining about your less than ideal circumstances and wishing to go back into slavery to be taken care of? Or are you Moses – trying to do what's right and follow God, but getting caught up in the world and falling short on a regular basis; are you at risk for losing your place in the Promised Land because you can't control your reactions to the shortcomings of others?

You alone are the master of your eternal destiny. God will lead you, but it's up to you to decide how you're going to react to negative events in your life. You alone have the power (with the help of the holy Spirit) to get control of yourself and stop giving in to the evil voices of the world. If it means that you have to change your friends or your job, do it! Offer them the opportunity to rise above the world with you, but if they decline, it may be time to move on – for your sanctification and salvation.

Lord Jesus: Strengthen me to react positively to the world and to walk away from negative people and their drama.

January 17

Then war broke out in heaven; Michael and his angels
battled against the dragon. The dragon and its angels fought
back, but they did not prevail and there was no longer
any place for them in heaven. Revelation 12:7, 8

I used to wonder how come there was so much unkindness in the world,
and then I read the book of Revelation. Then I read it again. And again.
And I'm still re-reading it. There's so much there to use to make sense
of the world, and understanding comes to those who ask for it.

At one time, Lucifer was an angel. Then he grew prideful because of his
beauty. (Ezekiel 28:11-17) When he was tossed out of heaven, one-third of
the angels went with him (Revelation 12:4a) and they were thrown down
to earth. So now we get to deal with them. I have no doubt that they are
here and attach themselves to people. The hard part is trying to decide
if my bad behaviors are my own or stem from an unclean influence. I
always assume that they're mine, but I ask to Lord to bind and remove
any unclean spirits that may have come to me once a week or so. Just in
case. They really are out there. Be careful who you shake hands with!

*Lord Jesus: Please bind any unclean spirits that have attached
themselves to me. Bind them and send them to the place of
darkness to await your day of judgment and set me free to be
the child you created me to be.*

January 18

O LORD, my rock, my fortress, my deliverer, my God, my rock
of refuge! My shield, the horn of my salvation, my stronghold,
my refuge, my savior, from violence you keep me safe.
2 Samuel 22:2b, 3

There was a time in my life when I didn't serve the Lord. I believed;
I even went to church. But I didn't have a personal relationship with

the Holy Trinity. I read the Bible; I was reading it from cover to cover. Some of it I understood – much of it I did not. And then life happened. Things got bad at home, and I found myself moving out and living with my mom. I was lost and didn't know how to fix the mess we had created. So one evening as I sat on the floor in my room, crying in despair, I cried out to God. I told Him I needed help, and He was the only one who could fix the problem. I looked around, and there was a Bible on the shelf. I pulled it out, opened it randomly, and the above Scripture was what I found. A sense of peace came over me like I had never felt before. God was speaking to me, telling me to lean on Him, and He would take care of me.

This passage changed my life forever. Since that occurrence, I worry about nothing. I leave everything to him, trusting Him in His providence and timing. My mom thinks I'm too casual about my income sometimes. And while I have been homeless and unemployed in the past, I've never slept in my car, never missed a meal, and never missed a payment on anything. And when I have questions or concerns now, I again resort to Scripture. I tell Him what's on my heart, open my Bible, and He gives me the answer – most of the time. Sometimes I'm thick-headed and don't understand, but it still works out. And it's a comfort knowing that he's in charge. Like I mentioned before – I don't always want to be in charge. Sometimes it's nice to just go along and enjoy the ride.

Lord Jesus: Open my heart to learn to trust you more.

January 19

"If you forgive others their transgressions, your heavenly Father
will forgive you. But if you do not forgive others, neither will
your Father forgive your transgressions." Matthew 6:14, 15

One of the hardest things in the world to do (if not THE hardest) is to forgive others who have caused us pain. My grandma told me she was afraid to let go and die at the end of her life. She had someone who had caused her great emotional pain, and she had not been able to bring herself to forgive this person. She knew this passage and was afraid to meet Jesus with her burden, but she just couldn't let it go. After she passed, when we were around her body at the funeral home, I asked her to come visit me in dreams. She came twice.

Her first visit was not a happy one. She told me she was in a place that was very cold and dark, she was naked, alone and being tormented: Purgatory. I had always suspected that a place like this existed even before I became Catholic, and this proved it for me. Her next visit was much more pleasant. I could see her wearing her favorite lavender dress and walking hand-in-hand with my grandpa. They were both smiling. She made it! But her soul had to spend time learning about the grievousness of her crime of refusing forgiveness.

Refusing to forgive someone does them no harm. It is our own soul that suffers from our inability to let go of hatred. The person she wouldn't forgive didn't suffer from her lack of forgiveness, she did, both here and on the other side.

Think of it this way: Jesus suffered a brutal beating and died on the cross so that you could have your sins forgiven by God. Think of all the crimes you've committed against him. What if He refused to give you mercy when you asked for it? Take up your cross as Jesus did and forgive those who have hurt you. Make a list: Column 1 is all the people you've hurt during your life and the deed that caused it; Column 2 is all the people who have hurt you and the deed that caused it. Which list is longer? Why are you hanging onto these all of these facts? Stop keeping score! Forgive, and let it go! You'll never have peace until you do.

Lord Jesus: Please grant me the grace to let go and forgive.

January 20
In peace I shall both lie down and sleep, for you
alone, Lord, make me secure. Psalm 4:9

I had trouble in my youth getting my brain to shut down at night, and occasionally I still do. But I found that, with my increase in faith and trust in Christ, I sleep better at night (provided I don't drink fluids all evening necessitating a trip to the bathroom in the middle of the night, at which time I begin to sing and then to stay awake). The Lord helps me to sleep by meeting my needs so that I don't have to lie down and fret over things that I failed to reconcile during the day. He is on the throne and in control, and I trust that everything will be taken care of in its own time, in the manner of His choosing.

Try to learn to let go of worrying and let God handle the things that are out of your control. You take care of the things that are delegated to you as part of your daily responsibilities of work, and ask for His guidance throughout the day. It takes some practice to get to this point, but then any task worth doing well always does.

Lord Jesus: Remind me to let you handle the things that I shouldn't, and show me how to handle the things that I should.

January 21
And do not be afraid of those who kill the body but
cannot kill the soul; rather, be afraid of the one who can
destroy both soul and body in hell. Matthew 10:28

So many people live in fear these days: unemployment, homelessness, germs, mass murderers, religious zealots, death, and the unknown. That's the biggest fear, isn't it: the unknown? Three or four hundred years ago, the biggest fear was likely contracting a disease. There weren't many so-called cures besides leeches and blood-lettings, treatments that were worse than the disease itself. (Seen any commercials lately for prescription meds?) It seems to me that people fear all the wrong things for the wrong reasons.

I personally don't like living in this world the way it is, but I'm not going to take myself out to avoid being killed by someone or something else. I don't think Jesus intended to try to reassure people who lived in fear of the unknown with this statement. Only faith in Him and His providence can remove that fear. I think He meant for us to anticipate death for Him – the death of a martyr. Most people will never have to face that threat, but there are many in the world today who do. Not every country in the world tolerates Christianity. Come to think of it, the good old US of A doesn't tolerate it too well either any more, despite the fact that many people came here for religious freedom.

The president of the United States can have you put to death, but only God can send your soul to hell for eternity. If it comes down to upholding your faith and dying for it or renouncing Jesus to keep your life, what will you do? I hope that I can remember that Jesus suffered great agony to rescue my soul from eternal damnation and be able to stand whatever pain I might have to endure because I love him, rather than deny him, save my physical life, and then be thrown into the pit for eternity.

Lord Jesus: Wake me up to the reality of whom or what I should fear.

January 22

The LORD, your God, is in your midst, a mighty savior; He will
rejoice over you with gladness, and renew you in his love; He
will sing joyfully because of you, as one sings at festivals.
Zephaniah 3:17, 18

God loves His creation. He especially loves the children that have a heart like his. He comes to us, saves us, and rejoices when we acknowledge Him and His Son. The Bible says there is more rejoicing in heaven over one sinner who repents than over 99 who didn't need to. (Luke 15:7) And it seems that God himself sings along. I love this idea. For some reason, I see God as an amazing operatic baritone, and *The Marriage of Figaro* comes to mind when I read this passage. He loves His children so much that He can't help but sing when they repent or do good deeds that bring glory to him.

I hope when I get to heaven that I can sing well. That has not been one of the gifts that I've been given for this life, unfortunately, even though I love to sing. I'm looking forward to singing along with Our Father as we work in the gardens of heaven. I don't expect that he'll work in the gardens, but he'll be singing somewhere, and we will all hear Him while we work.

Lord Jesus: May I always make you sing with joy.

January 23
Whatever you do, do from the heart, as for the
Lord and not for others. Colossians 3:23

Many people are very interested in what they can accumulate in their bank accounts, expecting to be paid for every little thing that they do. Others like to receive some form of recognition for all of their efforts. These are not the people that the Lord chooses. He likes people who don't worry about their accounts, who don't seek recognition for their every move, or who love to give just because they have something to give. These people are accumulating great wealth in their account in heaven, receiving payment from their true employer and Master, the Lord. You always give the best gifts to the one you love. If you truly love the Lord, you can't help but do the things that contribute to your balance in the heavenly Father's bank.

I love to do things for people without telling them and hope that they don't find out it was me. It's cool to sit back and listen to them talk all about something that was done for them, and they can't figure out who it was. It makes me feel good. One thing I like to do in the wintertime is clean the snow off a car close to mine when there's no one around, whether I know the owner or not. Try performing a totally random act at least once a week, and see how it feels. I warn you: it's addictive!

Lord Jesus: Lead me to people who need to be uplifted.

January 24
Before investigating, find no fault; examine first, then criticize.
Sirach 11:7

There is just one thing I would add on to the end of this verse: 'if necessary.' I get so aggravated with people who assume – including me. I've done it more than once in my life, and I'm trying to let that habit go. No, you shouldn't 'judge a book by its cover'; but in this day with so many crazy people running around, you can't be too careful either.

My practices today lead me to avoid those who seem potentially dangerous if I don't need help or if I would have to go out of my way to speak to them. I don't have a problem saying hello or thank you to anyone, but initiating conversation when unnecessary has been curtailed except in the grocery line. You just can't be too careful nowadays.

Now, having said all that, if you're in a position where you come into contact with someone who seems a bit off kilter or someone speaks gossip to you, I think we all know that everyone should receive the benefit of the doubt. Should being the key word, here. It's like I tell my kids: "Just because you can, doesn't mean you should." I also tell them to think about how they would feel if someone did the same thing to them. It comes back to 'love thy neighbor.' It's never safe to assume. Things rarely are as they initially appear.

Lord Jesus: Remind me to steer away from those who gossip and assume, and help me to avoid these bad habits in my own behavior.

January 25

Then he said to the crowd, "Take care to guard
against all greed, for though one may be rich, one's
life does not consist of possessions." Luke 12:15

I'm sure you've heard the old phrase that 'he who dies with the most toys wins.' I don't know how anybody could ever believe that, and maybe they don't. Maybe they just say it to sound stupid. The only ones who win when they die are those who have made preparations while here for going to heaven. There's probably a good chance that one who accumulates many toys in this life hasn't taken the time to accumulate wealth for the next one.

I would suggest that there are many ways to be rich without ever involving money; that being rich is a state of mind. Whatever you think denotes wealth is what you will strive to accumulate. I like to collect smiles, and I've found that the best way to get one is to give one. I like to do random acts of kindness or ones that can't be repaid. I like to take Communion to people in the hospital because they can never repay that act; only God can pay me for that one. And the looks of gratitude are priceless. Those experiences make me wealthy in a way that no thief can ever steal and the market can't destroy.

What makes you rich? Is it on the inside of you, or the outside? If the market crashed tomorrow, would your wealth be gone?

Lord Jesus: Help me let go of the 'things' of this world and accumulate true wealth.

January 26

The prophets prophesy falsely, and the priests teach
as they wish; Yet my people will have it so; what will
you do when the end comes? Jeremiah 5:31

Most of the prophets in Jeremiah's day were actually false prophets. They were telling the people that the Lord would never destroy Jerusalem because His temple was there. "Peace," they said, when there was no peace. The Lord himself was sending the Babylonian king to destroy the nation of Judah because of their sinfulness. They were worshiping pagan gods, sacrificing their children, practicing sexual promiscuity, and ignoring God.

Jeremiah was speaking the true prophecies that he received from God, while the temple prophets were speaking their own version of 'truth.' They were lying to the people and saying that the messages came from God. If I've learned anything in my lifetime, it's that you don't put words in God's mouth, and you don't use Him to your own advantage. God is not mocked, and he's not a marketing tool.

Many of the people of Jeremiah's day claimed they knew God, but they only knew *of* him; they didn't serve him. They cried out to Him when things got bad, but He didn't listen to their cries because they weren't His children. He sent the message through Jeremiah that they would be spared when the Babylonians came if they would give themselves up and surrender to them, but most of the people wouldn't hear it. They preferred to listen to the lying prophets who told them that Jeremiah was the liar and that they would be protected. I see this happening again today. Many preachers don't preach the promises of the justice and judgment of God; they only tell their congregations about the promises of prosperity. You can't have one without the other, and that has never changed.

When the Babylonians got to Jerusalem, they laid siege to it for two years. The city ran out of food and water and resorted to cannibalism.

This is what God does to those who turn their backs to Him and choose to live lives of idolatry and self-indulgence, chosen people or not. Given the nature of much of humankind today, it didn't surprise me when we started having droughts last year. What will *you* do when the end comes?

Lord Jesus: Show me your true prophets of today.

January 27

Then the dragon became angry with the woman and went off to wage war against the rest of her offspring, those who keep God's commandments and bear witness to Jesus. Revelation 12:17

If you've never read the book of Revelation in the Bible, I suggest you do so. Before you do, ask Jesus to open your heart and mind to understand His word. It's a book that requires presence of mind; I mean to say, you have to keep in mind that John wrote about what he saw in the images. Those images were of things and nations that didn't exist in his day, so he had to describe them in the context of what he knew. Some things are symbolic, while others are just his description in the vernacular of his day. For instance, Ch 12, v14 reads, "But the woman was given the two wings of the great eagle, so that she could fly to her place in the desert where, far from the serpent, she was taken care of for a year, two years, and a half-year." From earlier reading, we know that the woman is Israel. When the antichrist comes, he will try to destroy the people of the nation of Israel but they will escape from him in a plane – 'the two wings of the great eagle.' This is what happens to send the antichrist after the Christians (v 17) – 'those who keep God's commandments and bear witness to Jesus.' He will become enraged that the Israelites have escaped his grasp, so he begins to reach out to destroy the faithful of the Church.

Even though the US Constitution guarantees the freedom of religion, that freedom will come to an end in the last days. We're already seeing the beginnings of the squeezing now with the requirement that all employers provide health insurance with access to birth control, including churches and other Christian-owned businesses that don't support the idea of birth control. Eventually, we will be driven underground and running for our lives. (Luke 21:12, 17) I speculate that continuing drought will have the food in such short supply that people will sell their own family members out to the government for provisions. (Luke 21:16)

These are the things that are coming. Daniel wrote it and Jesus spoke it: Many of us will be handed over to the antichrist and will perish by his command. I think those days could be close, perhaps starting within the next five years or so. They could still be postponed if the people of this nation would change their hearts, turn to God and repent of their sinful ways. But truthfully, I don't see it happening. Better get prepared.

Lord Jesus: Be merciful to us, your children.

January 28

But Samuel replied: "Does the LORD delight in burnt
offerings and sacrifices as much as in obeying the LORD?
To obey is better than sacrifice, and to heed is better
than the fat of rams." 1 Samuel 15:22 (NIV)

When the people demanded a king 'like the nations around them,' the Lord was displeased. He wanted to be their only King and Master, but they wanted a man that they could see. The Lord initially made Saul king and sent instructions to him through the prophet Samuel. One of the commands that was given was for some settlements to be put 'under the ban.' This meant that everyone and everything was to be destroyed by fire.

At the battle with Amalek, Saul kept the king alive along with a large number of sheep and oxen. He told Samuel that the livestock were for sacrificing to the Lord, even though the Lord had said to kill them all.

And for his disobedience, he received the message above. He also lost his blessings from God. Samuel had the unhappy job of delivering the news to Saul that the Lord had rejected him as king. And if that wasn't bad enough, the Lord also sent a spirit to torment Saul.

I know how it feels to have the Lord remove His blessings because of disobedience. It's a tough thing to have to go through. You walk from one day to the next wondering, "What's going to go wrong today?" until you finally come to the point where you have to give in to whatever he's told you to do. Remember Jonah? He ran away: storm at sea, tossed overboard, swallowed by a fish. After three days inside the fish, he relented. I'd like to think it wouldn't take me three days in there to make that decision, but who knows. A heart that is hardened to God takes a long time to turn – and some never do.

Lord Jesus: Remind me of Saul and Jonah when I ignore your commands and requests.

January 29

"Take care what you hear. The measure with which you measure will be measured out to you, and still more will be given to you. To the one who has, more will be given; from the one who has not, even what he has will be taken away."
Mark 4:24, 25

This is a foreshadowing of what will happen at the final judgment. If you have believed in Jesus, been generous in giving, and merciful to others in your life, then generous will be the rewards you receive in the eternal kingdom in addition to the gift of eternal life with God and His Son. I try to be generous when I hear of others in need, but sometimes I find myself being lazy and selfish – not because I don't want to give, but because I don't take the time to pick up items for the food pantry, stop at the hospital to visit someone I know is there, or call someone who is having troubles at home that needs to talk. Do unto others....

If, however, you have not given to the poor, offered forgiveness to others, or only put money in the plate because you felt you had to, stingy will be the rewards that you receive – provided He gives you anything at all. Paul called it 'escaping through the flames.' And in the event that you have not given yourself to Jesus for His use, you should only expect to be tossed into the lake of fire for eternal damnation: "Even what he has will be taken away."

Lord Jesus: Open my heart and help me to be more attentive to the needs of others.

January 30

And the punishments came upon the sinners only after forewarnings from the violence of the thunderbolts. Wisdom 19:13

The book of Wisdom is not in the Protestant Bible, but it is in the Catholic Bible. I find it to be a very fine example of poetic writing. There are a few verses that I have struggled to understand, but I have no trouble with this one.

When God gets upset with us, for whatever reason, He always gives us a warning event or message from someone before He punishes us. This particular verse was attached to a discussion of the situation of the Israelites in the desert after leaving Egypt. They were constantly grumbling against Moses, and were frequently found challenging his authority. There were several occasions when God had to reprimand them, and sometimes He sent death into the camp. But there was no penalty that came without a forewarning.

He always gives us the chance to review and repent before He sends chastisement. The question is, are we paying close enough attention to recognize it when we are confronted with it? And are we willing to change our hearts and minds to turn and go another route?

Lord Jesus: Always continue to give me warnings when I'm out of line before giving me what I deserve for my transgressions.

January 31

For if God did not spare the natural branches, he will not
spare you either. See, then, the kindness and severity of God:
severity toward those who fell, but kindness to you, provided
you remain in his kindness; otherwise you too will be cut off.
Romans 11:21, 22

I wonder if God ever regretted choosing Abraham's descendants for His chosen people. No matter how many prophets He sent and how many times He punished them, most of them returned to lives of sinfulness and wouldn't stay faithful to Him. Backsliding is what they call it – when you start out good, but you just can't maintain it.

I don't think it would have mattered who He chose. Humankind has shown throughout history that they can't be trusted as a group. Even King David fell into sin for a time. But I think God knew from the very beginning how it would go. No matter what the lineage of the people, when they see someone as a threat, the most common reaction is to eliminate that threat. (John 11:50) And that was just what the Jews did – they killed Jesus to try to keep Rome from coming in and destroying their territory, among other reasons. Of course, they only postponed the inevitable. The Romans destroyed Jerusalem roughly 40 years after Jesus was crucified.

Many of the Jews of Jesus' days had hardened hearts. They wanted their own version of a Messiah – someone who would free them from the tyranny of the Romans and others who wanted them dead. They wanted a warrior, a political figure. What they got did not meet their perception of their needs. Instead of freeing the people from Rome, Jesus frees us from punishment for our sins; instead of a military warrior, Jesus is a prayer warrior; and the only thing Jesus had to do with the politicians was to poke them in the eye by pointing out their hypocrisy. Most of the Jews missed the boat because they wanted what they wanted, not what God wanted. And so do we.

Many people today just can't find time to go to church for one hour a week, but they expect God to be right there to help them whenever they want Him to be. They don't give to the church, but they expect to be taken care of when they lose their job. They don't give God glory for anything, but expect His blessings in everything. They don't pray to give thanks, but only when they want or need something. Is it any wonder that there are so many people out there who think God is dead when He doesn't give them what they want? They say they know him, but their actions tell another story. As the saying goes, sitting in a pew on Sunday doesn't make you a Christian any more than standing in your garage makes you a car.

Many of the Jews missed the boat when Jesus came, so God cut them off and offered us their place. But He expects us to continue to yearn for the right to that place. Faithfulness to Him is a must. Apostasy will get you cut off just as it did the Jews.

Lord Jesus: Show me the weaknesses in my relationship with you.

February

February 1

Woe to those who go down to Egypt for help, who depend upon
horses; who put their trust in chariots because of their number,
and in horsemen because of their combined power, but look
not to the Holy One of Israel nor seek the LORD! Isaiah 31:1

The one thing that the Lord asks of us is our reliance on Him for all
things. If we can let go of our preconceived notion of thinking that we're
in charge and let Him lead, guide, and provide, we will not want for
anything. It sounds like it should be easy, but we know differently. Our
tendency toward self-reliance drives us to depend on what we can see
with our own eyes and presume to know what God would have us do.
We cave to the lust of our eyes and our hearts, and also to the demands
of others.

This particular passage relates to a battle, but the implication is there
for all things in our lives. All too often we look to other humans to
solve our problems or give us the answers we want, and never seek the
wisdom or counsel of the Lord. It's really silly if you think about it:
asking a human of limited intelligence and vision instead of the Creator
of the universe who knows all people and their hearts, limitations, and
intentions. It should be a no-brainer, so why is it so hard? Perhaps it
is because we only use the five senses we're accustomed to rather than
reaching out to God with the sixth sense of the Spirit that He gave us.

Lord Jesus: Remind me to call on you rather than other people
when I need help.

February 2

For the time will come when people will not tolerate sound
doctrine but, following their own desires and insatiable
curiosity, will accumulate teachers and will stop listening to
the truth and will be diverted to myths. 2 Timothy 4:3, 4

I understand this passage very well. There was a time when I was distracted by the ideas of astrology and mysticism. The lure is similar to what you have in seeking the Spirit in the Church, but this doesn't come from God. The human heart is always seeking that which it cannot see or understand. Some people find their hope in the Blessed Trinity and the promises of the Bible, while others refuse to believe that the Bible can be true. Instead, they prefer to believe in things that God has warned against. I sometimes wonder if people would be more inclined to accept Christianity if they could buy their way in or be saved by works instead of grace.

There are many people today in the Church who like to dabble in the mystical arts, thinking that they are doing no harm to anyone by believing in New Age ideas. But the Lord was very specific about staying away from all forms of divination and 'naturalism.' The longer you spend thinking about a particular subject, the more you think about that subject and less about others. And this process is nothing new amongst the people of God. In Ezekiel 8 & 9, the Lord God takes Ezekiel by vision to the temple in Jerusalem from his captivity in Babylon. There He shows the prophet the abominations of the priests and elders worshiping images of snakes and animals inside the walls of the temple. There are also priests worshiping the sun on the portico and women worshiping a pagan deity in the outer court. All of this was happening within the temple walls. You'd think that the priests of God would know better – and do better! – but it seems they didn't. They brought destruction down upon themselves and the city.

The Lord calls His children to be holy and that includes staying away from so-called harmless practices. The Bible instructs us to guard our hearts. One way we do that is to not watch programs or movies or read material that will lead us away from him. After all, practicing something means we're trying to perfect it. Do you really want to perfect something that the Lord has told you not to do?

Lord Jesus: Turn me away from falsehoods; keep me in your truth.

February 3

Even in your thoughts do not make light of the king, nor
in the privacy of your bedroom revile the rich, because
the birds of the air may carry your voice, a winged
creature may tell what you say. Ecclesiastes 10:20

"A little bird told me." So goes the saying that I grew up with, but I didn't know until I read this passage where that saying came from. So what's the point? It's not considered proper for righteous persons to speak ill of anyone – even if the words spoken are true. (Note to self.) The time spent complaining about the poor quality of national leadership or the selfishness of the wealthy that don't support philanthropic causes could be better spent praying for those persons. The possibility also exists, of course, that you could be overheard and reported to those persons and then get into hot water – especially if you found yourself in a position where you needed their assistance or approval for something, like a job. Best just to keep your mouth shut, and then there are no worries of your sin getting you into even more trouble than having already committed it.

Another old saying comes to mind: "Do unto others…." If we leads by example, then there is nothing for others to complain about. Jesus says we are to be the salt and light of the earth, adding good 'flavor' and leading others out of the darkness. How can we be those things if we are busy complaining about things we can't change? Pray instead.

Lord Jesus: Please remind me to pray about things I can't change rather than complaining about them.

February 4

For everyone who exalts himself will be humbled, but the
one who humbles himself will be exalted. Luke 14:11

My grandma used to always say that sometimes you had to toot your
own horn. The older I get, the less I agree with that statement. Not that
I would dis- my grandmother, I just think we'd have to agree to disagree
on this one. I've never been much of one to take a lot of credit for things.
I prefer to work in the background and make others look good – like
they planned well for the event to come off so smoothly.

When I was young, I didn't know how to take a compliment. I would deny
that it was true or just blush and turn away. I had no self-confidence.
But having self-confidence doesn't necessarily make one feel like they
have to 'toot their own horn.' On the contrary – I would suggest that it
is those who are short on self-confidence that exalt themselves – that
they are fishing for a compliment. Or that they are potentially arrogant
or prideful.

Jesus says that those who humble themselves will be exalted. He's not
talking about that taking place here on earth. That will be when He
hands out the rewards in heaven. He also says that those who take credit
for their works here by 'tooting their own horn' have received, right here,
all they're going to get for that deed. That was the way the Pharisees
behaved, and not the way that we should. Sorry, Gran.

Lord Jesus: Remind me to give the glory to you when someone
compliments me on the works I do, because they're really your
works anyway.

February 5

Thus says the LORD, your redeemer, the Holy One of Israel:
I, the LORD, your God, teach you what is for your good,
and lead you on the way you should go. Isaiah 48:17

I haven't known many people who were natural-born leaders and easy to follow. Most of the ones I've been subjected to were quite full of themselves – the kind you don't want to be around, much less be forced to work with. I had a boss one time that said he didn't have an ego. Boy, was he deluded! He was so blinded by his ego, he couldn't even see it.

Okay. So let's say someone is born to be a leader. Even the top-most leaders still have to follow someone else: the highest military personnel still have to answer to the president in America, and the president is supposed to follow the desires of the nation's people. (I personally think we're off track here.) But if all leaders followed the Lord, wouldn't that be great? There would be no more wars; policies would be enacted that would care for those who need it; and everyone would have bosses that genuinely cared about the business and their underlings. That doesn't sound very realistic, does it? At least not in the world in which we live today.

The devil gets to control the world and all the people in it who have decided that the kingdom of God is not for them. And so until the time of the earth ends, we are subjected to following human leaders who aren't following the ultimate leader – God. And while we have to behave because we are children of the King, we don't have to like our earthly bosses. We do have to pray for them, though. Pray that they will be converted, perhaps because of our witness, our good example of Christian morals, and our work ethic as we follow *our* leader, the redeemer, the Holy One of Israel.

Lord Jesus: Lead me.

February 6

Many will come in my name saying, 'I am he,'
and they will deceive many. Mark 13:6

Jesus told the disciples how to know when the end times were drawing near, and one of the signs would be false Messiahs appearing on the scene. I don't consider myself old, but I've seen at least a couple in my life so far. The two that come to mind are Jim Jones and David Koresh. I'm not positive that Jones said he was Jesus returned, but I have read that Koresh did. And I can't help but wonder how people who know their Bible could fall for a charlatan like that. Maybe that's the key: they didn't know their Bible. Do you? Would you recognize a deceiver who says he is Christ?

I'm just guessing here, but I think we will all know without doubt when Jesus comes back. He isn't going to drive a car or gather followers in a bunker or have a bunch of teenage wives. He won't walk the earth like a man when He comes – He will return as the righteous judge, ready for war. Zechariah 14:4 says the Mount of Olives will part, and He will stand with one foot on either half of the mountain – not live in Waco, Texas with a bunch of guns.

People make Christianity so hard, but it's really quite simple. Jesus said, "Unless you turn and become like children, you will not enter the kingdom of heaven." (Matthew 18:3) He wants us to stop relying on our senses and our 'wisdom' and trust only in Him for everything. And the only way we'll know what to expect is to pray about it. To be childlike means to trust in Him as we would a parent for our home, our meals, and our protection; everything we need. Who do you go to when you have a need? Do you kneel down and pray, or do you rely on your own wisdom? Relying on ourselves or others will only lead us to grief. We will end up deceived in the end.

Lord Jesus: Teach me to trust you – completely.

February 7

This, rather, is the fasting that I wish: releasing those bound unjustly, untying the thongs of the yoke; setting free the oppressed, breaking every yoke; sharing your bread with the hungry, sheltering the oppressed and the homeless; clothing the naked when you see them, and not turning your back on your own. Isaiah 58:6, 7

When I was growing up, fasting was not something that was taught in the churches that I went to. As a matter of fact, I think I only know of one person who fasted in those days. Now, nearly everybody I know fasts from something for 7 weeks every spring during Lent.

Back in the days of Isaiah, the Jews complained a lot. They didn't like doing the things they were expected to do as part of their heritage – like fasting. There were two things that the Jews did when they were fasting that made their actions abhorrent to God, rather than drawing themselves closer to Him as the practice was intended: 1) their days of fasting were just like any other day except that they ended in fights, or 2) they simply laid at home in sackcloth and ashes doing nothing at all. Neither of these two produced the result that the Lord desired, which was that the individual was to draw near to God in prayer, with the fasting, and learn about Him and His ways. It was, and is, to be a time of contemplation.

If they had contemplated the ways of the Lord, they could have learned that what He really desires from His children is that they become more like Him. They would also have done the things listed in today's passage, because when you become more like Christ, those are the things you do – the things listed in Matthew 25 that will get us into heaven: feeding the hungry, giving drink to the thirsty, clothing the naked, and visiting the sick or those in prison (v 34-36).

When we fast, we give up rich foods. Some people go on only bread and water as suggested by Our Lady in her appearances at Medjugorje. Some of us have blood sugar issues and have to be very careful about the way we fast in order to maintain our health. There is always a way to have a dietary fast, but what the Lord really wants from us is fasting from our own evils that keep us from Him. He also wants us to show love – love for Him and love for our neighbor. If we could do that, everything else would be easy. No one would be hurting, because everyone would be taken care of.

Lord Jesus: Give me a heart like yours – one that deeply loves all people.

February 8

So I declare and testify in the Lord that you must no longer live as the Gentiles do, in the futility of their minds; they have become callous and have handed themselves over to licentiousness for the practice of every kind of impurity to excess. Ephesians 4:17, 19

Sexual promiscuity is nothing new. As it says in Ecclesiastes, 'there is nothing new under the sun.' But it seems that in the past twenty years or so, it's everywhere: billboards, tv shows and ads, pda, and scanty clothing on all shapes and sizes of persons showing off their wares and leading others into temptation. I wonder where it all started. Was it the 50's and Rock-n-Roll? The hippies of the 60's? Or maybe the drug scene of the 70's?

It doesn't matter who started it. It's up to each of us to stop it in our own life and discourage it in the lives of others, especially our children. If your attitude or actions draw someone else into your sins, you are responsible for their sins. Jesus said, "Things that cause people to stumble will come, but woe to the one through whom they come." (Matthew 18:7) Modesty is almost a thing of the past – I'd really like to see it return. It would be nice to not have to travel all over town to find a shirt or a pair of shorts that covers all that it should. Wouldn't it be nice to see human bodies treated with respect in all aspects of life?

And remember again that practicing means an attempt to perfect an action. Let's not practice impurity.

Lord Jesus: Help me change my attitude toward my body and treat it with respect.

February 9

But the just live forever, and in the LORD is their recompense;
the thought of them is with the Most High. Wisdom 5:15

The promises of God give us hope so long as we trust Him and allow Him to guide us. It isn't hard to restrain ourselves from sin and live righteously; it's simply a matter of deciding that that's what we're going to do. Unfortunately, many just don't want to. I know – I used to live that way. I knew who God was, but I didn't know Him personally. I didn't know enough to be afraid of spending eternity in hell. Now that I do, I thank Jesus every day that He rescued me from myself. I'm thankful that He thought enough of me to not give up chasing after me. He's thinking of you, too. Are you still running from him?

Lord Jesus: Thank you for rescuing me. Never let me get away from you again.

February 10

If anyone says, "I love God," but hates his brother, he is a
liar; for whoever does not love a brother whom he has seen
cannot love God whom he has not seen. 1 John 4:20

Jesus said, "By this everyone will know that you are my disciples, if you love one another." (John 13:35) One of the things I teach my kids in religious education class is that none of us is perfect, no matter how hard we try, and we have to learn the difference between loving someone and approving of their behavior. It isn't the same thing. We were put here to learn how to serve God willingly and faithfully and to love others – not to judge, not to get rich, and not to be politically correct. Just because I don't condemn you for your behavior doesn't mean I approve of your behavior.

It's easy to imagine loving someone that you can't see. But how real is that love when you can't figure out how to love the ones that God has put in your path? Part of our road to righteousness is helping others break free from sinfulness. When you accept that others aren't as far along their path as you are on yours, it becomes easier to speak out to show them where they are exhibiting a shortfall in their progress. And if we can't work up the courage to confront them or speak out, we at least need to have the courtesy to pray for God to show them their shortcomings. And then maybe He will forgive ours as well. This is how we love God: loving the ones that He has put in our path.

Lord Jesus: Help me to see beyond the surface into the lovable parts of people.

February 11

No discipline seems pleasant at the time, but painful. Later on, however, it produces a harvest of righteousness and peace for those who have been trained by it. Hebrews 12:11 (NIV)

We've all seen them at the store – the kids that throw tantrums and the parents that fail to control them. I haven't yet figured out if there are more of these than the well-behaved ones, or if it's just that you notice the screamers more. I know that if I or one of my siblings had behaved like that, we'd have gotten a good swat to the rear end – and did so more than once. Strangely enough, we didn't require a sound thrashing; the threat of a beating was typically sufficient. Maybe it was because we knew that our parents or grandparents meant it when they made a threat.

When I was married, I had two step-children. They had been 'let go' in their upbringing so that they were used to getting their way and not being held accountable. They knew that the threats of their dad were empty ones – that he would never follow through on them. I, on the other hand, always did. I suspect that's why we didn't get along very well most of the time.

Ironically, my step-daughter, after having a step-child of her own, told me that she remembered how I had tried to discipline her and her brother and finally understood why I had been such a hard-ass when it came to my administration of it. And while she didn't like it at the time, she finally appreciates me for it, because she now has understanding of why it is needed and that there are benefits to being able to control one's self. My step-daughter sees now that my intentions were not selfish, but rather honorable.

The Lord does the same thing to us. He is the Father – He is in charge whether we choose to recognize that fact or not. He expects a certain level of behavior when we claim salvation. And if we choose to be wayward, we should expect to receive discipline as a result of our choices. In the end, don't you think a swat from the Father will be worth taking?

Lord Jesus: Thank you for disciplining me to help me achieve righteousness.

February 12

The root of all conduct is the mind; four branches
it shoots forth: good and evil, death and life, their
absolute mistress is the tongue. Sirach 37:17, 18

The mind is the most powerful thing in the universe next to God. It drives everything that happens. Those with the strongest minds have the most sway and frequently do the most damage, because it seems that they work for the enemy of the Church: I offer as examples prayer banned from schools and ***Roe v. Wade.*** They want to take the words 'Under God' out of the pledge of allegiance and remove the Ten Commandments from all government buildings. If someone were truly moral and interested in the welfare of the people, they would want the Ten Commandments displayed so that all would have the opportunity to read and ponder their benefits. As it is, they show themselves to be amoral and thus not servants of God. There is only one other force to serve if it isn't the Holy One – it is the Adversary.

Alone, we cannot defeat the devil and his minions; our mind is not a strong enough weapon to fight that battle. We must call upon the holy Spirit to fight that battle for us. In the book of Daniel an angel appears to Daniel after he had prayed for understanding. The angel tells Daniel that he was dispatched from heaven right away to give him an answer to his prayer, but he was confronted by a spirit from the devil that fought to stop his arrival. In the end, the archangel Michael had to come and help fight the battle to allow the angel to continue his mission. This is what goes on in the spiritual realm all around us all of the time. The battle is raging for our minds and our hearts. If the devil wins, we could lose our place in eternity with God. Please don't let that happen to you or your friends and family. Pray for deliverance from the influence of these unclean spirits, for good minds bring forth life; evil minds bring only death and destruction.

Lord Jesus: Protect me in battle.

February 13
"Do not be afraid, just have faith." Mark 5:36

Fear does not come from God, it comes from the devil. It is a lack of faith and trust, and an unwillingness to let go of control – us thinking that we know what's best for us. When I was anxious in times past, the Lord would send me this verse. He doesn't have to now; it's stuck in my brain. And while I may not have much faith or trust in the people of this world, I know I can trust in my God because He sees the big picture. This does not mean that I always like what I get, but it does mean that I will always be taken care of.

What do you fear? Why do you feel this way? Some people allow their fears to dictate their life, and that is *no* life. I used to be afraid of water since I nearly drowned at a young age. I knew that fear was irrational, yet I could not control it. Only after I asked Jesus to set me free from my fears did I begin to experience freedom from my anxieties. Ask God to free you from bondage to your fears, and start living!

Lord Jesus: I trust you completely.

February 14
When a land sins against me by breaking faith, I stretch out my hand against it and break its staff of bread, I let famine loose upon it and cut off from it both man and beast. Ezekiel 14:13

There is a lot of sinfulness in this country today, and a refusal to acknowledge the Lord as Master. This country was founded on Christian principles and a belief in the Divinity and Providence of God. It is the only nation besides the original land of Israel that was dedicated to God from its inception, and yet every day we see God's people in America getting tossed under the bus and the Lord being thrown out of every public venue. I'm afraid that no amount of outcry will stop the downward slide this country is on. The only thing we can do now is pray for those who have yet to be converted and for those who have hardened hearts. We need a nationwide revival.

Last year was one of the worst years for crops in this country in a very long time. It falls into place with the beginnings of the birth pains that Jesus listed in His Olivet Sermon that outlined the time prior to the tribulation. From reading the 6th chapter of Revelation, it appears that the four horsemen may already be riding forth: the conquering power, wars, famine and disease.

I can't tell you how many wars and revolutions are going on around the world today, but it isn't just the Middle East that's warring among themselves. There are gang wars going on in the cities of America and other European nations, and murder rates are up nationwide (if not worldwide). Viruses are mutating and becoming antibiotic-resistant at alarming rates; bird flu and swine flu are still cropping up all over the world. And now we have lower crop production rates here at home due to floods and drought. Even when we have plenty of food available, the vitamin and mineral content is so low that our bodies are still not getting the nutritional values needed to keep them healthy. So even when we eat plenty of food, we're still starving to death.

As I perform my daily readings, the Lord keeps sending me back to this passage. I believe He is telling me that famine is coming to our country and to collect some food for emergency situations. And by doing so, I will also be able to help others. Sometimes His providence takes the form of a warning to get ready, not to just kick back and wait for Him to make a miracle.

Lord Jesus: I trust you to provide that which I need until you take me home.

February 15

To the angel of the church in Sardis, write this: "The one who has the seven spirits of God and the seven stars says this: 'I know your works, that you have the reputation of being alive, but you are dead. Be watchful and strengthen what is left, which is going to die, for I have not found your works complete in the sight of my God.' "Revelation 3:1, 2

These verses always give me pause when I read them. I can't help but wonder if I'm not doing things to the Lord's satisfaction. Evidently I'm not, or I wouldn't question myself. I think there's always something more I could be doing. And then I wonder how many people there are who fall into this category, but He tells me not to worry about them. I am responsible for me; I have to give an account for me; I need to take care of my own business. I know I need to pray more often and with more focus.

I used to think it would be neat to pass by my church on my daily travels and stop in, but I discovered that doesn't seem to work. The last couple of times I went to the prayer chapel, I decided to pop in for a brief visit as I was driving by. Big mistake. I found myself unable to focus and kept thinking about everything else that I needed to take care of before the end of the day. I need to make time to go there when I can turn things off. Otherwise, I think He probably just finds me annoying – like a bee buzzing around His head, noisy and flighty!

My greatest concern is that my works aren't complete – that somehow I have fallen into a trap and don't realize that I'm spiritually dead even though I may look alive to others. I don't do as much as I used to because I now have a full-time job and don't have the time available that I had before. It sounds like excuses to me. I wonder if it sounds that way to him.

Lord Jesus: Show me my shortcomings – help me rectify my life.

February 16

And the LORD, their God, shall save them on that day,
his people, like a flock. For they are the jewels in a
crown raised aloft over his land. Zechariah 9:16

There are many verses in the Bible that are 'feel good.' For me, this is one of them. I am humbled by and take comfort in the idea that the Lord thinks so highly of me. Here on earth, I'm a diamond in the rough, constantly being cut, shaped, polished, and perfected by the Master Jeweler. In heaven, I hope to be a jewel in His crown. The highest honor for any jewel is to be deemed so beautiful and perfect as to be placed in the headdress of the king and to be seen by all dignitaries who would come into His presence.

It is no light-hearted matter for me. I take my role as child of the King very seriously, because I don't want to disappoint Him. And it would be my greatest joy to be close to Him forever – on His head, or by His side.

Lord Jesus: Polish me and make me even more beautiful than I already am.

February 17
The God of all grace who called you to his eternal glory
through Christ will himself restore, confirm, strengthen, and
establish you after you have suffered a little. 1 Peter 5:10

No one is a big fan of suffering. But it is a fact of life that, if you are a child of God, suffering of some sort will come. There are many potential forms it could take: physical torment, emotional distress, temptations, or persecutions. And while we all shy away from distress, God allows situations to come to us that cause discomfort in order to make us grow. He knows that sometimes we will fall, because failure (for a human) is the greatest teacher. If everything came easy, we'd likely not have any appreciation for what we have. Also, Jesus died a horrific death to give us the chance to grow spiritually and reconcile us to the Father. There's no reason to think that we are so special that we wouldn't have to suffer a bit as well. (It's the polishing from yesterday's reflection.) And what kind of children would we be if He gave us everything, and we never worked for anything? Spoiled rotten, little brats would be my guess.

Jesus himself was tempted, just as we are today. How else could He have any idea how to help us combat spiritual terrorism if He'd never experienced it as a human? I do like His rebuttals to the devil, though.

He fought him with the one thing that the devil could not refute: the solid, unshakeable Word of God. (Matthew 4:1-11)

Lord Jesus: Lead me through temptations so that I can fall, grow, and be strengthened in your love.

February 18

I wish to remind you, although you know all things, that the Lord who once saved a people from the land of Egypt later destroyed those who did not believe. The angels too, who did not keep to their own domain but deserted their proper dwelling, he has kept in eternal chains, in gloom, for the judgment of the great day. Jude 5, 6

There was a time when I was part of the problem instead of the solution. And many times throughout the year I feel regret that I allowed my life to be that way for so long. It gives me some comfort, however, to know that, even when they lived in heaven with God, some of the angels were so ... gullible? full of pride? ... that they left heaven with Lucifer when he got kicked out. It's hard for me to imagine how that could happen; how anyone in the presence of God could become so unhappy or discontent that they would challenge Him or volunteer to leave.

When the LORD brought the Hebrews out of Egypt, He performed many miracles – not just in Egypt, but also along their route to the mountain. And despite witnessing the great and awesome power of God, many did not fear or accept Him. They turned their backs on Him when he didn't speak to them for just a few days. They didn't trust the One who delivered over a million men, women, and children from slavery in Egypt to provide them with water or food in the desert. How much easier it must have been for them to turn on Him than it was for the angels. And yet, despite both the angels' and the Hebrews' knowledge of God and His abilities, they still turned away from Him.

Lord Jesus: Please don't let me walk away from you – ever.

February 19

Elijah appealed to all the people and said, "How long will you straddle the issue? If the LORD is God, follow him; if Baal, follow him." The people, however, did not answer him. 1 Kings 18:21

The Hebrews were about to get a huge lesson in the power of God. The temple was all but forgotten, and the people were immolating their children (sacrificing them alive in fire) and engaging in all manner of illicit behaviors in the pagan temples. One of the foreign gods that was widely followed was Baal. He had over 400 priests around the Judean countryside when Elijah was the prophet there. He called all of those priests together and challenged them, as well as the people; but the people would not stand up for the Lord and walk away from their pagan practices.

We are a lot like this today. Many people refuse to give up their unclean practices when they become Christians. I don't know if they think they're acceptable to God or not, but the truth is, if He was fine with you the way you were, He would never have called you out. And we are called to continue to clean up our act and be separate from the rest of the world in our beliefs and practices. We are not to be engaging in racism, oppression, foul language, gossip, lying, stealing, misrepresentation, drunkenness, or idol worship (whatever your own personal idol is: sports, sex, money, drugs, fame, gaming, etc.). Even choosing to go to a sporting event on Sunday rather than go to church is idolatry. The list goes on and on.

As soon as Jesus rescues us, we are to begin to put unclean things out of our lives. But like the Hebrews, we want to have our cake and eat it too. They believed that so long as the temple was in their midst, God would protect them. They eventually discovered that was not the case. (See the book of Jeremiah.) So if it seems that God has lifted His hand of protection away from you, perhaps He has.

Lord Jesus: Open my mind to see me the way you see me, in all my uncleanness.

February 20

For the kingdom of God is not a matter of talk but of power.
1 Corinthians 4:20

Jesus talked a lot about the kingdom of God, but the way He made the biggest impression was showing it to people. He showed them through His healing of hundreds of people during His time of ministry, by raising the dead, and by casting out many demons from the afflicted. He showed them the Father through His treatment of the woman caught in adultery by forgiving her and telling her to stop sinning instead of stoning her as the law required.

Many miracles and signs were performed by the apostles after Jesus went back to heaven, and many signs are being done today in the world, if we would just stop and take the time to see them. Sometimes the power of God is not a great sign in the sky, but a still, small voice speaking to my heart. You can talk about God to someone all day long, but until you show them His power working in your life, they will not understand or believe.

Lord Jesus: Show the world your power through me today.

February 21

Remember your Creator in the days of your youth, before the
days of trouble come and the years approach when you will
say, "I find no pleasure in them." Ecclesiastes 12:1 (NIV)

When I was young, I didn't understand what was being said in Sunday school, and we never talked about Jesus at home. We said kid prayers at dinner and before bed, but I didn't really understand what they were for. Praise God that He never gave up on me! He had a plan that I needed to fulfill, and He wasn't going to let me stay away from Him forever.

What I know about him, He has taught me through Holy Scripture and life experience. He is the one who has taught me His ways, taught me what it means to be faithful (that's a 2-way street), and what kinds of things bring true pleasure. I'm not talking about intimacy or other physical pleasures like eating and drinking. I'm referring to those things that serve the Lord and bring joy to the heart and a sparkle to the eyes. If you haven't experienced this sensation, you're missing the point of life: finding joy in serving the Lord and your neighbor. Learning this at a young age forestalls the time when one has to look at one's life and no longer find anything pleasant in it.

You can serve the Lord and find joy every day of your life. And the earlier you start in life, the longer it is until you have to look around and see nothing of value. If you do it right, you never have to reach that point – you will always find something pleasant in each day, with or without health or wealth.

Lord Jesus: Thank you for teaching me about the true pleasures of life.

February 22
Jesus stretched out his hand, touched him, and said,
"I will do it. Be made clean." Luke 5:13

People today don't generally have a good grasp of what it meant to have leprosy in Jesus' day. It was basically the equivalent of a death sentence that would drive a person from the community to die alone. The person would have to stay away from people and call out, "Unclean!" as they neared others. And no one would touch a person with leprosy, as it was considered a communicable disease transmitted by touch.

There are two very interesting events taking place in this interaction between Jesus and the leper. First, the leper approaches Jesus, an action which is socially unacceptable for him. He doesn't ask Jesus to touch him, but asks only to be healed. And second, Jesus, being who He is, would have it no other way than to touch this man, once again breaking social norms. I think He touched him for several reasons: to heal him physically, emotionally, spiritually, and socially. The man needed to know that he was important enough for Jesus to acknowledge and care about. He needed to be shown the love of God, and Jesus wanted to show the people that the man was worthy of admittance back into the community.

The important thing for us to recognize in this interaction is that there is no one who is beyond the healing touch of Christ.

Lord Jesus: Heal the parts of me that are diseased, especially my heart and my mind.

February 23

Everyone who lives on milk lacks experience of the
word of righteousness, for he is a child. But solid food is
for the mature, for those whose faculties are trained by
practice to discern good and evil. Hebrews 5:13, 14

As we all travel our journey through life, we should be growing in knowledge and wisdom, gathering information, and learning how to apply it. We are expected to mature in our ways of thinking and behaving. (Note: You can still mature and be child-like.) And as we age, what we can eat changes. As babes, we start with milk, advance to soft cereal, and then receive pureed foods. At one, we finally get to smear birthday cake all over everywhere, and eat small or soft things that can be grasped by little hands. As we get older, our repertoire of opportunities grows into the many complex things that we eat as adults, like Porterhouse steak and enchiladas. But what if you stayed a baby all your life, living on nothing but milk? No rich and savory foods, meat or crunchy veggies, no chocolate or cashews.

This is an analogy for your spiritual life. God expects to give us milk when we're spiritual babes and more rich and tasty treats as we grow in knowledge and ability. You're expected to grow spiritually just as you grow physically, but many don't. They stay immature and can't get weaned from the basics so that they can get a piece of meat to chew on. That's what the deeper things of God are – big hunks of meat to gnaw on (or carrots, if you're vegetarian), spending time working them out, and making our spiritual muscles grow stronger. Some people never develop a taste for the meatier things in Christ – I pity them. They are missing out on so much!

Lord Jesus: Give me taste for more advanced spiritual food.

February 24

When we present our petition before you, we rely not on
our just deeds, but on your great mercy. Daniel 9:18b

There is nothing I can do on this earth to earn my way into heaven. Only by God's great mercy and grace can I get there. And the other part of that offer is the perseverance and loving-kindness of Jesus Christ. Jesus took the punishment I deserve for my evil actions while hanging on the cross. Crucifixion is one of the most painful and cruel ways to die, and yet Jesus took that pain for me. He gave me His righteousness in place of punishment. Hallelujah! Thank you, Jesus!

And even more amazing is the fact that He continues to offer us pardon for our shortcomings, even though we should know better while we fail to do better. My good deeds are like filthy rags in the shadow of the cross, and yet the Father and the Son still love me passionately.

Lord Jesus: Thank you for your sacrifice which saves me and your mercy which keeps me.

February 25

Examine yourselves to see whether you are living in faith. Test
yourselves. Do you not realize that Jesus Christ is in you? –
unless, of course, you fail the test. 2 Corinthians 13:5

Sometimes I think we take too much for granted when it comes to our
own behavior. There is a proverb that states, "There is a way that seems
right to a man, but in the end, it leads to death." (14:12)

I'm a stupid human when it gets down to it – I think I'm doing the right
thing much of the time, but when the situation has passed, I realize I
was out of line with Christ. Paul says we should examine ourselves. I
would suggest that I need to examine not just me, but everything that
comes from me: words, thoughts, and actions – and all before I let them
fly off into the world. I'm not good at that sometimes, although I have
made some improvements. And I always do worse when I'm tired and
cranky or my blood sugar tanks. I have realized that the best thing I
can do for everyone during those times is stay away from people and
keep my mouth shut.

Lord Jesus: Help me examine myself for needed improvements;
I need more of you in me.

February 26

When pride comes, disgrace comes; but with
the humble is wisdom. Proverbs 11:2

It's hard sometimes not to smile and laugh at someone who falls off their
pedestal. You know you shouldn't, but you can't stop yourself for that
brief moment when you first find out that someone gets what is coming
to them. Karma some call it. Regardless of the terminology, pride is one
of the biggest and oldest sins out there. The Bible tells us that Lucifer
suffered from pride in his own beauty. Vanity is what we call that today;
a lot of people have it and don't even know it. They think it's okay to

'show what you got' to the world and look your best while doing it. I gave that up a long time ago after many years of stupidity. I think of it now as false advertising. The real thing rarely looks as good as the packaging, and some people are shallow enough to walk away when they see all the flaws we hide under our cover of vanity.

Pride isn't just found in the treatment of our personal appearances. It's also found in our choice of career, car, home, spouse, friends, and toys. Pride leads to a fall. Be humble in all things and let God do the rest, because He exalts the humble, and humbles those who exalt themselves. (Luke 14:11)

Lord Jesus: Help me to see my true beauty and let go of pride.

February 27
And do not leave room for the devil. Ephesians 4:27

How many times have you said something like, "I hope I don't see so-and-so today," and then, of course, you always do? The devil knows every weakness we have even better than we know them ourselves, and he will exploit those weaknesses every chance he gets. I have learned that it's better to not say such things – it seems like they get acted upon less when I restrain myself.

One of the hardest things I've had to do in my life is learn restraint. If I open my mouth and let everything out that I think, ugly things can happen and feelings get hurt. If I followed every impulse, I'd weigh about 500 pounds. Self-control of our thoughts and actions leads to better relationships (as a general rule). It's when we let that unclean thought or visual cue get out of control in our mind that bad things begin to happen. Temptation is what the devil is best at, and if you give him a millimeter, he'll lead you straight to hell. That's why the Bible says to guard your heart – keep uncleanness from entering and gaining a foothold. And choose carefully what you watch and listen to, since what you focus on becomes what drives your life.

Lord Jesus: Be my focus.

February 28

He who loves [wisdom] loves life; those who seek her out
win her favor. He who holds her fast inherits glory; wherever
he dwells, the LORD bestows blessings. Sirach 4:12, 13

One thing that everybody seems to want these days is information; and with smart phones being what they are, there is virtually no limit to what a person can find out in a very short period of time. No more trips to the library, no need for encyclopedias or tutorial manuals. It's all online and waiting to be downloaded. The problem that I see with this is that it requires very little initiative, and I'm not sure that learning actually takes place. And what good is all of that information if you never do anything with it?

In the days before the internet, a person had to do research if they wanted to increase their knowledge. They had to really want the information enough to pursue finding it. Today, acquiring information is a very casual thing much of the time. You can have a genius IQ and hold all of the world's knowledge in one hand and still be the stupidest person in the world when it comes to common sense.

All of the knowledge of the world is useless if you don't learn how to apply it. This is the difference between knowledge and wisdom; information versus application. Wise people learn from their mistakes. They learn to succeed not because they always have the best ideas, but because they take different routes that lead them away from the mistakes of the past. Wisdom versus folly; restraint versus self-indulgence. Which ones do you think the Lord will reward?

Lord Jesus: Teach me to be wise.

February 29

"Rather, when you hold a banquet, invite the poor, the
crippled, the lame, the blind; blessed indeed will you be
because of their inability to repay you. For you will be repaid
at the resurrection of the righteous." Luke 14:13, 14

If you really are interested in scoring points that will get you noticed
by God, don't follow the crowd. Most people who have a dinner party
aren't looking for a reward, but an invitation to someone else's house:
you invite them, they invite you, you're all square, net gain zero if you're
keeping score - and a lot of people do. I used to be one of them. I always
thought in terms of who I owed or who owed me. I was miserable and
afraid of what someone was going to expect from me to even the score.

Life is so much easier now that I don't keep tabs on activities. When
you work to do things just because you can and it helps other people,
there is no greater feeling of contentment and joy. I work for God – He
is my boss. He pays my earthly wages through the job He lead me to.
And the way I say thank you is by using extra funds left over from my
pay to help others – sometimes it goes in the plate at church or to the
retreat center, sometimes for supplies for the food pantry or the local
home restoration bank. I love to give anonymously to organizations that
help others who never see that it was me and my mom dropping off items
that they will receive. It's how I repay God for taking care of me when
I was homeless and unemployed. He provided just what I needed every
day, and now it's my turn to supply others who find themselves in need.

*Lord Jesus: Thank you for helping me so that I may help others
in their need.*

March

March 1

Love justice, you who judge the earth; think of the LORD in
goodness, and seek him in integrity of heart; because he is
found by those who test him not, and he manifests himself
to those who do not disbelieve him. Wisdom 1:1, 2

I invited a man to go to church with me one time, a man who hadn't
been since he was very young. He told me that he didn't need God. He
is still alive today, doing his own thing. And God will allow him to do
that since He permits us to exercise our free will. But it seems strange
to me that someone who was raised in church and says he believes in
God would think that he is safe from eternal damnation for making a
statement like he did. I personally don't want to test God's mercy over
His judgment.

I'm curious what God's remarks to him will be when he passes from this
world. I picture him walking up to the pearly gates and meeting God
face-to-face. God asks what my friend can offer to the heavenly realm,
and my friend states his laundry list of qualifications and skills learned
here on earth. God then says to my friend: "We don't need those skills
here. I need people who know how to trust me and pray. Good-bye."
And off my friend goes to that other place. He believes he doesn't need
God here, and God may not need him there.

Lord Jesus: Thank you for convincing me that I need you.

March 2

Do not be led astray: "Bad company corrupts good morals."
1 Corinthians 15:33

It's true. I got mixed up with the wrong crowd when I was young and ended up a long way away from God. Even after my baptism at the age of 21, I failed to comprehend that my life was not worthy of salvation. I wasn't even trying to clean it up. I don't know where I would have ended up had I died during that time.

I don't subscribe to the 'once saved, always saved' theory. I think once He rescues us He expects us to make an effort to change our hearts and behaviors, hence the requirement of repentance. Jesus didn't say, "Be baptized and repent." It was the other way around. Change first, and then get baptized. I was obviously a bit out of order, but I had made the choice to believe, and so He continued to pursue me. I came around eventually. Maybe that's why He kept me alive – so that I could complete my commitment and fulfill the works He gave me to do. I would never have written this book if He had left me to my own devices, wouldn't be teaching children about Him and His mercy, and probably wouldn't have the wonderful job and opportunities that I have now, all because of one person's bad influence. Choose your friends carefully. If they don't lift you up and uplift you, you should be questioning why you're spending time with them. Cut that cord and set yourself free.

Lord Jesus: Protect me and my family from evil influences.

March 3

If I say to the wicked man, You shall surely die; and you do
not warn him or speak out to dissuade him from his wicked
conduct so that he may live: that wicked man shall die for his
sin, but I will hold you responsible for his death. Ezekiel 3:18

Donna Noble

One of the jobs that the Lord gave to the prophet Ezekiel (and gives to us as well) is the responsibility to tell others that they are living in a way that is unworthy of salvation. Rarely does this message get a good response from those who receive it. It's called being a watchman, and the Lord expects us to do this even if it costs us friendships or jobs.

Christians are being persecuted in America today, and many don't even realize it. Speaking out is oftentimes tantamount to cutting your own throat from a social perspective. But which would you rather have: no friends from here and God for eternity, or lots of friends from here in torment with you and no God for eternity? It's hard. When I confront someone, I start by saying that I love them and am concerned for their salvation, and it is not my intent to anger but to share my concerns with them. What they do with my statements after that is up to them. Their blood is then upon their own head. It's their choice to make.

Lord Jesus: Grant me wisdom to lead others out of sin and into your light.

March 4
In those days he departed to the mountain to pray, and
he spent the night in prayer to God. Luke 6:12

There are lots of lessons in the Bible that we easily overlook by just reading. It is only in studying each verse that we sometimes find the most profound teachings. Here we find Jesus going off by himself to be alone in prayer. I can really relate to this one. I like to go to the chapel to spend time in quiet contemplation and prayer, but sometimes I find that others are there and interfere with my peace. The rules are No Talking and Cell Phones Off while in the chapel, but sometimes folks forget. And Luke says Jesus spent the whole night in prayer. I wonder when He found time to sleep.

Even though Jesus was divine, He still needed to pray. How do we expect to be able to withstand the onslaught of the devil if we only spend 5 minutes in prayer before falling asleep and without finishing properly? That's not prayer – that's an afterthought at the end of the day. I should know – I've done it enough. Finding a half-hour or more to spend in focused prayer is a challenge for many people. I suspect that the biggest thing standing in their way is not responsibilities, but choice: they simply choose to watch TV or work at home without opting to spend time with Jesus. If you only spend an hour at church once a week without actively participating (you're just there), why would you think that constitutes worship or meaningful time together? That's what prayer is after all: worship and time together.

If all you're doing in your prayer time is asking for God to fix things and give you what you want, you're not doing it right. I like to thank Him first for all that He does for me, especially the things of which I'm unaware. Gratitude is a very rare and important gift these days. I've seen a question on facebook that says, "What if you woke up today with only the things you thanked God for yesterday?" Practice gratitude.

After thanking Him for His loving-kindness and gifts, I like to ask for His providence and protection for friends and family. Everyone knows at least one person who is in desperate need of blessings – pray for those people second. Third, pray that you receive wisdom and guidance, for most of the other blessings flow from these two gifts.

Last of all, share your burdens and give them to God to keep. As the saying goes: let go, and let God. He knows what you want, what you need, and what He plans to give you. Know that when you don't get what you want, He has something better coming. Don't sweat it! Just because you don't understand today doesn't mean you'll live in ignorance forever. I asked for His blessing when I wanted to marry my second husband and asked for a specific sign. I didn't get it. I decided to marry him anyway. My bad – He knew he'd never be faithful to me. He was gone after only

14 months. I should have prayed more and listened to His heart and not my own. Emotions lie to us; Jesus is the only one who won't.

Lord Jesus: Create in me a desire to spend quality time with you.

March 5

You shall return by the help of your God, if you remain loyal
and do right and always hope in your God. Hosea 12:7

No matter how far you fall, there is *always* hope for restoration with the Lord. You may be so far away that you think He can't hear your prayers, but that's just Him waiting for you to admit that you've fallen and are in need of mercy. That's the prayer He wants to hear before He's willing to answer any others. He will always be faithful to provide a way back for you if you genuinely want to return to Him.

It's strange, but sometimes when I'm wrestling with something, so caught up in the worldliness of it that I'm blinded by it, I hear a voice call my name. It sounds as if it's right behind me, but when I turn around, there's no one there. I have to assume that it is the Lord reminding me that He is always there to help, always there to give hope, and remind me that I never have to go it alone since I'm a child of the King.

Lord Jesus: Thank you for giving me hope.

March 6

For many, as I have told you and now tell you even in tears, conduct
themselves as enemies of the cross of Christ. Their end is destruction.
Their God is their stomach; their glory is in their 'shame.' Their
minds are occupied with earthly things. Philippians 3:18, 19

It saddens me to see the behavior of many of our young people today. They have no shame and very few scruples. They have no patience and expect everything to be easy – in their grasp at a moment's notice: they want what they want when they want it. They don't keep secrets, but tell all of their business to anyone who will listen. And maybe that's the problem – the ones who should have been listening as they grew up didn't, so they look everywhere else for the parents they wish they could have had.

Even more sad are the parents who act the same way – no shame, sharing all their business with people who don't have a need to know, and not paying any attention whatsoever to their kids. Then they wonder why their teens don't want to listen, mind, or have anything to do with them. The state of many families today is pathetic at best. Few and far between are the homes that have love and kindness in them, teaching of right and wrong, temperance, tolerance, and respect. A lot of people talk about how bad the world is today – I wonder what their kids are like. What did those parents teach their children? Womens' lib? Right to choose? Abuse and neglect? Or maybe they didn't teach them anything at all, but left them to learn about the world from the tv, internet, and video games. Frightening thought, isn't it? It goes on more often than you know. I've seen it. Obesity and lack of social skills is just the start of a life lost to someone else's selfishness and laziness.

I have kids that come to my Christian Initiation class who were born and baptized Catholic and have never been to church. That might not seem like a big deal to those of you who aren't Catholic, but it is in this church. When a child is baptized Catholic, the parents, god-parents, grandparents, and everyone else at the ceremony agrees to raise the child in the ways and knowledge of God and Jesus Christ. Clearly someone is shirking on their duties. Several someones. So what are you teaching your kids?

Lord Jesus: Help me teach my children about you, about right and wrong, and about good and evil.

March 7

Here is my servant whom I uphold, my chosen one with whom I
am pleased, upon whom I have put my spirit; he shall bring forth
justice to the nations, not crying out, not shouting, not making
his voice heard in the street. A bruised reed he shall not break,
and a smoldering wick he shall not quench. Isaiah 42:1-3

When I decided that I wanted to set a good example for others to
(hopefully) follow, this is the passage that set my standard. I wanted
to be like Melchizedek – pop onto the scene, deliver a blessing, and
drop back out. I wanted to show the Father's love by exhibiting humility
to others and putting their needs above mine. I wanted to show that
Christians are not crass, loud, or rude; they don't force their beliefs on
others or shove it down their throat. They're not in your face, but rather
gentle and encouraging. For someone who has been hurt by a fellow
believer or who is new to the faith, I try to build them up rather than
squash their spirit. If there is only a little flicker of flame left, it is my
job to fan it into a roaring fire, and that can't be done by force – only
with encouragement.

This is the prophecy of 'The Servant of the Lord' – Jesus. He is my
model.

Lord Jesus: Make me more like you.

March 8

We must consider how to rouse one another to
love and good works. Hebrews 10:24

Yes, we must. One of the hardest things for some Christians to do, it
seems, is to love others. But that is just what Jesus expects us to do.
He isn't talking about loving the people inside the Church, he's talking
about those outside. "I did not come to call the righteous but sinners."
(Mark 2:17) There is a whole huge world out there that needs to know

Jesus. They **don't** need to see us squabbling among the denominations. One thing that angers Him today is the fact that the church is so splintered. It is a sign of the times, however, that the church will fall prey to blasphemous teachings and practices that the devil has finally managed to slip in to the sermons. We need to upgrade our image and show more love for our 'neighbors.'

We may not be able to draw them into the Church today, but tomorrow the Lord may finally break through the hardened shell around their heart. And when that happens, they will need someone to turn to that knows the Lord. We need to be doers of the word, loving and helping others so that when the need for a mentor arises, the Lord will have someone for that person to turn to. Will you be that person?

Lord Jesus: Give me heart like yours to see the needs of others and the ability to love them unconditionally.

March 9

Before I formed you in the womb I knew you, before you were
born I dedicated you, a prophet to the nations I appointed
you. "Ah, Lord GOD!" I said, "I know not how to speak; I
am too young." But the LORD answered me: Say not, "I am
too young." To whomever I send you, you shall go; whatever
I command you, you shall speak. Jeremiah 1:5-7

It never ceases to amaze me that God designates common people like me to be His voice in the world before we're ever born. I believe that He has very specific plans for every person on the planet, yet some never figure out what their mission was to be. I know how it feels to live a life that is unfulfilling, one that is never satisfying. It's how I felt before I gave my life to God. And if I had never come to the realization that He had plans for me, I would have continued down the wrong track trying to fill my life with something meaningful and yet never succeeding.

Last year I had a boy in my class that was eight years old. Shortly after meeting him, I felt he would make a good priest. About three weeks later, he expressed to me that he would like to be a priest when he grew up. I wish I had had so much connection with God at that young of an age that I could have known what path I was to follow. I don't know how most people get off track or never make it onto the right track, but I'm glad that the Lord brought me back onto mine. I can't wait to see what else He has in store for me!

Lord Jesus: Help me find and stay on the path you have laid out just for me.

March 10

It was then permitted to breathe life into the beast's image
so that the beast's image could speak and have anyone
who did not worship it put to death. Revelation 13:15

'It' is the false prophet, doing what he is slated to do in the times of the end: performing miraculous deeds that will cause those who are *not* saved (and some who say they are) to follow the antichrist. This verse has sparked some interesting contemplation in my mind. I can think of a couple of ways that an image or statue could get someone put to death for not offering it worship: it could have an unclean spirit attached to it that would report to its superior any non-compliance, or it could have some kind of special computer and camera inside. And if those who are not saved think that the false prophet and the antichrist are God and/ or Jesus, they won't fight having an image put in their home. But those people aren't the ones they're after: it's those of us who know that they are false that won't accept the image in our homes, and hence will be put to death for refusing to comply.

Why would they do this? It is the working of the devil to set up a mock system like the one that God has. He seeks to be worshiped as God is; he has a front man that presents himself as a healer and speaker that points to the one who leads and saves, in imitation of Jesus. It is the unholy trinity: the serpent (devil), the beast (antichrist) and the false prophet. They speak only lies and know their ultimate fate. They seek to take as many down with them as they can.

I think there will be people who serve God who will also be doing miraculous things in the end times. How will you know who's who? Look at who gets the glory – that will tell you whom they serve. If their actions are uplifting and give glory to the true God, then they serve Christ. If they take the glory for themselves or for another human being, they are unholy in nature.

I've knelt before statues to pray before, and I tell you that I cannot lift my eyes while I do. I do not want to make the mistake of falling into a trap of thinking that a statue is capable of anything. The only thing a statue should be used for is to bring to mind the real thing. A statue or picture cannot walk, talk, hear or answer a prayer. So the next time you kneel down to pray, think about who (or what) you're praying to.

Lord Jesus: Awaken me to the truth of my worship.

March 11

"They trust in weapons and acts of daring," he said, "but we trust in almighty God, who can by a mere nod destroy not only those who attack us, but the whole world." 2 Maccabees 8:18

It's an awesome feeling to be a servant of the Most High God and His Son. There is nothing that is impossible for those who believe. And there are probably many more things that I could have in this life if I were to ask him, but I find that what I have is enough. If there is something that He wishes me to do, He tells me or leads me to another who is to be involved. And fighting Him is not an option. I have tried rebellion and avoidance and found that when He wants it done, He doesn't give up until it is done. And if he's on a timeline and I don't comply, He finds someone else that is more – agreeable. Even after everything I've seen, I still have trouble believing that He wants me for His own and His projects. It's that "I'm not worthy" mentality.

This particular passage was related to battle. The Maccabees were relying on the Lord to defend them, and their trust in Him is enviable. They truly knew who was in control – the God who created the universe, promised the land to Abraham's descendants, rescued them from Egypt, and delivered Jerusalem from the Assyrians by slaying 180,000 troops the night before a battle. This is their God. This is my God. Is He yours?

Lord Jesus: Remind me that there is no power greater than yours.

March 12

Ground that has absorbed the rain falling upon it repeatedly and brings forth crops useful to those for whom it is cultivated receives a blessing from God. But if it produces thorns and thistles, it is rejected; it will soon be cursed and finally burned. Hebrews 6:7, 8

As I was studying and contemplating recently, I perceived that the Lord shared something with me. I heard the still small voice say, "A stalk of wheat with no fruit will still be burned." When Jesus tells the parable of the wheat and the weeds (Matthew 13:24-30), He says that the saved are the wheat while the unsaved are the weeds. The farmer (the Lord) allows all of the plants to grow up together, and then they are to be separated at the harvest time (judgment day).

When Paul talks about the judgment day in his first letter to the Corinthians, he says that those who are saved but have only works that burn up will still get into heaven, but will just barely make it in. (1 Corinthians 3:14, 15) I guess that means they get singed?

If I understand correctly, those who profess a belief in Jesus Christ and have some works, but they aren't really good works (the works get burned up), will still get in to heaven. And those who profess a faith in Jesus but do absolutely nothing with it (stalk of wheat with no fruit) will be sent to hell. That sums up my understanding. Would you agree?

Lord Jesus: Help me to grow fruit on my stalk.

March 13
The LORD withholds no good thing from those who
walk without reproach. Psalm 84:12b

That isn't to say that everything that comes to us is good; troubles always come in this life, that's just the way it is. And that's good insofar as we need those experiences to learn. But the Lord's plans for us are to have good things in abundance – so long as we abide by His laws, love our neighbors, and live a clean life. Everyone falls sometime. The one who is without reproach will get right up, ask forgiveness of the Lord and whomever else he may have hurt, and get on with life. This is the life that the Lord wants for us.

Lord Jesus: Thank you for all your blessings in their many forms.

March 14
... even we have believed in Christ Jesus that we may be
justified by faith in Christ and not by works of the law, because
by works of the law no one will be justified. Galatians 2:16

When the Lord brought the Israelites out of Egypt, He gave them the law. Part of the law was the system of sacrifices. If you committed a sin, you had to go to the temple and make a sacrifice. When you had your first male child, you went to the temple and offered a sacrifice to buy him back from the Lord. There were rules governing all activities in their lives. There were animals you couldn't eat, rules for cooking, and activities prohibited on the Sabbath like travel, cooking, and transacting business. Rules, rules and more rules. And the worst part was that the Pharisees and scribes had fine-tuned the laws into even more laws. Jesus said they 'strained out the gnat, but swallowed the camel.' (Matthew 23:24) They made the laws harder for the people to follow and wouldn't lift a finger to help the people keep them. This was the world that Jesus was born into.

During His ministry, He said that He had fulfilled both the prophets and the law: the prophets by fulfilling all of their predictions about the Messiah; the law by negating the requirements for sacrifices by becoming the last sacrifice ever to be needed. He offered His spotless life as the sacrificial lamb to take away our sins, and all we have to do is believe. The law saved no one. As they said in the movie *Pirates of the Caribbean*, "They're more like guidelines." Works will not save you either, but it is expected that belief in Christ will result in works. If a person is truly a believer, they won't be able to keep from having good works.

Jesus said that the greatest law is 'to love the Lord, your God, with all your heart and all your soul and all your mind.' And the second is 'to love your neighbor as yourself.' If you can get even close to fulfilling those two laws, you will have all the others covered.

Lord Jesus: Thank you for sacrificing yourself for my salvation.

March 15

The bread of charity is life itself for the needy; he who withholds it is a man of blood. Sirach 34:21

Most of us have had a time in our lives when we had little or nothing. I found myself divorced, homeless, and unemployed at the age of forty. I had a plan to join some friends in North Carolina in their ministry, but the Lord told me at the last minute that that was not where He wanted me to go. He had another plan for me, one that would lead me into the Catholic Church (never expected that), and end up teaching children who were coming in as well. I had a unique perspective that allowed me to relate to where these kids were in their lives.

My brother was kind enough to let me live with him and his family while I got back on my feet. Had He not made that offer, it's no telling where I would have ended up. My point is this: Everyone needs someone else's help at some time in their life, and we who have been helped by God through the hands of others should be willing to pay that kindness forward. The writer of the book of Sirach says that a man who refuses to help others in need is no better than a murderer. In the eyes of God, you have done the same as doomed them to death.

Lord Jesus: Soften my heart; encourage me to want to help others as you would help them yourself.

March 16
"Nothing is concealed that will not be revealed, nor secret that will not be known." Matthew 10:26b

The judgment day will be a very interesting one. Everything that I have done will be replayed for me to see, and nothing will be left out: every good deed and private blessing I bestowed on someone else, every prayer I've said, every cross or hurtful word spoken, every sly activity, every time I hurt someone's feelings: everything. Now that I know this verse, I try to avoid things that hurt others but, being honest, I can't say I always succeed. There have been times when I forgot to pray for people that I promised to, times when I did what I wanted instead of what the Lord wanted, goofed off when I should have been working diligently at some project or other.

This passage is why I take responsibility for my actions even when they're wrong, because then it isn't concealed, it's not a secret to hide. When you hide things you leave the door open for the devil to slip in and create guilt, and frankly, I don't need any more of that. And this is one of the beautiful things about Confession – it's not a secret anymore for the devil to throw in your face.

Lord Jesus: Help me keep my activities above reproach.

March 17

Wealth is useless on the day of wrath, but
virtue saves from death. Proverbs 11:4

What are you cultivating in your life? Are you busy accumulating monetary wealth? If so, what good are you planning to do with it? If you're just hanging onto it for yourself and not sharing it with anyone else, God might think you're being a bit selfish. Is that what you want Him to think? If God has given you a long and fruitful life, shouldn't you share a portion of it with Him and His Church or some other charitable organizations?

One day your life will end. What if it is tomorrow? We're all only one heartbeat away from death. Make sure you've got some virtuous activities to endear you to God. Would you rather be wealthy here and not know for certain you're headed to heaven, or use your wealth here to make certain that you have a place there without doubt? Seems like a no-brainer to me. What do you think?

Lord Jesus: Show me opportunities to share the wealth you've given me.

March 18

Yet the archangel Michael, when he argued with the devil in a dispute
over the body of Moses, did not venture to pronounce a reviling
judgment upon him but said, "May the Lord rebuke you!" Jude 9

I have always found this verse fascinating. I had wondered what
happened to Moses' body after the Israelites left him on the mountain
and went into the Promised Land, and here it says that Michael came
to take care of it. I guess I can understand that since Moses was special
to God. What I don't get is why the devil would want it. It's not like he
could do him any harm. And if anyone would deserve to be cursed, it's
the devil, but Michael didn't do it. He did not want to show any sense of
independent activity, but handed the devil's rebuke to God to perform.
I suspect that Michael and Lucifer were close in heaven at one time. If
it were me in Michael's place, I hope that I could be so reverent to God
as to let Him handle a situation like that.

It's hard to go a whole day and not hear someone curse somebody else,
whether it be live or on television. And hearing it at home makes our
children more likely to grow up to do it themselves. It's not our job to
curse, but it is our job to point out when correction is needed. We are
called to rebuke our Christian siblings when they are out of line – but
not to curse them. Only God may do that.

*Lord Jesus: Grant me wisdom to speak when necessary and give
me the words to say.*

March 19

Because of the LORD's great love we are not consumed,
for his compassions never fail. They are new every morning;
great is your faithfulness. Lamentations 3:22, 23 (NIV)

It gives me comfort to wake up every morning and know that, no
matter what happens today, the Lord has more than enough mercy to

go around for all of His children to receive, a never-ending supply of mercy available to those who strive to keep His commands and regret the shortcomings of their days' activity. I am so thankful that the Lord doesn't carry over my faults from one day to the next when I ask His forgiveness. Hallelujah!

Lord Jesus: Thank you for your mercy and faithfulness.

March 20

I want you to insist on these points, that those who have
believed in God be careful to devote themselves to good works;
these are excellent and beneficial to others. Titus 3:8

It seems to me that a person who loves God should not have to be told to do good works; for if the Father's love is truly in your heart, you won't be able to stop yourself from doing them. It's what you do when you love someone since it brings joy to your own heart. It's like a game, doing things for others and seeing how long it takes for them to figure out that it is you. And if you play it right, they never do.

I state, with much disappointment, that there are those in the world who do no good works at all. I believe that these people do not know God, no matter what they may say. They are using their talents only for themselves and with no regard for the One who gave them those gifts and abilities. If you do nothing for anyone else, you do nothing for Jesus. And all that gains you in the end is a one-way ticket to hell.

Lord Jesus: Show me opportunities to perform good works for you and your glory.

March 21

Shadrach, Meshach and Abednego answered King Nebuchadnezzar,
"There is no need for us to defend ourselves before you in this
matter. If our God, whom we serve, can save us from the white-
hot furnace and from your hands, O king, may he save us! But
even if he will not, know, O king, that we will not serve your god
or worship the golden statue which you set up." Daniel 3:16-18

I love the faith of Shadrach, Meshach and Abednego. They loved God
so much that they were willing to give up their lives for His law. The
book of Revelation says that the antichrist will set up a statue and
force everyone to worship him. It's the white-hot furnace all over again.
Which one will you choose? I hope if it ever comes down to me having
to bow down before someone or a statue or get thrown into the furnace,
I hope I have the strength to choose the furnace.

It would be a good thing to learn to trust the Lord to protect and provide
for our needs before we get into a situation where we absolutely have to
have him, and there are a few who live this way now. Someday we may
all have to make the choice: trust in Christ and His grace and mercy,
or rely on the mercy of the antichrist. I'm thinking the second doesn't
seem very likely – a merciful antichrist sounds like an oxymoron to me.

Lord Jesus: Teach me to trust in you – no matter what.

March 22

"Because you have kept my message of endurance, I will keep you
safe in the time of trial that is going to come to the whole world to test
the inhabitants of the earth. I am coming quickly. Hold fast to what
you have, so that no one may take your crown." Revelation 3:10, 11

Some preachers out there are telling their flocks that they will be
raptured out before the tribulation starts. I disagree with that teaching.
It isn't an original tenet of the Church; it didn't come into existence until

the mid-1800's. My personal *opinion* is that it is one those 'doctrines of demons' that Paul spoke about. I have searched and searched the Bible for any passage that would support their position. The ones they quote are feeble at best. And this one says to me that He will let us go into the tribulation and protect us while we are there. That is a subjective safe, I need to add. According to Daniel, the antichrist will be successful in his efforts to kill many of the faithful. For some, it will be a test. For others, those who die will be an example of strength and perseverance.

Don't rely on someone else to tell you what's coming or how it is or isn't going to be. Check it out for yourself, and try to be prepared for anything that the Lord may send. Hold onto your crown.

Lord Jesus: Show me the future and my place in it.

March 23

For you show your might when the perfection of
your power is disbelieved; and in those who know
you, you rebuke temerity. Wisdom 12:17

America has turned away from God. We see it in the changing of the definition of marriage, in laws that do not allow Biblical teaching against homosexuality, in the removal of the name of God from the money, the Pledge of Allegiance, the courtrooms and schools, and the banning of the Ten Commandments and Nativity scenes from public places. Americans no longer believe in the God of the Bible. They have made Him into Santa Claus and Father Christmas – a loving and giving man who judges no one and allows His people sins of all natures. This could not be more wrong.

God is not man. And while He is a loving God, He also expects purity from His children, so he has to reprimand and discipline them. Judgment will fall heavily on those who lead others astray with their false teachings. And He will not fail to judge those who followed those teachings blindly without bothering to check them out for themselves. Remember the Bereans. (Acts 17:11)

Lord Jesus: Help me to understand you and the depth of your power.

March 24

According to the law almost everything is purified by blood, and without the shedding of blood there is no forgiveness.
Hebrews 9:22

I know how it is when you feel unclean – when you've sinned and you know it – when you feel distant from God for your transgression. Under the old law, I would have had to go to Jerusalem and make a sacrifice to make atonement for my sin. An innocent animal would have had to shed its blood and give its life in order for my sins to be washed away. I think this is sad – it seems so unfair. But that is the way God wrote the law. And even before the law was written God had Abraham sacrifice a ram in place of his son Isaac.

When Jesus gave His life as a sacrifice, He too was innocent. He shed His blood and gave up His life so that we could have our sins wiped away. He was (and is) the innocent, sacrificial Lamb of God. He washed away our sins with His blood. We have repentance and reconciliation with God because of His love and unselfish acts. He took away our sins and gave us His righteousness in their place. Revelation 7:14 says, "They have washed their robes and made them white in the blood of the Lamb." Is it time to do laundry?

Lord Jesus: Thank you for shedding your blood to make me clean.

March 25

Against the wanton people I came and I chastised
them; I gathered troops against them when I chastised
them for their two crimes. Hosea 10:10

Care to take a guess as to what the two crimes were? Murder and idolatry. Care to take a guess as to what two of the most prevalent sins in our nation are today? Murder and idolatry. Did you know that there have been over 55 million abortions performed in this country since *Roe v. Wade*? Did you know that that number would equal the combined current number of residents in 8 of the plains states? Children today are often seen as an inconvenience rather than a gift from God. And there are now more divorces inside the Church than outside.

I live in what used to be a fairly safe city. Now we have at least one shooting every week and many murders every year. The city of churches is fast becoming the city of murder. There is no respect for life at any stage for many Americans today. Many people worship their own life and desires to the detriment of others. How long do you think the Lord will let this go on?

Lord Jesus: Open my heart to see the depth of my own coldness and complacency.

March 26

"So you also, when you have done everything you were
told to do, should say, 'We are unworthy servants; we
have only done our duty.'" Luke 17:10b (NIV)

Rarely in the time that I have served the Lord have I felt obligated to do so. I don't see it as an obligation; I see it as a privilege. I do things for Him because I love Him and want to make Him happy. He is the husband of my heart. I do feel unworthy, though. I bet Billy Graham felt the same way when he got started, and look how many souls he saved. I don't expect to ever match his numbers. And if I save but one soul from the fires of hell, I will be happy. And if one is good, more is better. I will keep on trying, just because I love him.

Lord Jesus: I am unworthy – use me anyway!

March 27

The wrath of the Lord I will endure because I have sinned against him, until he takes up my cause and establishes my right. He will bring me forth to the light; I will see his justice. Micah 7:9

There is always hope when you know God and His Son, Jesus, so long as you are willing to admit that you have sinned and accept responsibility for yourself. He may be angry for a bit, as parents sometimes are, but He will come around when He sees you being contrite for your errors. He knows your heart even better than you do, so He knows when you're serious about your repentance. There is light at the end of that tunnel, just you wait and see. The time will come when justice will be served to those who wouldn't admit their sinfulness, but you will be safe from His judgment.

Lord Jesus: Please accept my apology for my waywardness, and remind me to be a better person.

March 28

Jesus answered them, "Amen, amen, I say to you, everyone who commits sin is a slave of sin." John 8:34

I have an interesting take on the history of the United States. One side of my family came from the south where they owned slaves; the other side ran a station on the Underground Railroad and helped the slaves escape. I like to tell people that my karma is balanced out when it comes to the subject of slavery. Personally, I find the idea of owning someone else for my profiteering to be abhorrent. If I hire someone that is paid, that's different – that's an employee. I know how it feels to be thought of as a possession, and it isn't a positive feeling. To be thought of as something less than the child that God created me to be is unacceptable.

We should never be a slave to anyone or anything. We should be in control of our own bodies, not letting our primal urges drive our thoughts and behaviors. Slavery is control. If you let something other than your brain direct you, that something is your master. You likely wouldn't live as a slave to another person – why would you be a slave to desires that will send you to hell? The only way I will be a slave is to be a slave of Christ. (Ephesians 6:6)

Lord Jesus: Help me get my sin under your control.

March 29
He who condones the wicked, he who condemns the just,
are both an abomination to the LORD. Proverbs 17:15

How do you know where to draw a line as you try to love your neighbor, when your neighbor is living in sin, without condoning his or her lifestyle? God hates sin – all sin. He also expects us to hate sins and not participate in them. So how do I disapprove of my friend who sins and love him as my neighbor? Paul says you don't. He says warn them several times, and if they refuse to repent, stay away from them. You don't have to hate them, just hate their sin and don't be tainted by their lifestyle choices. You can still love them, just pray for them from a distance. If you continue to remain too close, you may end up thinking that it's okay after all. Rare is the person who can remain friends with a sinner and keep themselves pure.

On the flipside, the Lord is equally unhappy with people who think that those who are righteous are not deserving of the same status as themselves. This is becoming more common in the world today. We see the double standard of certain groups who will not allow Christians to have Nativities on public lawns, but they can have pagan setups instead. It's becoming dangerous to be a Christian these days right here in America. You don't have to go overseas to suffer persecution, just put Christian symbols on your lawn during the Christmas season.

Lord Jesus: Help me see people through your eyes and guide me in your will for them.

March 30
Be angry but do not sin; do not let the sun go
down on your anger. Ephesians 4:26

It's okay to get angry, BUT – it isn't okay to stay angry. Being angry with someone else doesn't hurt them at all. It will, however, eat you up if you don't get rid of it. Have you ever been angry with someone? Do you remember how much time you devoted to those negative feelings? Did it make you tired? It wore me out until I realized that it was only hurting me and not them, so I finally let it go. Anger is sometimes classified as murder in the Church if you let it get out of hand and destroy your life, your marriage, or someone else's good character.

Paul wrote to the Ephesians not to hang on to anger. Somehow we have to learn how to exhale, release, and disengage that urge to rant, rave, and lash out at others when we are hurting emotionally. Anger makes us into the worst versions of ourselves. I don't like to live there, because that's no life. That's misery. I create enough of that for myself without adding anyone else's input. I've learned to exhale and forgive people when they act stupid or ignorant. You just never know what they're dealing with – maybe they just received divorce papers and they're trying to cry and drive at the same time; maybe they just had someone dump a huge pile of problems on their doorstep, and they aren't capable of dealing with all of those issues. It could be one of a million things making someone behave badly and ruin your day. DON'T LET THEM! Forgive and let God handle them. You have more important ways to spend your energy.

Lord Jesus: Help me to let go of anger and forgive.

March 31

Then Job answered the Lord and said: I know that you can
do all things, and that no purpose of yours can be hindered. I
have dealt with great things that I do not understand; things
too wonderful for me, which I cannot know. Job 42:1-3

It's hard for us with our human pea-brains to comprehend how ... big ... extraordinary ... powerful ... complex ... God is. I can't even find the right word for him. Nothing we have in our vocabulary is awesome, amazing, or massive enough to cover who He is and what He is capable of accomplishing. There is absolutely no limit to what God can do. He created the universe and everything in it; every emotion and feeling, our sense of humor, our very souls. He gave us our hair color, eye color, personality, and talents. He gave us the desire and drive to fulfill our individual missions.

If He really wants me to do something, He can make me do it. But He doesn't want to force me into anything; He wants me to choose to do His will. When He wants something done, He finds the perfect person to do it, and it is not our place to question His decisions. He knows every thought, fear, and desire and will use the one He deems fit for the job He has in mind.

Lord God: Thank you for showing us your great things.

April

April 1

The Lord will rescue me from every evil threat and
will bring me safe to his heavenly kingdom. To him be
glory forever and ever. Amen. 2 Timothy 4:18

The Lord doesn't see things as we do. We think that because we are
Christians that we shouldn't suffer. Here, Paul says that he will be
rescued from threats and delivered to the kingdom. It *doesn't* say that
we won't have to deal with evil, only that we will prevail in the end.
And all that really means is that we'll get to go to heaven if we don't
give up on God.

Jesus himself said that we would be persecuted and turned over to
authorities. (Matthew 24:9) That could be government, synagogue, or
spiritual authorities. I know that while I'm trying to write this book, it's
Lent. Bad timing, I know. I'm having trouble sleeping at night since
there is war going on in my dreams all night long: mental, physical,
spiritual, and emotional war all at the same time. It's distracting and
exhausting. And that's just what goes on at home. Then there's the
stuff that goes on at work: problems with shipping, warehousing, and
inventory mishaps. But as my brother says, God is still on the throne. I
say, if He lets something get taken away over here, He'll bring something
bigger and better over there. And for those who do not serve God but
make life miserable for others, 'even what they have will be taken away.'
(Luke 19:26)

Lord Jesus: Thy will be done!

April 2

For the people of Israel shall remain many days without king
or prince, without sacrifice or sacred pillar, without ephod or
household idols. Then the people of Israel shall turn back and
seek the LORD, their God, and David, their king; they shall come
trembling to the LORD and to his bounty in the last days.
Hosea 3:4, 5

I think 1800 years constitutes 'many days,' don't you? After World
War 1, some people decided to give the Hebrews back their Promised
Land, even though there were people living there. That last part I have
trouble with. I think there should have been a bit more preparation and
consideration done for the Palestinians living there, but they didn't ask
me. And I can't say honestly that I agree with everything the Israeli
government is currently doing, but I am happy that they are back where
the Lord wanted them to be.

Having said all that, I hope and pray that the Israelites are returning to
God now that they have their own land and the remaining temple wall. I
read several years ago that only about 25% of the Jews were religiously
active, and I can't help but wonder why that is so. After everything
that the Lord has done for them, you'd think they'd be more prone to
gratitude and have a willingness to honor him.

Hosea prophesied that they will return to God and 'David, their king'
in the last days. That reference to David is sometimes used in the Old
Testament to refer to the Messiah. So if we were coming close to the
end of days, we would expect to see conversions of the Jewish people to
Christianity. And it is happening. (See the following website for more
information on an organization that leads Israelites to Jesus Christ.
http://www.jewsforjesus.org/about-jews-for-jesus/categories) There's no
suggestion on how many might be needed to convert in order for the
fulfillment of all the end time prophecies to take place. Stay tuned!

Lord Jesus: Change the hearts of your people to draw them to you and our Father.

April 3

For the one whom God sent speaks the words of God.
He does not ration his gift of the Spirit. John 3:34

There have been many times in my life when I spoke to someone, and they responded with, "I really needed to hear that." Many times it seemed that the words that came out of my mouth were a bit goofy (at least to me). They weren't what I would normally have said, but they made absolute sense to the person they were spoken to. I don't take any credit for the words spoken; I believe it was the action of the holy Spirit. And I count myself blessed to be the occasional bearer of God's words to those who are seeking His help or guidance. In traveling my journey, I've learned that the only limitation of God's power in someone's life is the constraint placed on Him by the one whom He seeks to help.

Lord Jesus: Show me where I'm holding you back in my life.

April 4

The works of all mankind are present to him; not
a thing escapes his eye. Sirach 39:19

Back in the days of my youth, I was dumb – **REALLY** dumb. I thought I could go here, go there, and no one that had authority over me would ever know. I could get away with it! (Whatever *it* was.) That was before I knew the Holy Trinity. Now I know that there is no hiding of anything. And when I eventually got busted, it is probable that they made it happen. Yes, I went to the school of hard knocks. And a couple of lessons took more than one failure, I'm sad to say. Now, in my religious education class, I ask my kids: Would you do that if Jesus were standing right next to you? Because He is.

Fortunately, God is merciful. He wants to let go of those stupid things I did as a youth and forget they ever happened. Micah 7:19 says, "You will tread our sins underfoot and hurl all our iniquities into the depths of the sea." I like that – very much. It gives me peace to know that the sins of my past are forgiven and forgotten, never to be held against me. Now if I could just get the devil to stop bringing them up, that would be even better.

Lord Jesus: Remind me when I am tempted that you are there watching me at all times.

April 5

Therefore, if food causes my brother to sin, I will never eat meat again, so that I may not cause my brother to sin.
1 Corinthians 8:13

Paul was talking about the freedom that we have in Christ, saying that meat is just meat. If you give thanks for it, it doesn't matter where it came from, even if it was part of a sacrifice in a pagan temple. He knew that there is no other god but the Lord God Almighty, and food offered to other 'deities' was of no consequence. That wasn't true for all people at that time, however. Paul is referring to recent converts who had just left the worship of those deities and their temples where that meat was sacrificed – those who didn't have the strong faith that he had. They were, as yet, unable to make that separation. And some of those persons would fall into judgment of him for eating this meat, or live in guilt if they ate of it thinking that it was somehow tainted by its manner or location of cooking.

One of the hardest things that I have found to do is to be constantly aware of the image I project. It isn't right for me to present an appearance or behaviors that would cause someone else to judge me. If I do cause that to happen, I am just as guilty of the sin as they are, because it's my fault that they fell into sin. I used to enjoy saying and doing things that would shock people (not utilizing nudity or profanity) just to make people gasp. I thought it was fun. But when I read this passage I knew that I would have to give up that pastime. James wrote that the tongue is nigh untamable. And I have to say, it was one of the most difficult things I've ever had to do. Learning to think before speaking and only allowing things out that are positive or edited is tough.

Words and food aren't the only things that we have to watch out for. Anything that causes someone else to sin is offensive to God. It might be scanty clothing (especially in church), coarse language, a flamboyant lifestyle; the list is practically endless. Any time that someone judges somebody else, they're wrong; but that's in God's hands. My job is to try to prevent anyone from falling in to that trap because of me. It's not as easy as it seems since people are always so willing to stand in judgment of one another.

There are two corrections that we each need to make in our lives with regard to this passage: one, stop judging others based on first impressions; and two, stop doing things that are causing others to fall into sin. Any sin.

Lord Jesus: Help me be more sensitive to the image I present to the world that I may not cause others to sin because of my foolishness.

April 6
Then the LORD of hosts in his great anger said that,
as they had not listened when he called, so he would
not listen when they called. Zechariah 7:13

In the parable of the vineyard owner, Jesus told us how the Father goes out daily looking for workers for His vineyard – an analogy for the time of life when people come to salvation. And no matter your age when you come to him, all will receive the same payment: eternal life with him.

No matter whether you've served for your entire life or given in on your death bed, if God calls and you say 'yes,' you win. The day will come, however, when people will call to him, and He will not respond. When the end times come and we are confronted with taking the mark, if we give in so that we can eat, He will not hear when we call. If you're not saved at that time, yet you bypass the mark and then Jesus returns, I can't say for sure what will happen. Do you really want to find out just how much mercy He has?

I like that I gave in when I did, and to this day wish that I had done so sooner. Life with God is enormously better than what it was without Him. And so for now, I work to stay close to Him. Why? Because I want Him to listen when I call and answer me in my time of worship, praise, or need.

Lord Jesus: Thank you for continuing to call to me, even when I wasn't listening.

April 7

Show yourself as a model of good deeds in every respect,
with integrity in your teaching, dignity, and sound speech
that cannot be criticized, so that the opponent will be put to
shame without anything bad to say about us. Titus 2:7, 8

Oh, that everyone in the Church would be this way! Maybe then, people might be more inclined to join. I know some folks won't go to church because of the 'hypocrites' that they would find there. I wish I could tell them that they would be in good company, but that's counter-productive. So instead, I tell them that you're not supposed to go for everybody else; you go so that you and God can be together. He loves to hear our worship, and a lot of those who don't go to church don't worship either. They just muddle through life with no particular focus on God's will in the world and in their life.

Occasionally I see a bumper sticker on a car that has a Christian theme. They're most notable when the driver is speeding, cutting people off, swearing, or flipping off other drivers. I understand that these are some of the ones that are giving us a black eye and a bad name, but the only thing you can do is pray for them. I try to not give people ammunition against the Church because of me, but I don't always succeed. Fortunately, I've never been one to flip people off, so there's a plus. I'm still a work in progress, after all.

Lord Jesus: Show those who give you a black eye their own hypocrisy.

April 8

The sins of the house of Israel are great beyond measure; the land is filled with bloodshed, the city with lawlessness. They think that the LORD has forsaken the land, that he does not see them. I, however, will not look upon them with pity, nor show any mercy. I will bring down their conduct upon their heads. Ezekiel 9:9, 10

I remember when I was little and we lived in the country – we never locked our doors, and we left the windows open at night. My brother and I roamed the countryside never feeling like we were in any danger. When I was in college, I used to jog every day. I was all over town on my jaunts, and no one ever knew where I was. If I had disappeared, it would have taken quite a while to figure out that I was gone. When I first moved to the city where I currently live, I would walk my neighborhood early in the morning when it was dark. Today, I only walk in the daylight, and I'm never more than 5 minutes from home. It's a terrible thing to be intimidated by people you don't know. There seems to be no place of safety. Just yesterday evening, a young man in our city was shot in his car at an intersection – not because he was part of a gang, but because he wasn't. What kind of logic is that?

The Lord has not forsaken the land, the land has forsaken God. And one day His Son will return, and it will be too late for those who thought they had it all figured out but were wrong – those who think that the only way to solve a problem is with a gun, or that anyone who disagrees with them deserves to die. "Woe to those who call evil good and good evil." (Isaiah 5:20) The lord will do to them as they have done to others – they will receive absolutely no mercy.

Lord Jesus: Please help us find a way to create peace in our neighborhoods.

April 9

The light shines in the darkness, and the darkness
does not comprehend it. John 1:5

This follows yesterday's reading very well, for those who walk in darkness cannot comprehend the light. They have no conception of peace, joy, or true love. It's like a foreign language to them. How do people get so far away from good and right? And why is there so much of it today?

There is good and bad, light and dark in each one of us. I like to think that we are prone to good deeds unless someone teaches us otherwise as we are growing up. I wonder what would happen if no one was ever taught anything but good behaviors. Probably the same thing that happened in heaven: pride would show up in someone somewhere sometime and ruin it for everyone else.

I have noticed in the past 5 years that there is a polarization of society in America, perhaps even the world. There is less and less gray, more and more dark. If we are called to be light, then our lights must shine even more brightly to hinder the expanding darkness and to draw those who are not committed over to the side of the light. If we don't lift a finger to bring people to the light, then we have no right to complain about the ever-expanding darkness.

Lord Jesus: Give me strength to shine brightly in a world of darkness.

April 10

But now, thus says the LORD, who created you, O Jacob, and
formed you, O Israel: Fear not, for I have redeemed you; I
have called you by name: you are mine. Isaiah 43:1

The Lord calls to each one of us, for He created us all. Some just can't seem to hear His voice. I try to act as an amplifier to boost the sound and help those around me tune in. He longs to redeem everyone, to wash away their sins and wipe away their tears, to take away their shame and fill them with righteousness. And like it or not, we all belong to him. The only difference between one person and the next is how much each acknowledges Him and loves Him in return.

Lord Jesus: Help me hear you calling my name every day.

April 11

Then I saw a beast come out of the sea with ten horns and
seven heads; on its horns were ten diadems, and on its heads
blasphemous names. The beast I saw was like a leopard,
but it had feet like a bear's, and its mouth was like the
mouth of a lion. To it the dragon gave its own power and
throne, along with great authority. Revelation 13:1, 2

This is the organization from which the antichrist will arise, an organization that is varied in its constituents like the UN or the European Union or some as yet unknown, perhaps global, entity. Seven heads suggests that there will be seven divisions with the number of diadems (crowns) suggesting ten leaders in this organization. The names of these nations/states/divisions will be offensive to God (blasphemous names). The seven heads is an allusion to the perfection of God, but they will be as far removed from the nature of God as you can get.

The different animals represented could suggest the nature of this entity. The leopard could denote swiftness: intolerance of those who disagree with the tenets of the union who will be quickly eradicated for their 'treason.' I don't know if you've ever seen a bear's paw, but it's huge with really long claws that don't retract. They are truly lethal to any that have the misfortune to irritate the owner, again suggesting that anyone who disagrees with the policies of the union will be dealt a lethal blow. The mouth of a lion is likely the strongest amongst the hunting animals, able to crush the bones of anything it gets hold of. Again, this suggests the nature of intolerance and destruction for those who refuse to be subjugated by this union.

The power to govern will be placed upon the union by and for Satan (the dragon) to fulfill his purposes. Care to take a guess what that purpose is? Once again, he will try to destroy the Hebrew nation. But this time his scope is even wider than before. This time he will also be after the Christians. Since he knows that there are some who understand prophecy and are onto his games, he will try to cause them to lose their salvation by stealth. If these things begin to happen and you're not sure what's going on, turn to others who have Biblical knowledge. Test what they say by reading it yourself, because some with knowledge will fall prey to his wiles. (See Daniel 7:23-26.)

Lord Jesus: Open my eyes to the activities of Satan in this world.

April 12

For he who finds me finds life and wins favor from
the LORD; but he who misses me harms himself; all
who hate me love death. Proverbs 8:35, 36

This is from Proverbs, so the 'me' is Wisdom. So many people today seem to lack wisdom or even the simple ability to make good decisions. I don't know if they don't have the knowledge to make practical applications or if they're just too lazy to try. Some of it, I think, is from the breakdown of our family unit in this country. I'm not saying that all homes are this way, but there are some parents that just don't teach kids how to be good, productive adults. They don't want to deal with whining so they turn on the tv and let the kids play video games or watch movies or (God forbid) anything on primetime cable these days. Rare, it seems, is the home that teaches the children to read, work on logic or math problems, or even learn basic social skills. It starts with one lax person, and it escalates with every generation that follows; a vicious cycle that rarely ends, although for some it does end in murder.

Wisdom is not something to be overlooked, but something to be sought after; our seeking after the Lord will bring wisdom to us. It comes to those who seek it and ask for it, but often comes with unfortunate circumstances – much like the way patience is learned – the hard way. I've often heard it said in Christian circles, 'Be careful what you ask for, you just might get it – but not the way you want it.' Nevertheless, wisdom is good to have. It's a step closer to God for those who choose to not live in spiritual ignorance and prefer to seek after everything that leads to God. 'All who hate me love death' – spiritual death – eternity in hell, separated from God is what awaits those who prefer to turn away from God and His wisdom.

Lord Jesus: Give me wisdom to seek you.

April 13

This Melchizedek, king of Salem and priest of God Most High,
met Abraham as he returned from his defeat of the kings
and blessed him. Without father, mother, or ancestry, without
beginning of days or end of life, thus made to resemble the
Son of God, he remains a priest forever. Hebrews 7:1, 3

I remember the first time I read about Melchizedek. He's in the book of Genesis (14:18-20) and is the only person ever mentioned in the story of the early life of Abram (Abraham) that is a follower of God. He is King of Salem (Jerusalem) and a priest of God Most High, according to the scripture. There is no other information about where he came from or if he had family. He just shows up, blesses Abram and his flocks, receives a tithe of booty from Abram, and disappears from history. I love this story. It's the way I'd like to be when I serve – drop in, give a blessing to someone, and move on to the next needy soul. I don't really care about the tithe part. I'd rather they give whatever they have to offer to someone in need.

The reference to Jesus comes from Psalm 110:4. Even though Melchizedek only appears in three verses in genesis, he makes enough of an impact that David mentions him in a Psalm, and the writer to the Hebrews spends three chapters talking about him and comparing his service to that of Jesus.

I used to want to have a pie shop, and I was planning to call it Melchizedek's. The Lord had other plans for me, however. I'm actually living out a bit of the Melchizedek effect by teaching my kids in RCIA. I give them a blessing and send them on their way.

Lord Jesus: Thank you for using me to bless others.

April 14

By the sword shall all sinners among my people die, those
who say, "Evil will not reach or overtake us." Amos 9:10

I'm sure the older folks among us remember the saying, 'they have their
head stuck in the sand', while younger ones might relate to 'they need
an intervention.' Both are a flippant way of saying that someone is living
in denial. This is the way the Jews were when the Lord brought the
Babylonian army to their gates. They thought that because they lived in
the city of the King with His temple that they were safe from destruction.
That's the problem with people who think they are indestructible – they
nearly always find out they're wrong. The Jews were wrong, and so too will
be some people who sit in the pews every week when the Lord returns.

The opening chapters of the book of Revelation are letters that Jesus
had John write to the early churches. If you read them you'll find that
he wasn't very pleased with some of them. There were a lot of failings
by the people in those churches as there are in ours today, and Jesus
was telling them that they needed to clean up their act or be considered
as evildoers when judgment comes. Read those letters and see if they
apply to you. They certainly give me pause. Evil is everywhere today,
and the only safe harbor is Jesus.

*Lord Jesus: Help me get my head out of the sand so that I can
see clearly.*

April 15

Therefore, neither the one who plants nor the one who waters
is anything, but only God who causes the growth. The one
who plants and the one who waters are equal, and each will
receive wages in proportion to his labor. 1 Corinthians 3:7, 8

I really like to garden (even though I'm not very good at it), and there
are a lot of verses in the Bible that speak to the gardener in me. This is

one of them. When we garden, we like to think that we are the ones in control. We plant, we fertilize, we water, and aerate. Therefore, we must be the ones who are causing the plants to grow and produce fruits and blooms. What a delusion! Sometimes the best-growing plants are from the seeds that get thrown out on the ground and do what God created them to do without any 'help' from us.

This verse speaks about the spreading of the kingdom of God. He could make it grow without our assistance, but that's not how He wants it to happen. He wants us to speak up for Him and lead others to salvation. He leads us to people that He wants to grow, and we plant the seeds for Him. Then He sends someone else along later to water that seed.

We always have a choice as to whether or not we want to speak up, and the rewards we receive one day in heaven will be a reflection of how many times we followed His leading: more good works, planting, and watering – more rewards. I don't know what those rewards will be, but I envision that those with the most rewards will be closer to the throne in the kingdom. Sometimes I wonder how my rewards stack up against others', and I realize that there is no way to know because there have been so many people throughout history in service to the King. Regardless of where I will be and what I'll be doing, you'll still find me planting and watering in God's garden.

Lord Jesus: Give me the courage to speak out for you and tend your garden.

April 16
The pride of your heart has deceived you. Obadiah 3a

I think pride is a serious problem today. I know I used to have it pretty bad: pride in my car, my home, and even my looks. I thought I was all that and then some. The problem with pride is that it swells your head and closes your eyes so that you can't see how far away from God you've travelled. It settles in your heart and gives you a false sense of security that all is right in the world, and you're at the center of it.

It's okay to have a nice home and car or to be careful about one's appearance so long as those things don't become the most important focus in our lives. Pride will separate us from God if we are not careful. It's the sin that caused Lucifer and one-third of the angels to fall from grace. So tell me again: What's important to you?

Lord Jesus: I need you to be the most important 'thing' in my life.

April 17

But I now write to you not to associate with anyone named a brother if he is immoral, greedy, an idolater, a slanderer, a drunkard, or a robber, not even to eat with such a person.
1 Corinthians 5:11

Ouch! These are hard words when you're supposed to love your neighbor, but you have to take this in context. The people of Corinth were a pretty immoral group when Paul arrived there. The predominant career was prostitution, so there was an issue with getting those who were saved to separate themselves from the crowds they had been involved with for most of their lives.

If you haven't been Christian all of your life, you know how this goes. You usually don't want to be around the crowd you ran with before, but they keep calling and showing up at your door trying to drag you back into their lives of dissipation. And while you would like for them to convert to Christianity, the hold that the devil has on them is tighter than the one the Lord uses on His children. He will not force anyone to come to Him or stay with Him. The devil, on the other hand, will do everything in his power to not only keep your friends, but get you back as well. It goes back to the saying, "Bad company corrupts good character." Choose your friends wisely.

Lord Jesus: Place a hedge around me and my family to protect us from the tricks of the devil and those whom he uses.

April 18

You say, 'I am innocent; he is not angry with me.'
But I will pass judgment on you because you say,
'I have not sinned.' Jeremiah 2:35 (NIV)

Unfortunately I know some people who think they are going to heaven because they believe in Jesus and yet refuse to admit that their lives are full of sin. How one can read the Bible and know what it says is sin and still refuse to see those activities in their life as sinful is beyond me. I know that they accepted Christ at some time in their life, but it is clear from their actions that they don't know or understand him. He expects people who believe in Him as their personal savior to be devoted to Him and His purposes, not their own.

Confession only goes so far: repentance and remorse are required as well. That means not only are you sorry for your behavior, you plan to stop doing things the Lord doesn't like. Similarly, admitting your sin and not planning to change will get you nowhere. I call that intentional disobedience, and that's a whole lot more trouble than admitting you have a problem and working to change and failing miserably. It's all about the state of your heart, and only you and God know what that is. And after yesterday's reading, I'll be steering clear of you – just so you know!

Lord Jesus: Open the eyes of those with hardened hearts so that they can see their sin through your eyes.

April 19

They clothed him in purple and, weaving a crown
of thorns, placed it on him. Mark 15:17

Two of my favorite things in the world are roses and black raspberries, and I have both of these types of plants growing at my home. The roses have to be pruned as the blooms die in order for new growth to come on. The raspberries only produce fruit once on their canes and so are cut off at the end of their growing season, necessitating that I spend a fair amount of time working with all of them. I use natural biostimulants to promote good health in my plants, and so these plants, both of which have thorns, get very thick stalks on them. Their thorns also get wicked long and hard. Occasionally, I have the misfortune of stabbing or snagging myself on one of these thorns. If you have never experienced this, you are missing an excellent opportunity to have a greater understanding of what Jesus went through when they placed the crown of thorns on His head.

It is commonly believed that the plant that the Roman soldiers used to weave the crown of thorns was from the jujube tree. A tree that you may have seen that could help you envision the branch used to weave the crown is the honey locust (or thorny locust). This tree has thorns that grow out of its branches and its trunk, some reaching a length of up to 8 inches. I can't imagine being speared with one of these thorns. Just getting snagged by one of mine creates excruciating pain. And woe be to me if the tip breaks off and festers in that wound. It can take up to 2 weeks for that tip to soften up and come out if you can't manage to find it and squeeze it out sooner. Wood splinters got nothin' on these babies.

Having these thorns in my garden and discovering just how painful they can be has given me one more thing to be ashamed of and yet thankful for in the suffering of my Lord Jesus.

Lord Jesus: Thank you for taking my punishment and giving me your righteousness in its place.

April 20

When I say, "My foot is slipping," your love, LORD, holds me up.
When cares increase within me, your comfort gives me joy.
Psalm 94:18, 19

The Lord is faithful to those who show themselves faithful. He may test you occasionally, but He won't let you fall so far that you can't get back. The tough part is keeping your faith in Him when He is letting you drop for that short period. Know this: When you hit the bottom, you'll find Him there waiting for you. Open your eyes and see Him and His mercy. He's waiting to draw you to His side and bless you with peace and joy and comfort. That is His gift to you when you give yourself as a gift to Him.

Lord Jesus: Catch me as I fall!

April 21

Beloved, do not trust every spirit but test the spirits to
see whether they belong to God, because many false
prophets have gone out into the world. 1 John 4:1

Have you questioned my spirit yet? You should. You should question everyone's spirit these days. The times are dark, and many would try to convert you to the side of the enemy by coming to you as a wolf in sheep's clothing. If the message doesn't adhere to the unadulterated word of God, don't trust it! My intentions are good, but I see things differently than a lot of people. I think that I'm an out-of-the-box kind of person most of the time. I like to think that there are things that go on in the universe that are outside the writings of the Bible, but I won't mention those things to you because they aren't appropriate to what I want to do here. My intention is simply to try to get you to open your eyes and see Jesus and the Lord God more clearly. Those other issues only muddy the waters and lead people astray.

Lord Jesus: Help me to stay focused on you and your truth.

April 22

When you make a vow to God, do not delay its fulfillment.
For God has no pleasure in fools; fulfill what you have vowed.
Ecclesiastes 5:3

I always feel bad if I agree to do a task and something comes up that makes me unable to complete my plan on time, or worse, not at all. One of the things I teach my kids is that they should only make promises that they can keep. Yes, there are extenuating circumstances sometimes. I'm not talking about those times; I'm talking about making a promise that you have no plan to fulfill.

People don't like to be treated that way, and I suspect God likes it even less – especially if you agreed to do something in order to get a blessing from him. As this verse says, He doesn't tolerate fools. If you make a promise to the Creator of the universe, how can you justify not keeping it? And why would you test His patience when you know He could take your feet out from under you without notice? Do you not fear the Lord? 'Fulfill what you have vowed.'

Lord Jesus: If I have failed in a vow, please show me so that I can make it right with you.

April 23

And do this because you know the time; it is the hour now
for you to awake from sleep. For our salvation is nearer
now than when we first believed. Romans 13:11

I suspect that every generation has thought that the world was in such a horrific state that it could end with the Lord's return during their lifetime. True there has always been war, famine, and disease, but only during the last hundred years have the Jews returned to the Promised Land. By the way, did you know that there was approximately 2000 years between Adam and Abraham (by Biblical genealogical records)? 2000 years between Abraham and Jesus? And it's been about 2000 years since Jesus. Coincidence? I don't think so. I'm pretty sure that God is well aware of timelines and such since He is a God of order and not chaos. He doesn't do random. Everything has a perfect time and season, but we have to guess and wonder since He doesn't share all the intimate details. I think He sometimes gives different people clues, but He doesn't give everything to one person. I believe He wants us all to share our encounters in order to put together the bigger picture – like a puzzle.

On a different tack: I was watching a program on PBS about travel in Israel. They showed the Western Wall, all that is left of the temple in Jerusalem. They also showed an archaeological dig in the northern part of the country. They believe it is the temple of Samaria. The guide said that, as they excavate, they are building a replica of what they find. I always wondered how the Jews would get the temple mount away from the Muslims so that the end times could be fulfilled. Now it looks like they don't have to. They'll have a temple. And even if it isn't the one where God visited His people, it will be one located in Israel. Let's hope they don't put a golden calf in it like their ancestors did.

Lord Jesus: Help me to prepare for the troubled times preceding your return.

April 24

The eyes of the LORD are upon those who love him; he is their mighty shield and strong support, a shelter from the heat, a shade from the noonday sun, a guard against stumbling, a help against falling. He buoys up the spirits, brings a sparkle to the eyes, gives health and life and blessing. Sirach 34:16, 17

Trust is an amazing thing to those who can muster the courage to engage in the practice; for when we realize that the Lord is the provider of all things and that He is in control of all that comes to us, we recognize that there is nothing that can harm us beyond what He will allow. And

He only allows events that are designed to make us stronger. Will some things hurt? Of course they will. How can one learn compassion or patience or perseverance without suffering?

The problems arise when we forget to check in with him, and then go off on our own. That's when the serious troubles come. It's good to remember that He is still there where we left him, calling to us to return, waiting to wipe away our tears, and forgive our transgressions. He is a loving Father, calling even to the most hardened of hearts to come to Him and give up their waywardness. There is nothing that He won't forgive for the truly penitent. And with that forgiveness comes the sparkle in the eyes, and life and health and blessing.

Lord Jesus: Thank you for reconciling me to our loving Father.

April 25
Some, by rejecting conscience, have made a
shipwreck of their faith. 1 Timothy 1:19b

It's interesting to watch the social war playing out in the media today. The liberal left would have us all be equal at every level, even when those levels are unequal by God's standards. They say they are raising the oppressed to a higher level, when what they are really doing is dragging us down to theirs. God is very clear in what He says is sin. Marriage is a man and a woman. There wasn't marriage before the law, there was just people being together. And even after the law was written down for the Jews, not everyone did what was prudent. Solomon could have used fewer wives (than 700) and no concubines (instead of 300) and been far better off. The pagan wives he had were the source of his downfall and the eventual split of the nation of Israel.

Why have I put this here? Simple: one of our Congressional leaders who says he is Christian and was against same-sex marriage, recently learned that his son is gay. He has now changed his political position to suit his son's sexual orientation – even though the Bible says that the son's behavior is wrong. As Paul wrote, the Congressman has made a shipwreck of his faith. Not only is his son living in sin, he has brought his father into that sin. The father has refused to follow his God and refused to ask his son to repent. Please don't misunderstand me: I don't dislike gay or lesbian people – I have friends that are. But I don't hide the fact that I disagree with their choices. And I expect them to honor my choices as well. And in the interests of loving my neighbor, I would tolerate civil unions for the health benefits that would become available to partners; just don't call it marriage.

Lord Jesus: Speak to the hearts of those who misunderstand and think that your mercy is approval.

April 26

For, as I watched, that horn made war against the holy ones
and was victorious until the Ancient One arrived; judgment
was pronounced in favor of the holy ones of the Most High, and
the time came when the holy ones possessed the kingdom.
Daniel 7:21, 22

The antichrist will make war against the holy ones, and he will be victorious against them. There will be open warfare. The conditions we are living in now are laying the groundwork that will enable him to be blatant in changing the laws that will allow him to oppress and murder those who refuse to follow his reign of evil. His will be the eighth beast empire on the earth. He will be the worst of all the tyrants to ever walk this earth. Think Hitler was bad? Not compared to this guy. Hitler slaughtered millions – this guy will likely have hundreds of millions. Anyone who refuses to worship him and his likeness will be put to death.

This will go on until Jesus returns, and then the tables are turned. Jesus slays all the evil ones with sword of his mouth. I believe that sword is the word of God. When he speaks, all who followed the beast will realize (only too late) that they were duped. They made the wrong choice – an eternal choice that can't be undone. I think it will be a bittersweet day: bitter that so many were lost to evil, and sweet that we will be alive eternally with Christ and God.

Lord Jesus: Speak your word to us now so that we may hear and believe before it is too late.

April 27
They strengthened the spirits of the disciples and exhorted
them to persevere in the faith, saying, "It is necessary for us
to undergo many hardships to enter the kingdom of God."
Acts 14:22

How important is it to you to have someone who is willing to support you every day and keep your spirits up? How long does it take for you to get down and depressed if you don't have that person there on a regular basis? Have you considered having an accountability or prayer partner? If not, you should. Having someone that will lift us up in prayer and be a sounding board in times of change or temptation is imperative for someone striving to remain faithful to their spouse, family, Savior, and the commitments made to each of them. Encouragement and hope are two facets of life that are necessary if we are to continue to endure life here on earth.

Jesus said that temptations would come. Each of us needs someone to help us fight them off, not just the holy Spirit. If we have someone to talk to regarding the struggles that we are undergoing, we can find a source of support that we can see clearly and hear. Hopefully that person will be the voice of the holy Spirit speaking and not the one through who the temptation comes. This is why I recommend having a prayer partner that is the same gender as our self. Too many times the devil has gotten into a male/female relationship that was perfectly platonic and ruined more than one marriage.

Each of us can be the voice of hope for someone, but make sure that the relationship is a healthy one. There should be give and take by each of the persons. A situation where one person is always taking from the other is not healthy and will lead to the loss of a friend. If you find yourself always feeling drained after having been with someone and there seems to be no likelihood for a change in the circumstances, step away. You can lose your own hope and peace of mind in a relationship like that.

Lord Jesus: Help me find someone that I can support and who will support me on my journey to you.

April 28

Because it became lofty in stature, raising its crest among the clouds, and because it became proud in heart at its height, I have handed it over to the mightiest of the nations, which has dealt with it in keeping with its wickedness. I humiliated it. Ezekiel 31:10, 11

When the Lord spoke these words to Ezekiel, He was referring to Egypt. But when I'm thinking about the state of our nation before I open my Bible to read, this is where I frequently end up. This is the state of America – puffed up with pride for all the wrong reasons. I think it's okay to be proud of our military personnel giving up their time and their very lives to defend the freedoms of our nation and others. I don't think it's okay to be proud to be Americans because of what we own or who we think that we are.

There are many places I would like to go and see in this world, but I hear too many horror stories of people who went and were murdered or kidnapped just because they were Americans. The world at large has a view of us as a people that isn't true for most of us. It's the 1 or 2% making the other 98 or 99% look bad. Americans are often seen as extremely wealthy and arrogant with too much time and money on their hands. I don't know about you, but that description certainly doesn't apply to me. If I were able to go to even one of the places across the world that I would like to, it would be because I had saved my nickels and dimes for many years to get there. I don't like being judged and pigeon-holed into groups that I personally find disappointing or even disgusting.

Lord Jesus: Please lead us away from pride and wasteful spending habits.

April 29

From his fullness we have all received grace in place of grace, because while the law was given through Moses, grace and truth came through Jesus Christ. John 1:16

Saved by grace. Grace for the moment. There but by the grace of God go I. All of these sayings apply the graces offered to us by God the Father and Jesus Christ. But what is grace?

Grace is always a Divine gift that enables someone to endure, persevere, or be protected. When I need strength, I ask God for the grace to endure. When I need more faith, I ask for the grace to believe. Salvation is a gift given through grace: God enables a person to believe the gospel and be saved. Grace is not something that can be earned; it only comes as a gift to those who have been called by God to salvation. And really – would you turn down a gift from God?

Lord Jesus: Thank you for providing me with the graces that I need to endure each day.

April 30

The more I called them, the farther they went from me.
Hosea 11:2a

You know that someone doesn't love you when you call out to them, you know they hear you, and yet they don't answer or acknowledge your effort. This is what happened to God when He sought the attention and repentance of the Israelites. He sent prophet after prophet to them, but instead of listening to the message, they called the prophets liars and killed many of them.

A lot of people today are receiving messages from the Lord and sharing them publicly. These prophets are getting this same attitude from many folks as a reception for their efforts, although no one has yet been killed that I am aware of. Somehow, people today look at their life and don't see that some of the things they do are sinful; only the devil could have blinded them so well. Perhaps they are part of a group that has no concept of evil or the afterlife; whatever they want to do is okay so long as it hurts no one else. Sex, drugs, and rock-n-roll, as my old friends used to say. But sex does not come from God – love does. And addictions don't come from God – moderation does. Rock-n-roll – I think that came from Elvis Presley.

The point is, there are plenty of messages coming from the Lord these days. Give them a listen with an open mind and apply what is being said to the world around you as well as your own life. If you hear that still small voice speaking to you in your contemplation, make sure it's the Lord that you're hearing. We know that the devil masquerades as an angel of light, and he'd really love to keep from losing his control over you.

Lord Jesus: Open my heart and my mind to hear you speaking.

May

May 1

I called to the LORD with my mouth; praise was upon
my tongue. Had I cherished evil in my heart, the
LORD would not have heard. Psalm 66:17, 18

Many are the times when I have called upon the Lord for His help,
and He assisted me. Sometimes He delayed His answer, and I wonder
if it was because I was distant and cool in my relationship with Him.
I wasn't being intentionally absent, but sometimes I let the world get
between us. I often don't do a good job of keeping myself close to Him
when life gets demanding of my time. And the further I let myself drift
from Him and the more unclean things I harbor in my heart, the longer
it takes to get an answer – if I get one at all.

It's easy to offer praise when times are good, but how often have I taken
time to praise Him when I'm busy and tired? It's also easy to call upon
the Lord when we are struggling, but how often do we offer praise for
Him in the midst of our troubles before we ask Him for assistance?

Lord Jesus: Forgive me for my absence and cold-heartedness.

May 2

"If the world hates you, realize that it hated me first. If you
belonged to the world, the world would love its own; but
because you do not belong to the world, and I have chosen
you out of the world, the world hates you." John 15:18, 19

All over the world today there is a double standard. While nearly everyone enjoys seeing a person stand out and be radically different, the only ones who are accepted by the world at large are the ones who exhibit worldly traits. Jesus was radically different, and the authorities hated Him for His teachings. Why? Because He was undermining their positions of status, pointing out the flaws in their teachings, and (according to their view) threatening to change the beliefs handed down by Moses. In fact, He was fulfilling Moses' teachings and prophecies and leading the people back to the way of life that God intended from the start.

Today, if Jesus were to come, He would receive the same treatment – possibly worse. People have become so hard-hearted that they can say they follow Christ without adhering to His teachings in any way, shape, or form. They love their lives of sin and won't let go of their pleasures. They show up at some church on Sunday and engage in the social event that they've turned it into. I'm not saying all churches are this way, just some, so choose your worship center carefully. If all they preach is prosperity and good times, you need to move on. If the blood and sacrifice of Christ, repentance, and sanctification are not being taught, that church is dead. Get out! And when Jesus does come, these are the ones who will knock on the door and say, "Let us in," to which He will reply, "Away you evildoers. I never knew you" (Matthew 7:23).

Christianity isn't a choice of which sins to keep. It's a life of sacrificing all sins and drawing near to God the Father, God the Son, and God the Holy Spirit. It's a life that many will condemn for its exclusion of the hardened sinners – not because we don't want them, but rather because we won't tolerate apostasy and false worship. They talk about Jesus, but they don't really know him. If they did, they would change their behaviors. As Jesus said, "They hated me without cause." (John 15:25)

Lord Jesus: Keep my heart tuned to you and your word.

May 3

When his children see the work of my hands in his midst, they
shall keep my name holy; they shall reverence the Holy One
of Jacob, and be in awe of the God of Israel. Isaiah 29:23

Before I gave my life to God, I can't say honestly that I knew him. I
didn't understand Him or His purpose. And I can't say I ever had a
Sunday school teacher who checked with me to find out if I was learning
what they were trying to teach. God and Satan were simply names in
a story that was way bigger and longer than my mind could grasp at
that age.

Now that I have had close calls and first-hand experience with the Holy
Trinity, I have true understanding of what it means to be a Christian.
And the people who have entrusted their children to me expect me to
be able to explain the Father, the Son, and the holy Spirit in a way that
is meaningful and will at least start their kids on their journey with a
better foundation than I had. I hope and pray, every day, that I don't fail
them – for the children's sakes. I have to be able to tell them who God
is, how He works, what He expects, and how to communicate with Him
so that they will (hopefully) not make the same mistakes that I did in
my ignorance. At least they know where to look for answers. I want the
kids to have awe and reverence for the Father, the Son, and the holy
Spirit in order that they may keep them holy and be able to recognize
their works when they see them.

Lord Jesus: Help me to see the works of your hands so that I can
recognize you in my life.

May 4

Know this first of all, that in the last days scoffers will come
to scoff, living according to their own desires and saying,
"where is the promise of his coming? From the time when
our ancestors fell asleep, everything has remained as it
was from the beginning of creation." 2 Peter 3:3, 4

One thing there has always been plenty of throughout history is people who scoff at others for their beliefs. It's a reflection, I think, of those who lack imagination and can't see beyond their own nose. As an example, I give you Noah: I can just see the sinful men that God wanted to extinguish sitting on a log with their flagons of wine, laughing raucously, and deriding Noah for building such a huge boat on dry land. I wonder if they began to rethink their disbelief when the animals started showing up to ride along and the flood waters began to rise. Or perhaps they stood outside the door pounding to be let in.

I'd bet that everyone throughout history that has had an outside-of-the-box idea that was bigger than most people's dreams experienced this same kind of derision: Galileo, Columbus, Isaac Newton, Marie Curie, or Lazarus. Lazarus was dead until Jesus restored him. Do you suppose that there were people who met him later that weren't there that day who said it was just some kind of trick? I'd bet there were.

And so it will be until the end. Scoffers will come who won't believe in anything they can't see or touch. But that doesn't mean that it won't happen. It just means that they will be caught in their acts of self-indulgence right up to the end. The sign of the Son of Man will be seen in the heavens, people will be transformed right in front of their eyes, and it will be too late – just as the day that Noah went into the ark and the Lord closed the door.

Even today I hear Christians saying that there is no reason to think that Jesus could come soon, despite the fact that we're witnessing the signs that Jesus himself listed as indicators being manifested daily (Matt 24).

And the Jews are back in the homeland. There has never been a better time for a second coming.

Lord Jesus: I believe; help my disbelief!

May 5

When I brought you into the garden land to eat its
goodly fruits, you entered and defiled my land, you
made my heritage loathsome. Jeremiah 2:7

Have you ever done something nice for someone only to have them turn around and take advantage of your kindness and then turn their back on you? It seems that some people lack the ability to be grateful for those who bring blessings into their lives, while others simply are so self-centered that they only see someone for the value of what they bring to the table. It's what I learned at a very young age: some people are givers (me) while others are takers. The Toby Keith song comes to mind: "I wanna talk about me-e-e...." It would be an even cuter song if it wasn't so true about so many people!

The Israelites were this way with God. Despite everything He had done for them (freed them from slavery, gave them a spacious and bountiful land, protected them from hateful neighbors), they just couldn't remember that they had a part in the covenant that their forefathers (who didn't keep it either) had sworn at Mount Horeb after leaving Egypt. God promised to protect and provide blessings so long as they remained faithful to him, and curses would befall them should they forsake him.

When they arrived in the Promised Land, they were supposed to kill all of the native people and destroy their paganism, but they didn't do it. In the end, what God had warned them about came true: they turned from honoring Him to worshiping the pagan gods of the land. They had sex in the temples of these false gods and burned their children alive in sacrifices to them. Is it any wonder that God felt it necessary to thin out the herd? I bet He was having flashbacks to the days of Noah, regretting that He had made them. The promise that He had made to Abraham would stand, but He found it necessary to remove the cancer from among His people and start over.

Lord Jesus: Help me understand the delicate balance between giving and receiving, and the difference between just honoring your name and sincerely serving you and your kingdom.

May 6

The spirit of the Lord GOD is upon me, because the LORD has anointed me; He has sent me to bring glad tidings to the lowly, to heal the brokenhearted, to proclaim liberty to the captives and release to the prisoners, to announce a year of favor from the LORD and a day or vindication by our God, to comfort all who mourn. Isaiah 61:1, 2

I have been unsure of many things in my life, and sometimes I was apprehensive. Rarely was I fearful, for fear does not come from God. And while He always knows what is best, He rarely seems to let me know ahead of time what that is. But when He called me to step up my game and get into ministry, I wasn't surprised.

I wanted to be sure that I understood what I was feeling with regard to this leading, so I did what I've done for many years when I've needed guidance from Him: I asked. I made the statement, "Lord, if this is what you want me to do, tell me." Then I opened my Bible and started reading. The above scripture is the one He gave me, and in ignorance and faith, I accepted His call. Little did I know where it would take me.

I had always gotten very nervous when I had to get in front of a group and speak and, of course, that's what He wanted me to do. I ended up being the pastor in a small church that was affiliated with a food pantry/ mission, and every Sunday He used me to deliver His messages to the small flock that He had given me charge over. I spent many hours giving out food, sitting with ill parishioners at home and in the hospital, and leading others to hope and spiritual restoration. It wasn't an easy time in my life, but it was gratifying at a level that I never suspected existed within me.

Lord Jesus: Open my heart; enable me to hear you calling me to that special mission that you have for me.

May 7

I do not nullify the grace of God; for if justification comes through the law, then Christ died for nothing. Galatians 2:21

One of the hardest things to teach to my kids is the concept of grace. Most of them are young enough that they don't really understand the process of animal sacrifices and the need for redemption, so grace is almost undefinable. I think it was the same for the Hebrews when they came out of Egypt. They knew about 'gods', and some still knew about God from the time of Jacob and Joseph, but the idea of being governed by special laws was something unfamiliar to them.

After God brought them out of slavery and gave the laws to the Israelites, He knew that that system wouldn't exist forever. Two thousand years before Christ, in the days of Abram, God knew what the plan would be and how He would change the laws that He would later give to the people. They needed to understand what the process was so that when Jesus came they could make the conversion from the law and the sacrifices to the grace of God with Jesus becoming the ultimate, pure, sacrificial lamb.

But many didn't want that change. The phrase 'If it ain't broke, don't fix it' comes to mind, and I suspect that's how many of them felt. Jesus said that He came to fulfill the law and the prophets. Only those that were truly attentive to God's expectations would get the message and be converted from following the law to living a life in Christ. What many wanted was a warrior king who would deliver them from the tyranny of oppressors, not a loving pacifist who wanted to rescue them from the forces of the devil and from their own evil hearts.

Today, instead of trying to live in accordance with over five hundred guidelines in the law, you only have to remember two: love God, and love your neighbor.

Lord Jesus: You are the sacrificial lamb whose blood washes away my sins. Thank You!

May 8

So we are always courageous, although we know that while
we are at home in the body we are away from the Lord, for
we walk by faith, not by sight. 2 Corinthians 5:6, 7

Paul is someone that I would strive to be like, but I don't think I have the fortitude that he had. I have found, however, that courage comes out when you need it. It's not necessarily something you know you have, but there it is, just in time. It takes a certain level of courage to be a Christian in these times, though. Every time we turn around, we're shoved into an ever-decreasing realm of freedom. And until we are taken to be with the Lord, we have to trust that, no matter what the world does to us, God is still in control, and He won't allow anything to happen without His permission.

One of the parables that Jesus told was about the wheat and the weeds (Matthew 13:24-30). In the story, the workers (angels) wanted to go out into the field and remove the weeds (sinners), but the farmer would not allow them to for fear that they might uproot and destroy the wheat (righteous ones). All were allowed to grow to the fullness of the harvest time, and then they were separated. The wheat went into the barn (heaven), and the weeds went into the fire (hell).

If you are a Christian and walking by faith, trusting in God and not yourself, you are wheat. Here on earth, while we live, we wish to be away from the evils of this world and be with the Lord in heaven, but we must fulfill the purpose for which we were sent. I believe that there is someone for everyone to rescue, one grain of wheat for each weed. Have you found your weed?

Lord Jesus: Lead me to the one that you want me to rescue.

May 9

"Whoever has my commandments and observes them is the
one who loves me. And whoever loves me will be loved by my
Father, and I will love him and reveal myself to him."
John 14:21

When you love someone, you want to please them. Even Jesus. So if we love Jesus and want to please him, how come we spend so much time doing what we want instead of what He wants? "What does He want us to do?" you ask. Is it so hard? He wants us to fulfill the greatest commandments: love for God and love for neighbor. How does watching hours of TV or getting drunk on the weekend show love for either God or our neighbor? How about videos or computer games or working lots of hours without any thought for the kingdom? If you want to spend time on facebook, at least do some service while you're there. And if someone gets offended and wants to unfriend you, let them go – it's their loss. If they can't accept that you are Christian, maybe you're better off without them anyway.

Jesus gave us only one command – love one another. Everything we do should show love to someone. I can't say I'm always successful, but He always points out my shortfalls so that I am aware of my failings. It takes striving every moment to live this life that we are called to. And it isn't always easy, but it will be worth it in the end. As a gauge, count up each day how many things you do that aren't loving in some way, and then see how many tics you have at the end of the day. I know I would do better if I didn't have to drive anywhere. Nevertheless, I take full responsibility for my own bad behavior – I am the only one in the end who will have to account for it.

I have discovered that the more conscious I am of what I do, striving to be the child Jesus wants me to be, the more He speaks to me through the holy Spirit and directs my steps to be a better representative for Him.

Lord Jesus: Reveal yourself to me in the trials of each day, showing me how to love others more.

May 10

The earth is polluted because of its inhabitants
who have transgressed laws, violated statutes,
broken the ancient covenant. Isaiah 24:5

Wouldn't it be neat if you could walk up to a tiger and pet it like a housecat? Or reach out and take a songbird from a branch and have it serenade you from its perch on your finger? There might be a few rare instances where this is possible now, but mostly the relationship between man and nature is one of fear, antagonism, and abuse. The primary motive? Greed, of course; profiteering off the natural stores of fossil fuels; skins, horns, tusks and fins; fishing without restraint until the oceans and rivers are empty; genetically altered grains; and pollution and garbage. It is amazing to me that, now that we have the new recycle toters in our city, we have almost no trash going out from our house each week. Nearly everything we have goes in the recycle.

Big corporate America doesn't like me much. I like wholesome food grown from God's seeds. I don't use Styrofoam (petroleum-based) if I can help it. I filter out the fluorine in my drinking water. I like mom-and-pop shops for as many of my purchases as I can make. I like to be able to see the people whose pockets I line, and if I don't like their attitude, I shop elsewhere. I like to deal with people who believe like me, who treat people with respect (until they no longer deserve it), and who aren't out to make a buck, but rather a friend. For me, profits flow to those who are fair and friendly.

I don't know when it started exactly, but somewhere in the late 19th or early 20th century the people of our nation and the world took off down the path that leads away from God in very large numbers. And I know that the churches are full of hypocrites and sinners, but that is no excuse for not teaching children the basics of morality and the spirit of fairness. The effects of this trend are clear to see: hospitality is all but dead; it isn't safe to open your front door to a stranger, much less leave it unlocked; and the condition of the water and soil across the globe is appalling. But the saddest thing to me is the plight of the children: parents ignore them or leave them alone; they are kidnapped or fall into gangs or drug use or die from being left in a hot car for hours; some are murdered by their own parents or the live-in boy- or girl-friend. Why? What caused humanity to become so selfish and disrespectful? Are we so busy or selfish that we can't find time for those we are supposed to love and serve? Are we so absorbed with work that we can't let it go for the evening and spend time with our families? If you don't want that child, there is someone out there who does. Don't kill it – take it to a fire station. They will see that someone cares for the child you don't want.

God said that the earth was polluted in the days of Isaiah. I wonder what He says about it now? Isaiah prophesied an end to the nation of Israel because of the conditions of their hearts. What do you suspect He might be planning for our nation if we continue down this path?

Lord Jesus: Cleanse our hearts and our land.

May 11

"You know how to judge the appearance of the sky, but you
cannot judge the signs of the times." Matthew 16:3b

I know from experience that we only see what we want to see much of
the time. It seems to be a common human condition to want to avoid
that which displeases us or makes us feel unhappy or scared. And just
because we choose to ignore those things doesn't make them any less
real or threatening.

So it is with the state of the world today. There are many things going on
that smack of the end times in an uncanny fashion. And while I believe
that we are very close, I know people who think I'm being an alarmist. "It's
always been this way," they say – just as Peter predicted. (2 Peter 3:4) All
I know is that I'd rather be ready and wrong than wrong and unprepared.

It's a bit scary to read, but a good book to prepare you for what the
tribulation times could be like is <u>One Second After</u>, by William R.
Forstchen.[4] His story is a tale of what happens after an EMP bomb,
a possibility that is even closer to becoming truth than when I read
the book, given that North Korea and Iran are creeping ever closer
to rocket-borne nuclear capabilities. Look around and assess what
you see – not what you don't want to see – and then decide if some
cataclysmic preparations are order.

*Lord Jesus: Help me to see and understand the things going on
in the world today.*

May 12

But Moses said to God, "Who am I that I should go to Pharaoh
and lead the Israelites out of Egypt?" Exodus 3:11

Is it insecurity or fear that keeps us from serving the Lord when He
wants to send us on a mission? Probably both. We know from reading the

Bible that many of the prophets were put to death for prophesying things that the people, especially the kings and priests, did not want to hear, and so we fear speaking out for the Lord. Moses lived in fear of returning to Egypt since he had murdered an Egyptian guard – that's why he left. We also have a hard time believing that God would want someone like us (me) to speak for him. Why would the Creator of the universe want a little nobody/sinner/chicken like me to be His mouthpiece? Why indeed?

There isn't a single person on this planet that is without sin, so there is not one person that is better than another. Each of us has a unique background that gives us a special insight to something that the Lord wants us to share with a group of people. Moses may have murdered an Egyptian soldier and run from justice, but he also had a unique relationship with the pharaoh's household – he grew up there and is likely remembered by someone, possibly even pharaoh. And this is where Pharaoh's head trash (and Moses') and the court magicians come into play.

Moses is just another man to pharaoh, not a follower of God when he ran off 40 years ago, and he likely had some training in the mystical arts from his time as a member of the royal family. Pharaoh probably put off some of the miracles of God as magical tricks. Aaron, Moses' Hebrew brother and a slave, went with Moses to Pharaoh to speak since Moses is thought to be a stutterer. (Exodus 4:10)

As the Lord began to destroy the food supply and infest the people, the Bible says that Pharaoh was ready to let the Hebrews go, but the Lord hardened his heart and stopped their release. Why? Maybe He wasn't done proving all that He wanted to teach the people and Pharaoh. Stories about what happened in Egypt traveled before the Israelites to the Promised Land. The people there were afraid of them and their God (Joshua 2:9-11), a useful fear for when the Hebrews eventually arrived in Canaan.

So: Why can't God use you? Sinner? No problem. Stutterer? No Problem. Afraid? No problem. The only thing stopping God from using you is your own head trash. Let it go. Look at what happened to the disciples when the holy Spirit came to them in the upper room. They became apostles and "spoke boldly in the name of the Lord." (Acts 4:31) Why me? Why not me?

Lord Jesus: Remove my head trash and the fears that prevent you from using me.

May 13

Tell the rich in the present age not to be proud and not to rely on so uncertain a thing as wealth but rather on God, who richly provides us with all things for our enjoyment. 1 Timothy 6:17

Many people have strived all of their life to accumulate a large nest egg for their retirement. I hope they get to enjoy it. Here is something else to keep in mind, however: the Federal Reserve is printing money at an alarming rate. It is supposed to be fed into the economy through the banking system as consumer loans. The banks however, are not loaning the money to their members – they are buying stocks for a fast cash profit, driving up market prices[5], and setting up the economy for an even greater fall than the ones we experienced in 2007 and 2008. Can you and your money survive another failure in the economy like that? Or worse, what if the economy collapses completely? What will you do when all of your hard-earned funds are just numbers in a dead computer file?

When the slide begins, there will be runs on the banks by people trying to get as much of their money out as they can. But banks today only allow about $2500 to be withdrawn without a one-week notice to bring in more funds from the Fed. If you have $10,000 in your combined accounts, you can only get $2500 of your money and will likely never see the rest of it again. This is what happened in the crash in 1929 and also in Greece in 2012[6].

A lot of people think I'm crazy for my views, but I am absolutely certain that the economy cannot continue on the path it is on. Reconsider how you're storing your funds. They might be more valuable stored as emergency food supplies and other stores of preparedness items. Pray to God to show you what to buy and where to store it for safe-keeping. He is the only one who will never lead you astray. And keep this fact in mind: the next year of Sabbath rest on the Jewish calendar, the **Shemitah** (pronounced Shmeeta), starts in September 2014 and ends in September 2015. This is the seventh year proscribed by God in the law when there is no farming, people eat whatever grows on the land, and debts are wiped away. (Lev 25:1-7) Did you know that your money is a debt for the bank? And the last **Shemitah** started in 2007 and ended in 2008. Sound familiar?

Lord Jesus: Show me what's coming and how to prepare.

May 14

You did not step into the breach, nor did you build a
wall about the house of Israel that would stand firm
against attack on the day of the Lord. Ezekiel 13:5

This is a verse that the Lord sent me to get me moving when I *knew* that I wasn't doing as much as I should to serve and speak out. He wants His children to rescue others from harmful practices, intercede in prayer to strengthen the works of the holy Spirit, beg for mercy for them, step into the breach to defray His wrath, and bring blessings to those most in need. This was the calling of the prophets – to step onto the front lines of the battle, speak the word of the Lord, and rescue the spiritually dying; in essence, to be a watchman.

When the Lord called to Jeremiah, the prophet was very young. Jeremiah objected that he wasn't old enough. The Lord told him that he was to speak out whether people listened or not, and He told Ezekiel the same thing. It's not for us to decide if they will listen, but whether or not we will carry their blood on our head for not speaking up. We have to relieve ourselves of the obligation to do whatever it takes to change someone's mind. We have to give people the information they need to make an informed decision about heaven and hell, and then keep on teaching them how to get stronger in their faith. God calls it 'building a wall that will stand firm against attack.'

How long had you been a Christian when that attack came that you were finally able to withstand? It took me a long time. I didn't have any reinforcement personnel in my life. I was trying to do it on my own, and I was failing miserably. And this goes back to what I said before about having a prayer/accountability partner. No one is meant to walk this journey alone – that's why we have the Church. And not everyone in the Church is a Christian, so choose your associates wisely. The Church is not safe from infiltration by unclean spirits.

Step into the breach. Rescue your friends and family. Build a wall around them to keep them safe to the end. And never lose hope. The day of the LORD will come, and no one should be caught off guard.

Lord Jesus: Show me how to rescue and keep safe my family and friends.

May 15
They are to slander no one, to be peaceable, considerate,
exercising all graciousness toward everyone. Titus 3:2

I don't know anyone who fits this description – not even me. Why is it so hard to hold my tongue and refrain from yelling and saying bad things about people who zip around me, cut me off, slam on the brakes so that they can turn, and make me slam on my brakes too? The problem with this scenario is that I shoot myself, not them, when I act that way. I need to be more forgiving when it comes to my driving behavior. And let's face it – occasionally, I'm the one doing something stupid that people yell at me for. Granted, I don't do it on purpose, but I have no way of knowing that they are any different. It's not like I'm in a big hurry; I rarely run so far behind that I would chance dying instead of making it safely to my destination.

So the question remains: Why am I so angry at people who are obviously rude and disrespectful? Maybe because they get me to act like them when I know I should be forgiving, no matter what. But that's not how we're wired, is it? Somewhere in our journey through sanctification we have to learn to practice what we preach and bless instead of curse – or at least learn to keep our mouth shut.

So here is your challenge for today: try to go the whole day without yelling or getting mad at anyone. And remember: one breath at a time. Be a good example of what a Christian should be. Why? Because you never know who is watching. You may be the only Christian they ever meet – be a good one – peaceable, considerate, and gracious to all.

Lord Jesus: Help me to hold my tongue and bless those who distress me.

May 16

Do not the tears that stream down her cheek cry out
against him that causes them to fall? Sirach 35:15

I remember the first time I read this verse. It isn't in the Protestant Bible, so I wasn't young when I came across it. But it really speaks to me since I am divorced, and it wasn't my idea. It's okay. I'm glad now that he's gone since I found out afterward who he really was. I cried so many tears up to the time that I found out those hurtful things; and then I cried some more, but those tears were for disappointment. I asked God how someone could make so many promises and then break every one of them? How could someone treat their spouse with so much disdain and never speak a word of their feelings or misgivings? Why? Why? Why? And I even asked the ex to tell me before he filed, but he refused.

It doesn't matter now that he's married and divorced again. I can finally say that I've let it go after ten years. And I wonder what God will say when the ex stands before Him and has to give an account for all the tears he made me and others cry? The Lord holds all of those tears in His hands. He knows where each one came from and who caused it to fall. For me, it's now 'forgive and forget'. The forgiving was easy after knowledge came. The forgetting is the hard part.

Lord Jesus: Help me remember the lesson and forget the one who caused me to learn it.

May 17

"Do not think that I have come to bring peace upon the earth. I
have come to bring not peace but the sword. For I have come to
set a man 'against his father, a daughter against her mother, and
a daughter-in-law against her mother-in-law; and one's enemies
will be those of his own household.'" Matthew 10:34-36

Jesus didn't meet anyone's expectations of what the Messiah would be when He arrived. Even after He had taught the disciples for three years, they still wanted to know, as He was ascending back into heaven, "Are you at this time going to restore the kingdom to Israel?" They were still thinking with their flesh and not their spirits. He had brought the kingdom to them; all they had to do was accept what He taught them and give up their old ways of thinking.

Sometimes it's a good thing to give up our old ways of thinking – that's how we grow in sanctification. But some people don't want to let go of their sinful pleasures and find excuses to stay just the way they are. Others will change the way they think, but support the wrong ideals in the name of love. It's hard to know how to love someone who lives in sin when they have professed a belief in Christ; when we know that they should be giving up their sins, but they persist because 'God wants them to be happy.' I haven't found a single verse that says that. And Jesus certainly didn't promise that we would be happy. He said we would be persecuted because of him. I can't help but wonder: Did they really get saved? Can't they see that the Bible clearly teaches against those behaviors? That's right – they haven't read the Bible. They are relying on someone else to tell them what's in it. Don't make that mistake – read it yourself. These are treacherous times. You can't afford to be wrong about what God expects in this day and age.

The days are coming when the families of the world will split into those who support the government and its progressive policies and those who support the teachings of Jesus. The two sides will be polar opposites when it comes to their ideals about church life and worship, gay marriage, abortion, contraception, and social programs. Jesus said that we are not of this world if we believe in him, and those of the world will hate us. Sounding familiar yet?

Lord Jesus: Help me to change the hearts and minds of those around me to accept your teachings.

May 18
Blessed is the one who does not walk in step with the
wicked or stand in the way that sinners take or sit
in the company of mockers. Psalm 1:1 (NIV)

Back in the days of my youth, there was a group of us who were barflies – always out looking for the next party or the coolest bar to hang out in. I travelled with this lot and was always out of my element. I don't know why I ended up in that group, but I was never happy with the party scene. First of all, I don't like crowds; second, I was always the worst introvert that was ever created. People who know me today would never guess that I was so socially awkward. I guess that's why I didn't get away from that group for so long – I knew that I was accepted with them, even though I wasn't happy with the lifestyle. What was interesting, though, was that when I was in a bar I would bring up God and Jesus in conversation. I would ask people if they thought that they were real and if they had met them. I got some really interesting answers, but what I got mostly was strange looks. And the crazy thing was that I didn't even go to church then, I had not gone for many years, and I wasn't saved. Guess He was at work on me even through those really dry years.

I spent ten years in a relationship that took me to bars and parties, got me arrested once and cost me a huge chunk of my collegiate grade-point average. I was never truly happy. I wanted out, but I couldn't figure out a way to extricate myself. I kept falling into the ways of the wicked and spending time with sinners. I was always depressed and unhappy knowing that there was a better life for me somewhere else, although I was stymied as to how to find it. Many of the people I hung around with (mostly the guys) were more than happy to stay in that life, a dead-end trip with no promising future. I didn't understand it then, and I don't understand it now. The girls who wanted more from life dumped them and moved on. The guy I was with wouldn't allow me to leave or stay gone. I considered suicide – I had lost hope. Interestingly, my mom was watching a profiler tv program one day, and I heard one of the characters describing a sociopath – the traits were an exact description of the guy I couldn't get away from. Happily, in an answer to prayer, another man came along and rescued me.

Listen to the voice of experience: if you are in a relationship that causes you to be subjected to a lifestyle that you feel is wrong, GET OUT OF IT! You are not meant to be there. The Lord may not like divorce, but neither does He like fornication, abuse, oppression, or perversion. His mercy is great, and He doesn't like it when His children suffer at the hands of sinners who will likely never become believers. Get out, and repent of your former way of life.

Lord Jesus: Thank you for rescuing me from a dead-end life and for giving me hope and a future.

May 19

And Mary kept all these things, reflecting on them in her heart.
Luke 2:19

I love Mary! Every morning when I wake up, with eyes closed, I like to envision myself in heaven saying 'Good morning!' to Jesus, the Lord God, and the Holy Spirit. One day, as I was performing this morning ritual, Mary showed up, and she's been there ever since. She didn't speak, she was just there. She's a tiny little lady, barely five feet tall. Sometimes she wears all white, sometimes a blue dress with a white mantle and veil. As I would address the Trinity, Jesus would be to my left and she would be to His left. And then one morning something else happened. After my greetings (I added her to the list), Jesus took a step backward, took His mother by the shoulders and moved her next to me, and then stepped into place at her left. There was no explanation, but I got the impression that He wanted me to get to know her. And that's where they continue to appear to me each morning for their greeting.

I figured the best way to get to know her was to start praying the Rosary. I had put it off thinking that I didn't want to be a 'Marian.' What I discovered in the Rosary is Jesus at a much deeper level that I thought I could never reach. Yes, Mary is there as well. And I have a new-found respect for her. She accepted the motherhood of the Messiah despite the fact that she could have been stoned for having been pregnant outside of marriage; her husband could have left her alone; and knowing that her Son would be grossly mistreated and murdered someday.

I like to contemplate what life with Jesus was like for her, and this verse has always been one of my favorites, even before I began the Rosary. For me, I think one of the best days for her was the wedding feast at Cana. I picture her standing in the background out of sight after she has sent the servants to her Son so that He can fix the shortage of wine. It was the height of embarrassment and one of the greatest social gaffes to run out of wine at your wedding feast, and it would seem that this family was so important to Mary that she risked alienating Jesus to get

Him to rectify the problem by the only means possible – a miracle. And He did not disappoint her. I never really stopped to think about how much He loved her. She was likely very young when He was born, maybe only about 15 years old. They basically grew up together. A closer relationship between mother and son is unlikely – they are the paradigm for the perfect mother and son in my mind.

Things she stored up in her heart for contemplation: Gabriel's visit, her time with Elizabeth, the birth of Jesus, the shepherds' arrival, the prophecies in the temple at His presentation, His first personal prayer, challenging the scribes in the temple at age 12, His first day of work with Joseph, His baptism, the day He manifested himself in the synagogue, His wisdom teachings, and all of His miracles.

Lord Jesus: Thank you for sharing your mother with me.

May 20
After the earthquake there was fire – but the LORD was not in the fire. After the fire there was a tiny whispering sound.
1 Kings 19:12

If the Lord were prone to shouting, everyone could hear him. But that's not how He likes to operate. Learning how to be quiet and pay attention has been a big challenge in my life of faith. Trust came easily; tithing is a no-brainer; and sharing what He has done for me is almost second-nature. But praying every day in a meaningful way and waiting for the recognizable response is a whole 'nother matter.

I suspect that the reason that the Lord chooses to operate in this fashion is that He is looking for people who are truly interested in hearing from him, those who want to be close to Him and enjoy a relationship with Him. For those who just say, "Help me!" in times of crisis and don't speak to Him otherwise, I think He turns a semi-deaf ear. He does not want us to call Him when we do stupid things that put us in peril and then expect Him to rescue us. This is what Jesus intended when He quoted the scripture to the devil from the parapet of the temple: "Do not put the Lord your God to the test" (Matthew 4:7, Deuteronomy 6:16). He wants full-time disciples, not part-time or fair-weather friends.

There is a saying that travels around facebook that reads something to the effect that, if you're looking for the Lord during a trial in your life, remember that the teacher is always silent during a test. You can look for Him in the storm, the earthquake, and the fire, but you'll likely only hear Him after the turmoil has passed. While you're struggling to pass your test, also remember that He only allows what you can successfully withstand. However, the test is designed to expand your limits, so expect to struggle and grow from the experience. 'What doesn't kill you makes you stronger'.... (Sounds like Kelly Clarkson in my head.) I know people who take offense at that statement. They don't think that a loving God should put His children to the test. But Jesus said that troubles come to those who follow Him. If you're not undergoing any tests, then you're no threat to the devil; he already has you where he wants you. The question is, are you where you want to be? In the devil's pocket? Or in Jesus'?

The Lord has promised to punish those who are complacent (Isaiah 32:9; Amos 6:1; Zephaniah 1:12; Rev 3:16). This is something He continues to tell me repeatedly in my seeking after His will. It's time to get off of the fence and pick a side. And be sure to listen for that still, small voice – it will lead you where you need to go.

Lord Jesus: Teach me to be quiet so that I can hear your voice.

May 21
"Watch and pray that you may not undergo the test. The spirit is willing but the flesh is weak." Mark 14:38

Jesus said this to Peter, James, and John in the garden of Gethsemane between His first and second requests to the Lord God to take away the need for Him to die on the cross. He had to wake them up to say it. They were clueless as to the events that were coming in just a few short minutes, much as we are throughout much of our lives. We walk around with our head in the clouds and are oblivious to the potential or impending disasters that lie ahead in our lives. Jesus wanted them to be 'prayed up', in touch with the Father so that they could be led to do the right thing when the time came.

I believe that, as the Divine Son, He knew when He agreed to come here to fulfill the role of Messiah that the cross would have to happen. But as a man, the idea of the suffering that He would have to endure to finish His mission was horrifying. He had His own test to pass; the disciples' tests were yet to come. It is unclear which test Jesus is referring to here. We know that He told Peter that Satan had asked to sift the disciples. Jesus knew Peter was going to fail, and told him to turn back and strengthen the brothers afterward. (Luke 22:31, 32) Failure isn't the end of salvation unless you allow it to be, and Jesus prayed that Peter would not lose his faith along with his test.

Is this the test Jesus is referring to in the Mark citation? I don't have a definitive answer to that question. But we can apply this directive to our lives. We can pray for the strength to bypass the test before the brunt of the trial arrives. Is this possible? Nothing is impossible for God, and the only determiner I can see for this scenario is your relationship to him. It is His decision to set aside conditions if He believes you can see and learn the full lesson without struggling through the mire. It can't hurt to ask, but don't be surprised if the answer is 'No.' After all, that was His answer to His own Son.

Lord Jesus: Thank you for passing your test and enduring a horrifying death so that I could be saved.

May 22

Things of the past I foretold long ago, they went forth
from my mouth, I let you hear of them; then suddenly
I took action, and they came to be. Isaiah 48:3

It surprises me how many people refuse to read the book of Revelation. They are afraid of what it says. The past 2 days I have talked about tests. The worst and greatest test to come through all of history is outlined in the book of Revelation. It is a guide to the things that the Lord will allow to happen, the culmination of centuries of sinfulness brought to an end. Yes, the events are terrifying, but this is no excuse to not read them and be prepared.

Jesus said that when the end comes, it will be as in the days of Noah: people will be eating and drinking and getting married right up until the end comes. He's saying that there are those who will be oblivious to the end of their lives and their impending judgment. I think a lot of people think they will have time to clean up their act before He arrives. But how will you know when he's coming if you can't recognize the signs? And how will you avoid the beast if you don't know how to recognize him? It's just like Noah: he spent 100 years building the ark and likely warned the people to repent. And then the rain came, and the Lord closed Noah and the animals in the ark. I see those same people standing outside beating on the side of the boat begging to get in, but it's too late. They didn't heed the warnings from Noah, so they died for their sins.

Jesus said that the day would come like a thief in the night and catch people unaware. (Matthew 24:42-44) But He is not talking about us Christians. He gave us the signs in the Olivet Sermon that will tell us when His arrival is near. (Matthew 24:4-35) Those who will be caught off guard are the ones who don't know or serve him. God tells us through the prophet Isaiah that He has foretold what would happen. He will suddenly take action at some point and cause those prophecies to be fulfilled. Will you be ready?

Lord Jesus: Thank you for prophets and prophecies.

May 23

Keep yourselves in the love of God and wait for the mercy of
our Lord Jesus Christ that leads to eternal life. Jude 21

There is an old adage that says, 'Absence makes the heart grow fonder.'
The idea behind this is that a person has become so enamored with
another that they pine for them more and more as the time between
visits passes.

Jesus feels this way about us – He longs for the day when we will return
to His side in heaven. But do we feel the same way about him? We should.
There is no more important person to the Christian than Jesus. If it weren't
for His sacrifice, there would be no salvation and no hope for our future.

So here is the challenge: how close are you to Jesus? Do you visit Him
in prayer? Do you visit Him in your mind and see Him smiling and
welcoming you with a big hug like a brother you haven't seen in ages?
That's what I see when I visit Him in prayer. He longs for the times that
I come to see Him. And having that relationship with Him makes it
easier to approach with head hung in shame when I fail to do the things
I should, or do things that I should not, and say, 'I'm sorry.' I need Jesus
and His mercy. I need His love. I need the hope that comes from our
relationship as I await His promised return. Thankfully, I have it.

Lord Jesus: I long for your love and your presence.

May 24

Am I then to punish your daughters for their harlotry, your
daughters-in-law for their adultery? You yourselves consort
with harlots, and with prostitutes you offer sacrifice! So must
a people without understanding come to ruin. Hosea 4:14

I recently had a booth at an outdoor event for my business. There were
other vendors up the way who were handing out 'goodies' to kids in order

to get attention. I did not witness the event that started the fracas, but I heard a young child scream out a very ugly and profane statement. I don't know if it was aimed at her mother or one of the vendors. Nevertheless, the idea that one so young could explode in such anger and say such horrible things is appalling. The mother screamed back, "You are so embarrassing!" As if she had no idea how the child could say something like that in public. I suppose the mother might not be the one whom the child learned the statement from, but she likely learned it at home. Kids don't just pull such foul language out of thin air.

It's pretty obvious that the wrong morals and principles are being taught in this home. I feel for the child – she will likely never change from what she is now. Her personality is already developed, and I would not be surprised to see her face on the evening news broadcast in a few years. It really gets me how people can't figure out how their kids go so wrong when this kind of stuff goes on.

The Lord said through the prophet Hosea that such people who are living in sin and teaching their sins to their children will come to ruin. This was in the 8th century b.c. So I guess it's true – history does, in fact, repeat itself.

Lord Jesus: Help me to see what I'm teaching my kids.

May 25

In this is love: not that we have loved God, but that he loved us and sent his Son as expiation for our sins. 1 John 4:10

How much does God love us that He sent Jesus to die in order for us to be reconciled to himself? Additionally, how much does Jesus love us to give up His place in heaven and come here to live as a man: hungry, thirsty, trips to the latrine, exhaustion, disappointment, betrayal, torture, and murder? He experienced the full range of human emotions and physical needs, and yet He persevered. I always wonder if He made it through because of His prayer life, or if it was His extraordinary power because of His divinity. Maybe both? Regardless, the amount of love exhibited by both our Father and His Son is beyond my comprehension. I always try to love others, but I frequently fail. Thankfully, they never do.

Lord Jesus: Teach me to love as you do.

May 26

A jealous and avenging God is the LORD, an avenger is
the LORD, and angry; The LORD brings vengeance on his
adversaries, and lays up wrath for his enemies. Nahum 1:2

If you haven't read the whole Bible, you should. It is very enlightening; full of miracles and amazing people who were rewarded for trusting in the Lord. And not everyone who was rescued was one of His chosen people. For instance, Rahab was a prostitute in Jericho who assisted the Israelite scouts when they came to see what was in the Promised Land. She knew by looking at them that they didn't belong. As reward for helping them, she and her family were spared – everyone who was in her home when the Israelites attacked the city. She also became an ancestor of Jesus and a part of our salvation history. This gives me hope!

Throughout the Bible, the Lord God destroys His enemies or sends them packing, even if those enemies are His own chosen people. He doesn't like sharing our attention with things or people that are keeping us from Him. The first Commandment is the Lord telling His people that He will not tolerate His children following other gods or making images and bowing down to them. He wants to be number One in every life, the first one we turn to and our last line of defense. For many people, God is far down on the list of priorities after such things as spouse, kids, work, vacation, or entertainment. He doesn't mind if we recreate so long as we remember Him faithfully, both while we're home and while we're away. And just because you're on vacation doesn't excuse you from church.

If God is far down on your list, remember that He is jealous and that He just may rearrange your priorities for you if you can't move Him up the list on your own.

Lord Jesus: Help me to understand how to rearrange my priorities to move you up the list.

May 27

Do you not know that your body is a temple of the holy Spirit within you, whom you have from God, and that you are not your own? For you have been purchased at a price. Therefore glorify God in your body. 1 Corinthians 6:19, 20

Before I became Catholic, I did not understand why the Catholic Church always used crucifixes rather than an empty cross. I kept thinking that they were keeping Jesus there when we know that he's not. I don't think I ever questioned anyone about why this is so. And if they covered it in RCIA class, I must have been distracted. But what I have discovered in my seeking after truth is that, for me, Jesus on the cross keeps the cost of my salvation ever in the front of my mind. His sacrifice was a horrifying experience that He went through for me to be saved because He loves me that much.

He did it for you as well. Have you thanked Him for it lately? What else do you do to show Him that you are grateful for His compassion and faithfulness? When you professed your belief in Him as Savior, did you walk away and not think any more about Him, as I did? I'm ashamed to say that now, but I do so in order that you can see that there is hope for anyone.

When we become a child of God, we are called to live a different life than we did before. Some take longer to get there. The important thing to recognize is that, if you're still breathing, He is ready to bring you to a life that gives glory to Him. And when you live for him, He gives you more peace than you could ever imagine. (John 14:27, Philippians 4:7) If you are saved, you no longer belong to yourself – you belong to Jesus. Would an outsider know that from watching you every day?

Lord Jesus: Never let me forget the price of my salvation.

May 28
For blest is the wood through which justice comes about.
Wisdom 14:7

I was really surprised when I first read this verse. The book of Wisdom is quite old, and yet here is a reference to the cross. Or is it? It isn't the gavel from the courts like we use today. Back in those days, a sandal was handed over to secure an agreement. And they didn't have courtrooms – the elders gathered and sat at the gates of a town.

The Romans were known for their cruel assassinations of rebels in the empire. One of their favorite methods of execution was crucifixion. Sometimes they cut down trees and made crosses out of them, and other times they simply nailed the hands of the convicted person to the branches and their ankles to the side of the tree. The person would hang there until dead from starvation, hypothermia, or wild animal.

It's hard to think of the wood of the cross being blest. But I believe that if that wood was capable of any sentiment at all, it cried out in agony over the nailing of our Lord and Savior to it. Then it rejoiced that the deliverance of all creation would soon come to pass. Soon, of course, is relative: from Adam and Eve until the day Christ was resurrected, some 4000 years, there was anticipation in all wild, created things and the chosen people of God for the sign of their deliverance. Some recognized it, some did not.

The wood of the cross was blessed to have the Savior of the world hung upon it. Jesus was blessed because He persevered to hang upon it. Be blessed yourself by kneeling before it to pray and learn of the one who died there to save you.

Lord Jesus: Teach me the truth of your sacrifice upon the cross.

May 29

I, then, a prisoner for the Lord, urge you to live in a manner
worthy of the call you have received. Ephesians 4:1

Everyone whom the Lord calls is to set themselves apart from the practices of the world, to be in the world but not of the world. We are called to become like Christ. I somehow don't think that Jesus was partying every weekend and getting drunk, complaining about His neighbors, stealing office supplies from work, or amassing large amounts of stuff to fill a house that was bigger than He needed. Oh yeah. He didn't have an office or a house or stuff. He did drink some wine, but no one ever said He got the least bit out of control. Everyone was His neighbor, and He always tried to uplift people and improve those whom He met.

The only people He ever said bad things about were the scribes, Pharisees, and Sadducees, and that was because they were hypocrites. They weren't living up to their call. They were supposed to be leaders of the people – examples for them to follow. There were a couple who heard His call and answered (Nicodemus and Joseph of Arimethea), but most just plotted how to kill Him before He could destroy their comfy life of apostasy. That is not the life we are called to as Christians. We are to be examples of good living: helping others, caring for the needs of the homeless and destitute, and generally loving our neighbors – all of them.

Lord Jesus: Show me my calling and help me to fulfill it.

May 30

For thus said the Lord GOD, the Holy One of Israel:
By waiting and by calm you shall be saved, in quiet
and in trust your strength lies. Isaiah 30:15a

What is faith? Ten years ago I would have had a very different answer than I have today. Isn't it interesting how time and life change the way we perceive things? My answer today would include the words from the scripture for today: patience (waiting), peace (calm), a contemplative spirit (quiet), and trust, along with forgiving, understanding, joy, and kindness. In summary, it's the fruit of the Spirit – the gifts that come as a result of living and loving and losing and seeking. It's trying something only to find out it's a waste of time and effort except for the lesson learned.

Isaiah is an interesting character and the perfect prophet for this passage to come through. He served the Lord 'naked and barefoot' for three years, when naked was the height of disgrace. I prefer to think he wore a loincloth, but I really don't know for sure. Either way, he had to really trust God to suffer such disgrace in the community. (I wonder what his wife thought.) And of course his message wasn't palatable to the people. He spoke the word of the Lord that condemned the people for their sinfulness and predicted the exile to Babylon.

Believing that Jesus is Messiah is not enough – you have to continue the conversion. Put your faith to work and learn the fruits of the Spirit, and therein you will find your sanctification.

Lord Jesus: Open my heart to learn from your Spirit.

May 31

It forced all the people, small and great, rich and poor, free
and slave, to be given a stamped image on their right hands
or their foreheads, so that no one could buy or sell except
one who had the stamped image of the beast's name or the
number that stood for its name. Revelation 13:16, 17

It surprises me how many people there are that refuse to acknowledge
that there are evil forces in the world. It seems that some believe that
if you acknowledge their existence you give them power over your life.
The way I see it, if you don't acknowledge them, you can't get rid of them
because they are there whether you acknowledge them or not.

Someday, the greatest evil in the universe will take control of this
planet in the guise of a man. My guess is that the same ones that won't
recognize demonic spirits won't recognize this guy either, at least until
this event mentioned in Revelation happens. It will then be hard to deny
who is in charge at that time.

When Jesus taught His disciples about the end times (Matthew 24 and
Luke 21), He talked about the birth pains: famine, disease, and war.
We already have those things in the world, but by the time the antichrist
takes over, the global conditions will be catastrophically bad. He will
seek to control the world's people and eliminate black market activities
by requiring the mark that will allow us to transact business. It isn't too
hard to imagine. The technology exists now that will allow you to walk
through an RFID station in a grocery store and be charged for every item
in your cart without going through a checkout lane. It's not just an id tag,
it's a locator. If you take it, you will not be able to hide from his forces. If
you don't take it, you won't be able to buy food or medicine or be treated
at a hospital. You won't be able to work. If you are planning to keep away
from this mark, you'd better start stocking up now – just in case.

***Lord Jesus: Show us the condition of the world through your
eyes so that we can be ready when the lawless one comes.***

June

June 1

You became haughty of heart because of your beauty; for the sake of splendor you debased your wisdom. I cast you to earth, so great was your guilt; I made you a spectacle in the sight of kings. Ezekiel 28:17

This particular verse is in the 'Against the King of Tyre' section of Ezekiel. The Lord sends me here when He wants to tell me that He is planning to allow a strike against a nation. And if you read the whole section, you'll find that, while this may be about the king of the island nation of Tyre, it is also where we learn about Satan when he was an angel. Check it out sometime.

Vanity is a sin (one that I used to have in abundance) that leads many people away from the Lord. There are many who would say that it is harmless, but I think the Lord disagrees. He made me just the way He wants me to look: hair color, eye color, nail color and bone structure. Spending excessive time and money on changing the way we look takes away from assets that we could be using in service. If I want to be a curly-topped platinum blonde, how does that edify my neighbor or give glory to God?

I'm not talking so much about an occasional or minor change to one's appearance for fun. I'm talking about the constant use of makeup; frequent haircuts, color and highlighting; fake nails and fill-ins on a regular basis; over-flowing closets; or spending hours every week at the gym or working out in some manner because of an anorexic fixation. I have to question why you think you need all of these fixes to your appearance. Who are you trying to impress? And why do you need to?

And if you think you need all of these things to make you look good, then maybe your problem isn't your appearance – maybe it's your self-esteem. And where does it end?

I'm glad to say that I outgrew my self-esteem shortage and am now finally comfortable in my own skin. It doesn't matter what people think of your appearance. You can't make everyone happy, so stop trying. Please the Lord – He's the only one that counts. And remember what happened to Lucifer when he let his vanity and pride get out of control.

Lord Jesus: Grant me understanding that allows me to be content with the attributes you have given me.

June 2

Rather, their thoughts were rendered dull, for to this present day the same veil remains unlifted when they read the old covenant, because through Christ it is taken away. To this day in fact, whenever Moses is read, a veil lies over their hearts, but whenever a person turns to the Lord the veil is removed.
2 Corinthians 3:14-16

Paul spoke in his day of those whose hearts were veiled by their adherence to the old covenant. They did not accept that God had sent His Son to rescue the world, and so their hearts were hardened against their own salvation.

There was a time when I tried to read the Bible, and I couldn't understand it. Then I was saved. And after that, the day came when I truly desired understanding and asked to receive it. The Lord is faithful to reward those who seek to understand Him and His word, and He grants insight to those who ask for it. He lifted the veil that shadowed my heart's understanding.

There is so much more to life than just going through the motions; in all things, but especially in our spiritual lives. Reading the Bible, understanding it, and learning to apply it in everyday use has been one of the greatest joys in my life. It's interesting how a given passage comes to mind when something happens in the course of a day.

I have discovered that each of us is our own greatest obstacle in our journey to salvation and sanctification. We can only grow as far or as fast as our heart and mind will allow. It is our own head trash that veils our heart and stops us from receiving God's graces. Let go of the limitations in your mind. Reach out to God and allow Him to open your heart and mind to receive grace, wisdom, and understanding, and you'll soon find that the possibilities for your life are endless.

Lord Jesus: Open my heart and mind to the possibilities that stem from my faith in you.

June 3
God's way is unerring; the LORD's promise is tried and true;
he is a shield for all who trust in him. Psalm 18:31

According to the website Bibleinfo.com[7] one person has claimed that there are 3573 promises in the Bible[8]. I haven't counted them myself, but I claim each one – the promises for abundance and the promises for condemnation if I fail. Why do I claim the latter? Simple: there cannot be God's blessings without acknowledgment that He will withdraw those blessings if I walk away from Him and His kingdom. (Deuteronomy 28: 15, 16)

There are a lot of preachers these days who preach about God's promises for abundance, but they forget to tell their congregations that there are conditions for receiving His blessings. First, you have to be saved – not just believing that Jesus is the Son of God and Messiah, but accepting Him as your personal Lord and Savior. James wrote that even the demons believe in God, but that knowledge will not save them. On the contrary, they shudder because they know they stand condemned. (James 2:19) Second, you have to continue to recognize His lordship and serve Him once you're saved. (James 2:20-24) And third, you should be undergoing a constant process of self-examination for the purpose of sanctification which is growing in holiness and letting go of sinful behaviors.

Getting saved and then continuing to lead a life of willful sins brings greater condemnation upon one's head than if you were never saved at all. (See 2 Peter 2.) Why do you think the dominant thought in the book of Proverbs is 'the fear of the LORD'? That phrase appears in the book 14 times.

For those who believe and desire to grow in holiness, God is a shield. What does that mean? A shield is an instrument of war, one which deflects the strikes from the adversary's sword or stops arrows. It is protection from things that cause death. God is our shield when we believe and trust in His promises – all of them.

Lord Jesus: Thank you for protecting me.

June 4

As you enter a house, wish it peace. If the house is worthy, let
your peace come upon it; if not, let your peace return to you.
Matthew 10:12, 13

This is one of the things that Jesus directed the seventy-two disciples to do when He sent them off to preach the kingdom to the communities of Israel. I can think of nothing that I want to carry with me and give to others more than God's peace, so why can't I remember to do it?! I certainly want people to bring peace to my home when they come to visit. The sad thing to me is that Jesus knew that the disciples would go into homes that would not be worthy of receiving His peace. And in those instances, the peace wasn't lost or wasted, it returned to the one who sent it out.

How much money do people spend every day just trying to find peace? They may call it something else – love, food, purpose, comfort, or happiness – but what they really want is peace in their mind and peace in their heart. There's only one thing that fills that peace void in every life, and that is Jesus. Only with faith in Him can a person find true peace.

Lord Jesus: Be my peace.

June 5

Rejoice not when your enemy falls, and when he stumbles,
let not your heart exult, lest the LORD see it, be displeased
with you, and withdraw his wrath from your enemy.
Proverbs 24:17, 18

It's really hard to not feel some joy when someone who has tormented me gets what's coming to them. When I was married, my husband cheated on me with a woman at work. Later on, after he divorced me to marry her, I found out he cheated on her, too. (If they'll cheat with you, they'll cheat on you.)

It was natural for me to feel joy when I heard that she was getting what I thought she deserved, but there was a sad element to the whole affair, as well: he just couldn't keep it to himself and be faithful to one person. He was also really good at misrepresentation, so you didn't find out what he was all about until it was too late.

The really sad part, to me, was that he was a preacher. And while I was happy to find out that the church where we had both served had released him from his ministerial position, I found it hard to gloat over that one as well. He wasn't teaching people everything they needed to know (I never heard him preach on adultery once), nor was he living the life that Paul tells Timothy that the leaders of the church need to practice. (1 Tim 3:1-10) And through it all, he said that he had not sinned. I had to step away when he told me that. I was afraid of a rogue lightning strike.

I knew about this verse when I heard all the scuttlebutt about these two. And yes, I did experience some elation, but I tried to keep it brief. First of all, the fact that he was destroying more lives was sad; second, the Lord deals out vengeance for His children and knows better than I what will affect someone most; and third, I wanted them both to get what they deserved in as much measure as the Lord was willing to hand them, so I backed off and let Him handle the situation.

Most people want to take the vengeance themselves, but I will tell from this experience and others, that the Lord does it better than we ever could. He knows what will repay best, and we don't have to get our hands (or souls) dirty to see that it happens.

Lord Jesus: Grant me the grace to let you handle the vengeance and not gloat when my enemy falls.

June 6
So they left the presence of the Sanhedrin, rejoicing
that they had been found worthy to suffer dishonor
for the sake of the name. Acts 5:41

Oh that there would be people like this today! How many people do you know that would be willing to step up and take condemnation and flogging for being a Christian? Or maybe even suffer death?

Here in the U.S. laws are being passed judicially that allow for the freedoms of those who aren't Christians to be recognized. The right to freedom *of* religion also allows for the freedom *from* religion. But that guarantee was intended to protect a personal choice, not ensure that each group or denomination would be free from witnessing others exercising their rights. And so the Christians have let their rights slip away in the name of tolerance.

The same is happening with freedom of speech. It is now against the law in Colorado to speak against or oppose homosexuality in any way.[9] It appears that we have had to give up our rights in order for others to gain theirs.

The day will come, and is not far off, when the government will try to close the churches in America. I believe all other forms of organizations that do not support or expound Christian values will be allowed to continue (including mosques and covens), but we will be forced underground unless something changes. Perhaps you think this is extreme. If so, watch the news tonight and read the global headlines on the internet, and then tell me you think I'm crazy.

Lord Jesus: Strengthen my spirit to support you and your word - no matter what.

June 7

The LORD said: Since this people draws near with words only and honors me with their lips alone, though their hearts are far from me, and their reverence for me has become routine observance of the precepts of men, therefore I will again deal with this people in surprising and wondrous fashion; the wisdom of its wise men shall perish and the understanding of its prudent men be hid. Isaiah 29:13, 14

This verse is for my ex, the preacher. When I confronted him about his adultery, he said he didn't have any – the Lord gave him that woman, she was the wife of his heart – despite his still being married to me. (I know – he's sick.) His heart could not have been close to the Lord, or he would have recognized when I challenged him that he was in the wrong. You have to wonder, was he ever really saved?

I see lots of stuff like this going on in the world, in the Church. It makes me disappointed and cynical sometimes. I know we're all sinners and are supposed to be trying to increase in holiness, and yes, we all fall down sometimes. Yet I can't help but wonder when I see some people and the way they live their lives if they have any inkling what it means to be a Christian. They come to church every week, but they seem to park their faith at the door when they leave. And then there are those who come to church and never sing any songs or pray the prayers. They don't wait for the priestly blessing at the end or even stop at the pew to kneel and say 'Thank You' to Jesus for his sacrifice that they just took part in when they received Communion. And many of them have children, so what are they teaching them about church?

I try not to judge, yet they give me plenty of ammunition. I pray for them to receive an awakening to the Spirit that they appear to be lacking. And just as in the days of Isaiah, the Lord will step in and 'deal with this people in surprising and wondrous fashion.' That doesn't sound good to me. And I hope that my own faith and works will keep me safe in the troubled times to come when He steps in to wake people up.

Lord Jesus: If I'm only going through the motions, please show me.

June 8
...since he is not the God of disorder but of peace.
1 Corinthians 14:33

You can tell a lot about a person by the things that go on around them. Chaos is rarely a sign that God is present. In this verse, Paul was talking to the Corinthians about what was going on during their worship services. Evidently there were some who were speaking in tongues, but they were all speaking at the same time; and there was no one to interpret, so no one was being enlightened or uplifted by the events.

I've been in churches where there was some praisin' goin' on and some tongues were heard, but I don't recall it getting out of order, so I have not experienced that kind of service. Of course there is the other side of that coin, as well. As I mentioned yesterday, I've seen people who come in at the last minute, set through the entire service, don't participate, and then take off as quickly as they can 'escape.' You wonder why they even come. By the way: I think God loves to hear you sing, even if it isn't your gift. Saint Augustine said, "When you sing, you pray twice." I can use those extra prayers!

Back to the issue of order: if you find yourself having to deal with someone who is constantly surrounded by chaos, watch your back. You never know who or what may be following in their wake.

Lord Jesus: Grant that I should praise you with joy and order.

June 9

It (the beast) was allowed to wage war against the holy ones
and conquer them, and it was granted authority over every
tribe, people, tongue, and nation. Revelation 13:7

Years ago, I read a book (I can't remember the author or title) where the author stated that he believed that the Lord was going to protect all His people from the reach of evil during the times of the tribulation. I found that strange. Could he have read the book of Revelation and still held that belief? If so, he was obviously deluded. It clearly says here that the holy ones will be subject to the antichrist and be defeated by him. At least some of them will be. This is supported in the book of Daniel:

> Those who have insight among the people will give understanding to the many; yet they will fall by sword and by

flame, by captivity, and by plunder for many days. Now when they fall they will be granted a little help, and many will join with them in hypocrisy. Some of those who have insight will fall, in order to refine, purge, and make them pure until the end time, because it is still to come at the appointed time. (Daniel 11:33-35)

And this control will be global, encompassing all people. No one will be safe from his wrath in any nation on earth unless they are hateful to the covenant between Christ and his followers. (Daniel 11:30, 39)

If we are alive during these times of trouble, we may all have the chance to find out just how strong our faith is. Jesus said that those who try to save their life will lose it (Luke 17:33), and for those who are ashamed of Him in this life, He will be ashamed of them in the next one. (Luke 9:26)

Lord Jesus: May my faith never fail you.

June 10

And all the trees of the field shall know that I, the LORD, bring low the high tree, lift high the lowly tree, wither up the green tree, and make the withered tree bloom. Ezekiel 17:24a

It amazes me how many people think they have the right to control others. Or maybe it's not that they think they have the right, perhaps they're unaware of their malady and just can't help themselves. Either way, I can't stand it when people try to force me to do something or tell me how to do this or that or live my life. Constructive criticism is one thing – that I can handle. It's the ones who think they have the answer to everything, but can't get their own house in order that irritate me. Their sentences always start out, "You should…." or "You need to…." but they often want you to tell them what to do to fix their problems. Their vision looking out is 20/20, but their interior view is totally blind.

In the end, it doesn't matter what any one of us tries to do, because the Lord is the one who has the ultimate control and the last word. Some things He will allow, and others He won't. He may allow you to fall on your face today so that He can pick you up tomorrow. Or He may let you lay there until you ask for His help. He always has a way to get us to follow His leading, some just take longer to get in step with His plans. He raises up those who are humble and recognize that He is in charge. And those who think they are wise will get their attitude adjusted at some point, because He brings the arrogant to their knees in due course. He may be saying 'trees' in this passage, but what He really means is us. We are the trees, and by our fruit we will be known.

Lord Jesus: Bless the roots of my tree.

June 11

And from your own group, men will come forward perverting
the truth to draw the disciples away after them. Acts 20:30

From the very beginning of Christianity, the Church has been warned against false prophets. The most frequent warning from Jesus to His followers was for them to be unlike the Pharisees, scribes, and teachers of the law who were proud, hypocritical, and most often looking for praise for themselves. They were firmly under the control of the adversary. Having spent time in ministry, I can tell you that some of the church leaders today are no different.

These false leaders may act like they know the way to the Father, but doubt their motives. They are often very charismatic, and strange things may happen around them. One common result of their activities is schisms and the splitting of congregations. In my time of contemplation, the Lord has imparted to me that one of the most distressing things to Him regarding the Church is the high number of splits (schisms, sects, and factions) that have torn the Church apart. Paul warned against quarrels over words in both of his letters to Timothy (1 Tim 6:3-5 and

2 Tim 2:14, 15) and instructed him regarding false teachers who would come against him and try to change the meaning of the gospel to suit their own ends: that is the beginning of a split.

If you are in a congregation that you think may be suspect, pay very close attention to the sermons you receive every week. There will be an underlying thread that will tie them together. If that thread is the Lord Jesus Christ and salvation by His sacrifice and blood, you're probably okay. You just might not be receiving the spiritual food that you need, and a move to a different church may be in order. But if the most common thread is a fixation on money or something that is questionable in its holiness, perhaps you need to approach the governing body and address your concerns to them. If they kick you out, you're better off anyway. And if you're *really* offended, you can report them to the national administration office of your denomination. The important thing is to separate yourself (and family and friends) from someone like this. They are not leading their flock to heaven but down a path to destruction.

People get led astray by the voice of the adversary and think it is the voice of God. Always question what you think you hear: if it is in violation of any of God's laws or does not give Him glory, it isn't from Him. Pray for those people who have obviously been misled.

Lord Jesus: Show me the heart of my pastor.

June 12
See, I am sending an angel before you, to guard you on the way
and bring you to the place I have prepared. Exodus 23:20

It comforts me to know that God has angels out there in the world fighting some of the battles that the devil is throwing at me. He so loved the Israelites when He brought them out of Egypt that He sent his angel ahead of the throng to assist them and get them to the Promised Land.

All of the gifts and promises that He made to the Israelites are ours as well. We are his children by adoption when we accept Jesus as Lord. He becomes our Brother, our Father, our Savior and our Advocate. He pleads our case when we fall. The devil stands before God and says, "Look what your child did! He(She) is mine now!" But Jesus says, "No. They are mine. They have repented, and they are forgiven." So not only do we have angels to help us, but we have Jesus and the holy Spirit as well. There is no excuse for someone to die in sin once they have been saved, but some people fall away and stay away.

Know that your angel is there to lead you and to help you. Your angel watches over you 24 hours a day. They don't take vacations. Thank them when you have a close call – just in case they were the one who protected you by making you late to work and avoiding that bad accident, or getting that phone call out of the blue that made your life change for the better. You never know what's going on in the spiritual realm; simply know that it is controlled by God, and followHhis lead.

Lord Jesus: Make me aware of my guardian angel.

June 13

Likewise, teach the older women to be reverent in the way they live, not to be slanderers or addicted to much wine, but to teach what is good. Then they can urge the younger women to love their husbands and children, to be self-controlled and pure, to be busy at home, to be kind, and to be subject to their husbands, so that no one will malign the word of God. Titus 2:3-5 (NIV)

When I was young, I'm ashamed to say I was nobody's role model. I certainly didn't fit the above description. But as the Lord began to work on me, I found myself wanting to be a better person, a better woman, a respected role model. Some may think I've made it. I would say that I'm just a bit further along the path to sanctification than I used to be.

Sometimes we learn things on our own, but other times find us in need of a swift kick in the seat of the pants. It is important to know and exhibit the qualities listed above to keep the Church from falling into condemnation (by the world or by the Lord) and if you want your children or grandchildren to be honest, earnest, productive members of society.

I think that the reason that there is so much crime and divorce today is because women aren't teaching their daughters how to be pure and chaste; nor are they teaching their sons how to respect women. And this is not something new – it has been going on for several generations. The Ten Commandments are all but forgotten when it comes to teaching kids what they need to know in life. I recently heard one of the children on my street tell another child that he would sue him, because his mom said that he could sue anyone and get away with it. Mind you, these kids are only 10 or 12 years old. What kind of man is the child with the sue-happy mom going to turn out to be? Probably not the kind I'd want my daughter to marry.

So how far are you from being the 'ideal' woman (or man, as the case may be)? Where can you make improvements right away? More importantly, what changes do you need to implement to make your home a better place to live and raise a family?

Lord Jesus: Show me your ideal of what I should be.

June 14
Who can say, "I have made my heart clean, I
am cleansed of my sin"? Proverbs 20:9

Have you ever met someone who is so self-righteous that you just wanted to puke? They act like they have no sin, but when you get to know them you find that they're skirting the edges of immorality at every turn and have their fanny perfectly balanced on the fence that separates clean and unclean. And you can't reason with these people. They know the Bible, and their activities *aren't* sinful. Not mortal sins anyway.

If you have to justify your actions to make them palatable, they're wrong. No discussion. Am I sin-free? Not a chance! I simply learned a long time ago that I can be forgiven if I just get off the fence, take responsibility for my mistakes, and pray not to do them again. I've said it for years: If someone says they don't sin, they're a liar. It's just that simple. No one is perfect no matter how hard they try. I know; I tried. I am so glad I gave that up! Only Jesus was perfect. And while I model myself after Him, I will never be able to achieve His perfection.

There's just one thing I'd like to know: how did He keep his thoughts so clean? I see people who murder and destroy other people's lives (slaughter in a movie theater and an elementary school), and I think that they deserve some great punishment. But that is not my job to do. Only God knows the proper judgment to be placed on someone. I have to ask forgiveness for those thoughts – they come to me before I can stop them. And while someone else may commit a truly heinous crime in my estimation, God sees all sins the same: sin is sin. Period. Some people simply have more of them.

Lord Jesus: Help me to see my own sins and not those of others.

June 15

"But I tell you that everyone will have to give account
on the day of judgment for every careless word
they have spoken." Matthew 12:36 (NIV)

How many times have you gotten a little huffy and said something that you immediately wished you hadn't? You knew right away that you were out of line, but you walked away without apologizing. Those moments and statements are the ones that do the most damage to others. In this verse, Jesus is telling us that we will be judged on 'every careless word' that comes out of our mouth in our lifetime. I think that the judgment will also include those hurtful things never spoken but thought to ourselves.

This verse has certainly made me more aware of the things that I say and think. I try to stop them from coming on and am usually successful in the verbal arena; not so much the thoughts, though. That's always the tough part – stopping a thought before it does any damage. And while my thought doesn't hurt anyone else, it hurts me because God knows about it. He knows my sometimes hateful and cruel heart – the one that gets tired and cranky and just wants to be left alone sometimes.

Since I started writing this book, I've had to re-evaluate myself – several times over. I still have lots of room to improve my behavior on my quest to holiness, and that is part of being human. The important thing is that I'm consciously working on improving myself, and these careless words are a sticking point for me. I need to work harder on my patience, tolerance, understanding, and forgiveness. Only then will I be able to make progress toward eradicating the careless words from my life.

Lord Jesus: Help me stop my 'careless words.'

June 16
For it is love that I desire, not sacrifice, and knowledge
of God rather than holocausts. Hosea 6:6

I've often wondered why there had to be blood and sacrifice for forgiveness in the Old Testament. It probably was stated at some time, but I don't recall reading it. Nevertheless, I wonder if the Israelites were supposed to feel more remorse for their sins knowing that an animal had to die for them to be forgiven. If so, God may have underestimated their hardness of heart since one of the reasons that He destroyed Jerusalem was because the Jews were sacrificing their own children alive in pagan rituals.

What God really wanted from them (and us) is mercy for others, adherence to the law, and love and faithfulness to Him rather than ritual observances. He wants us, not our money. He wants our service to others in His name rather than worrying about church and organizational doctrines. He wants our worship all the time wherever we are, not just in church on Sunday.

It's a lifestyle, not a religion. I don't have any use for religion, which is made by man. A life of faith in Jesus Christ is not a religion, no matter what some people say. And please do not misunderstand: it is important to attend church – it's where we are fed the word of God and offered opportunities to share and minister to others; it's where we sing and offer our thanks and praise as a community; it's where we get our spiritual batteries recharged; and it's where we deliver at least a portion of our tithe. Our Pastor always said 50% of your tithe to the church, and 50% to charity. Why? Because God desires love and mercy, not sacrifice. Charity is mercy to others, and the portion that goes to the church supports programs that acknowledge Him in the world – the two things He desires most.

Lord Jesus: Teach me how to please God in my worship and my service.

June 17

They drove out many demons, and they anointed with oil
many who were sick and cured them. Mark 6:13

There's something you don't see much anymore! When I say to someone that I think there's an unclean spirit involved in a situation, why does that person look at me like I'm crazy? Jesus drove out unclean spirits from people all the time, so why do people think that aren't unclean spirits anymore? And yes, I realize that there are times when folks are just plain nuts and that's all there is to it, but sometimes Jesus said that illnesses were caused by spirits. Could this be the reason that many people aren't healed today? Are they being treated for symptoms rather than the root of the problem?

You don't see too many anointings, either. They do it in the Catholic Church, but I can't tell you if many people are healed as a result. There are some miraculous occurrences, but I don't know all the details to know how anointing and prayer place in the events. I *do* know, however, that it won't work if you don't try. And it certainly can't hurt. Everyone needs healed from something.

Lord Jesus: May I receive your anointing of healing.

June 18

To the person who pleases him, God gives wisdom,
knowledge and happiness, but to the sinner he gives the
task of gathering and storing up wealth to hand it over
to the one who pleases God. Ecclesiastes 2:26a

Who do you try to please on a daily basis? Spouse? Boss? Friends? Yourself? Do you have a problem saying No to people? I used to until I realized that it was detrimental to my own health. It cost me my dignity, my money, my happiness, and my peace of mind. I knew it had to stop, and I was the only one that could make it happen. I trained myself to say No, and it is an ability that I would not give up for anything on earth.

The ability to say no applies especially to activities in the church. Once they find out you have a servant's heart, they ask you to do everything: cleaning, committees, driving folks around. It can get to a point where your service works take over your life. That can be fine if you have nothing else to do – no job, no family, no other responsibilities. But who does that apply to? No one I know.

You don't have to be involved in every activity that you're asked to join. Pick the one area that you know God has called you to, and stick to that until a new passion comes to you. At my church, I've been a greeter, helped plan a mission, taken Communion to the homebound and to those in the hospital, and taught religious education to 6th graders and children initiates. I know that the Lord has put it upon me to teach the children. I don't want them to have the misunderstanding and lack of life application skills that I had as a youth, so that is my passion. They need to know who Jesus is, why we should love and serve him, and how to pray and grow in holiness.

Think about life as it would be without faith: the acquisition, storing, and utilizing of things and money. There is nothing else to work for. (This is a general rule: there are always exceptions.) Is this all that you're accomplishing in your life, an accumulation of stuff? Do you want a life that means more? Are you working for things to pass on to someone else when you're gone, or are you working to please God so that all good things come to you? Occasionally, I go through my stuff and give a bunch of it away. If I haven't looked at it or used it in over two years, it goes unless I have a peculiar reason for keeping it. I have an aversion to keeping things that have no use (it's just clutter to me), and much of it is donated to organizations that serve the Lord.

Lord Jesus: Teach me how to please you.

June 19
"'Sir,' the man replied, 'leave it alone for one more year, and I'll dig around it and fertilize it. If it bears fruit next year, fine! If not, then cut it down.'" Luke 13:8, 9 (NIV)

Mercy: God's greatest gift. Some would say it is grace, but I say there would be no grace if God had no mercy. Grace saves me, and mercy keeps me. This parable is about mercy. The owner of the vineyard is ready to dispatch a non-bearing tree, but the vinedresser asks for one more season to try to turn it around. God owns the vineyard, and Jesus tends the trees which are us. This particular tree represents a person who has not been saved. God is ready to move on, but Jesus wants more time to work on this one.

As Christians, we are expected to bear fruit as a sign of our conversion. Jesus said that you will know the tree by its fruit: good trees, good fruit; bad trees, bad fruit. And every tree that doesn't bear good fruit is cut down and thrown into the fire which is eternity in hell. (Matthew 7:16-20)

Jesus is tending to each of us every day. Do you hear the sound of his voice? And what do your fruits look like? Are they good or bad? Do you even have any? Is this the year that God says, "Enough! Cut it down!"? I hope not. He is merciful, but even he has times when he draws the line. Remember what happened to his chosen people when they turned to false idols and child sacrifice.

Lord Jesus: Show me how you see my fruits.

June 20
And he went out to meet Asa and said to him, "Hear me,
Asa and all Judah and Benjamin! The LORD is with you when
you are with Him, and if you seek Him he will be present
to you; but if you abandon him, he will adandon you."
2 Chronicles 15:2

God will never walk away from you if you are earnest in seeking Him every day. I can't imagine how hard it is for Him to sit idly by while someone who used to love Him and has walked away from their relationship gets into trouble. It's like a mama bird letting the baby bird flail around while it's learning to fly. The difference in the two scenarios is that you can get back to God after your flailing if you want to – so long as you seek Him with love and earnest repentance. But the mama bird takes off once the babies learn to fly, leaving them alone and on their own.

Just because you're chosen and special today does not mean that you will be tomorrow. The qualifier here is that ***not*** being special is your own choice – He will never drop you if you are truly trying to be a better person. So then the questions are, "Am I truly seeking to be that better person? Am I seeking His will? Has my heart changed to try to be more like His? Have I abandoned the hedonistic practices that I used to indulge in?"

The Bible is the Christian's textbook. If you haven't read it, how can you know the guidelines you're supposed to be observing? Don't rely on others to tell you how to live your life unless you know for a fact that they know and live out the rules themselves. And even then – it's always better to read His words yourself. The Lord may have a special message He wants to share with you.

Lord Jesus: Remind me to stay close to you so that I never stray from your side.

June 21

Yet for us there is but one God, the Father, from whom are
all things and we exist for him; and one Lord, Jesus Christ,
by whom are all things, and we exist through him.
1 Corinthians 8:6 (NIV)

I believe that God created us as friends for Himself and His Son. We are His – all of us. According to Genesis, He walked in the garden and visited Adam and Eve. It must truly break His heart when He hears people say that He doesn't exist and that those of us who believe in Him are deluded and foolish. But we'll see who's deluded and foolish on the judgment day when He delivers the rewards that each of us has earned. Paul wrote earlier in this letter to the Corinthians that each believer's works will be tested by fire: if their works are burned up, they will still be saved but they will have no offering to make; if their works survive and are refined, they will receive a reward. (3:11-15)

You can't earn your way into heaven. Only by believing in the Son of God can you be saved. The rewards I refer to are our works that will be offered as a sacrifice of incense, a sweet savor to the Lord, when we reach the eternal kingdom and upon which (I believe) our proximity to the throne will be determined. For instance: I see Billy Graham being really close to the throne based on the fact that he saved so many souls. Someone who was saved on their deathbed and has no works as a result of their faith will be on the outer edge of heaven and will still be filled with joy at being there. I think we will all be given an opportunity to serve close to God at some time in heaven, but some will get to stay close to the Father and Son all the time – like Pastor Graham. These thoughts are not Biblically based – they are just my thoughts of how things *might* be. Keep in mind – I've been wrong before.

Lord Jesus: Lead me to more opportunities to gain rewards for the eternal kingdom and bring you glory.

June 22
"Come to terms with him to be at peace. In this
shall good come to you." Job 22:21

I am not a big supporter of the 'prosperity' movement within the Church. I think there are too many people who are focusing on the money side of things. They teach people that by being Christian and believing in God, He will automatically reward you with wealth. I know a lot of people who are good Christians that have next to nothing, and others who just go through the motions, don't tithe and have every material thing you could ever want. Which ones will be heading to heaven? Only God can answer that question. My point here is that you shouldn't become Christian or go to church just to be well-off financially. If you love God and seek Him,Hhis wisdom, and His will for your life, He will reward you with what you need (and maybe some of what you want).

I have not lived a perfect life. I've had both sins of commission and omission. But I have never been without unless I chose to. I was homeless and unemployed for a while back in 2005, but I never once had to sleep in my car or outside in the weather. And I never once missed a meal unless I chose to not eat for some reason. In 2009 I had to go into business for myself doing bookkeeping. I did not have many clients, but I did have a bit of savings and a few friends with small companies that could not afford to pay big CPA firms for the work they needed done. All of my bills were paid on time in the two years that I was self-employed and again, I missed no meals. My savings was wiped out, however. And just when I needed a full-time job, He provided one.

He has been faithful to fulfill every need I've had since I turned my life over to Him. So what is true prosperity? I guess it depends on your perception of what it is that you need. And no matter what the truth of your need is, the one thing that will always ensure that you have it fulfilled is trust in God.

Lord Jesus: I trust in your providence for all that I need.

June 23
"Should anyone press you into service for one mile,
go with him for two miles." Matthew 5:41

I'm sure you've heard 'go the extra mile' before, but did you know that this is where it came from? This verse is from Jesus' teaching during the Sermon on the Mount. He was suggesting radical new ways to look at a life of faith, and one of the ways that He was encouraging change was related to a practice enforced by the Roman militia. The soldiers would frequently force locals to carry their gear when they had to travel. They would basically grab someone, no matter what they were doing, and press-gang them into service. Jesus was telling the people that they should not only carry the gear for one mile (happily), but go a second mile without being forced or even asked.

The second problem with this activity was that many of the Jews hated the Romans and wanted nothing to do with them – they were unclean Gentiles and also cruel overlords. Talk about willing service! You can maybe begin to see why so many of the leaders of the Israelites disliked Jesus so much. He was not only telling people to refrain from being hypocrites (as the leaders were), but also to serve the ruling nation willingly and almost without question.

It's the fall of Jerusalem to the Babylonians all over again. In the fifth century b.c., the Lord spoke through the prophets and said that the people would be blessed if they would acquiesce to Nebuchadnezzar and go into bondage without a fight. He told them they would be provided for and be safe if they would simply go quietly, but the people didn't believe the prophets. They also didn't believe that the Lord would allow the city to fall because the temple was there. And so they starved and ate their own children because their hard hearts would not allow them to see the truth of God's word and the heinousness (in His eyes) of their own actions. So if the Lord is telling you to do something, even if you don't want to, perhaps you should rethink that bit of disobedience.

Lord Jesus: Where can I be of more service to you?

June 24

Jonah began his journey through the city, and had gone
but a single day's walk announcing, "Forty days more and
Nineveh shall be destroyed," when the people of Nineveh
believed God; they proclaimed a fast and all of them,
great and small, put on sackcloth. Jonah 3:4, 5

In all of the stories in the Old Testament, the Ninevites are the only ones to heed the word of the Lord when he sent a servant warning of destruction to their city due to sinfulness. From the king down to the animals in the stables, all were to fast without food or water, repent of their sins, and pray for God's mercy. And they did. The city of more than 120,000 people was spared along with their livestock. God gave them forty days, and it only took them one. Oh that people today would be willing to see that they have strayed so far from the true path and seek his mercy and grace!

If you only had 40 days to live, what would you do with it? Would you sin it up? Or pray and fast for mercy?

Lord Jesus: Teach me to pray and fast.

June 25

"For it is from within, out of a person's heart, that evil thoughts come—sexual immorality, theft, murder, adultery, greed, malice, deceit, lewdness, envy, slander, arrogance and folly. All these evils come from inside and defile a person."
Mark 7:21-23 (NIV)

This is Jesus informing the Pharisees that their judgment of Him was once again incorrect. They believed that for someone to eat without washing their hands meant the that person was unclean and so was the food. Jesus tells them that what is in your hand goes into your mouth, down to your stomach, and out to the latrine. It's just a pass-through. The condition that causes true uncleanness is related to a different organ – the heart.

If you could see someone's heart and the list of things that were its greatest desires (clean and unclean), would you want to? It would certainly make things easier when getting into a relationship with someone. It would only take about 15 seconds to read over the list of things that were important to the one you were contemplating as a mate to find out if you were compatible. Chances are pretty good that a lot of divorces could be avoided if this were possible. Unfortunately, those whose lists we need to read are the ones that will lie about what is on it.

I made it my prayer for a while that Jesus would show me people's hearts. What I discovered about people that I thought I knew was quite interesting. Most of them were pretty much as I thought, but there were a few who turned out to be completely selfish and ruthless. He has given me the gift of spiritual discernment – he shows me people's hearts – what they are despite the way they act. It is a great gift to have – being able to know a person's heart before they ever open their mouth. And it works in most cases, but not all. I can't read some people because they are consciously shielding their true self and intentions. Those are the ones I avoid. They have nothing to offer me, or anyone else most likely.

Lord Jesus: Show me people's true selves – show me their hearts.

June 26

For I take no pleasure in the death of anyone, declares the Sovereign Lord. Repent and live! Ezekiel 18:32 (NIV)

Remember when I said I thought that God made all of us to be His friends? I use this verse to support that position. And Peter said that the Lord is delaying his return as He waits for many to repent. (2 Peter 3:9) Meanwhile, more and more children are being raised without any knowledge of Him. I think all schools should teach comparative religions, and then all children would have at least some knowledge of God and His precepts. Then when they get older they would have at least some chance of finding their way to Him. Some people grow, live, and die without ever having been taught anything about Him. Sad. As a result, they frequently have no hope in anything beyond what they can see or touch.

Lord Jesus: Show me the way to a penitent life.

June 27

And this is my prayer: that your love may increase ever
more and more in knowledge and every kind of perception,
to discern what is of value, so that you may be pure and
blameless for the day of Christ. Philippians 1:9, 10

The gift of discernment: if you don't have it, it's almost impossible to explain. It's a feeling or an impression of someone, something, or a situation that comes like a flash. It may be a picture or a movie. Sometimes it comes as a feeling, a smell, or a physical sensation, possibly pain. No matter how it arrives, it is the holy Spirit giving you a lot of information in your heart or your mind (or both) in a split-second. It is for your direction or protection, or for the assistance of someone else. I often find that I have repeated instances where a person keeps coming to mind. I occasionally find out what their circumstances are, but mostly I've learned that they simply need prayer.

In today's passage, Paul is telling the followers in Philippi that he hopes that they will grow in love as a result of their increase in knowledge and insight. He also hopes that these increases will cause them to have better discernment of the actions which will reflect a life of holiness. If you don't have knowledge, insight or discernment, you can get it. You need only be earnest in prayer when asking God to grant you the gifts that will help you understand how best to serve His kingdom.

The hard part of having the gift of discernment is occasionally knowing what goes on in others' lives without being told, or knowing in advance what is going to happen to someone. For instance: I had a friend who had a daughter in high school. I was visiting their home in the month of September, and the Spirit told me: "She will be pregnant in less than six months." And she was. I didn't say anything to her parents at the time. Sometimes these impressions don't come to pass. I have to assume that the information is based on the path that someone is on at the time I get the message. People do change course, after all.

Some of the messages that I get are political, regional, or global. Sometimes they pertain to one person, other times to a whole group. It is difficult to know which ones to act on and which to let go of. And this is when you have to pray all the more for wisdom.

Lord Jesus: Give me the gifts that I need to discern my role in your plan and help others.

June 28
Be merciful to those who doubt. Jude 22 (NIV)

One of the hardest things I've found to do is put up with people who are insecure. You likely know someone like this: can't make decisions on their own without asking everyone else what to do; would rather have you tell them what to do than decide on their own; can't go anywhere alone, always needs a companion. I confess I don't understand this kind of person. I prefer to be independent, make my own decisions, fall on my face and get up and start over, and take responsibility for my failures. I'm not afraid to fail, not afraid to get lost – sometimes I do it on purpose just to see what else is out there.

I guess the big issue here is trust – or rather a lack of it, aka doubt. Some people have never had to stand on their own and never wanted to. Perhaps they don't have faith that they can find their way out of a 'lost' situation. Doubt is a crippling affliction that does not come from God. It makes a person ineffective in nearly all applications of the principles of faith. They may doubt themselves, or God, or their worthiness of receiving God's graces. Understand this: *No one* is worthy of the grace of God – that's what makes it grace. No person can earn graces or salvation. God offers them to us, and we accept or decline.

Doubt is normal to a certain degree. We can't see God, and so sometimes we struggle in the life of faith. But so long as we remain true to His precepts, He will remain true to us. So in your daily dealings with people, remember to ask yourself: is my issue with this person a result of doubt, or is it simply a difference of personality and gifts? If you suspect doubt, pray for the person to be released from the weakness that cripples them and be kind to them.

Lord Jesus: Help me to understand people's differences, and remind me to be patient with those who are not as far along in their spiritual growth as I am.

June 29

Their deeds do not allow them to return to their God; for the spirit of harlotry is in them, and they do not recognize the LORD. Hosea 5:4

Gone are the days when a small business owner in America could pick the clients they wanted to do business with. The Jezebel spirit is destroying the Christian landscape, and not only in the business realm. Everywhere we turn we are expected to accept and promote the factions of society that disbelieve the word of God, while their groups are not expected to do anything for us. And not only are they exempt from giving us our equal rights, they are supported by the government in their efforts to take us down. Listen to the words of Jesus given to John in His revelation of the end times regarding this spirit of harlotry:

> "To the angel of the church in Thyatira write:
>
> These are the words of the Son of God, whose eyes are like blazing fire and whose feet are like burnished bronze. I know your deeds, your love and faith, your service and perseverance, and that you are now doing more than you did at first.
>
> Nevertheless, I have this against you: You tolerate that woman Jezebel, who calls herself a prophet. By her teaching she misleads my servants into sexual immorality and the eating of food sacrificed to idols. I have given her time to repent of her

immorality, but she is unwilling. So I will cast her on a bed of suffering, and I will make those who commit adultery with her suffer intensely, unless they repent of her ways. I will strike her children dead. Then all the churches will know that I am he who searches hearts and minds, and I will repay each of you according to your deeds.

Now I say to the rest of you in Thyatira, to you who do not hold to her teaching and have not learned Satan's so-called deep secrets: 'I will not impose any other burden on you, except to hold on to what you have until I come.'

To the one who is victorious and does my will to the end, I will give authority over the nations—that one 'will rule them with an iron scepter and will dash them to pieces like pottery'—just as I have received authority from my Father. I will also give that one the morning star." (Rev 3:18-28 NIV)

Notice he says that he is upset that we tolerate the Jezebel spirit. There are Christians across this nation today who are going to jail for not serving people whose beliefs disagree with their own. To them I say, "Be strong, and keep the faith!" To those who tolerate and stand back and allow these things to happen, I offer this from Rev 3:1,2.

These are the words of him who holds the seven spirits of God and the seven stars. I know your deeds; you have a reputation of being alive, but you are dead. Wake up! Strengthen what remains and is about to die, for I have found your deeds unfinished in the sight of my God.

It's time to wake up and smell the coffee.

Lord Jesus: Help me to recognize those who have a Jezebel spirit and stand strong against them.

June 30

In those days John the Baptist appeared, preaching in the
desert in Judea saying, "Repent, for the kingdom of heaven is at
hand!" It was of him that the prophet Isaiah had spoken when
he said, "A voice of one crying out in the desert, 'Prepare the
way of the Lord, make straight his paths.'" Matthew 3:1-3

John was sent in the spirit of Elijah the prophet who slaughtered the
priests of Baal and heard the voice of God as a still small voice from
the cave. John came in spiritual strength and power and for the purpose
of preparing the people for the arrival of his cousin, Yeshua, Jesus
of Nazareth. It was his sole purpose in life to fulfill this mission – to
prepare the way of the Lord. He baptized the people to wash away their
sins so that the idea would not be totally new to them when Jesus came
speaking of spiritual baptism.

I used to think of Billy Graham as our modern-day John the Baptist,
and when he became elderly and retired, I prayed that the Lord
would send someone to take his place. There are a lot of very popular
evangelists and teachers in our country, but none of them, in my mind,
could replace his charisma and thirst for souls. And then I saw Rabbi
Jonathan Cahn. He is a Messianic Jew who speaks the words of God
with full understanding of their meaning. He didn't have to study the
Hebrew language and try to translate it to us; he speaks the language
already. And he is of the priestly line, as was John the Baptist whose
father Zechariah was himself a priest in service at the temple when the
angel of the Lord appeared and told him that John would be born to
herald the coming of the Christ. And a herald is what Rabbi Cahn is
as well. If you haven't yet read his book *The Harbinger*[10], you really
need to do so. It will give you a very different view of the world that we
are living in.

Lord Jesus: Prepare a way in my heart for your arrival.

July

July 1

Say this to him, says the LORD: What I have built,
I am tearing down; what I have planted, I am
uprooting: even the whole land. Jeremiah 45:4

This message from the Lord was for Baruch, Jeremiah's secretary. It was near the time of the end for the land of Judah and the city of Jerusalem, and Baruch was complaining because he was weary from much groaning. He was tired of being tired, hungry, and persecuted. Everything that the Lord had tried to build for His chosen people was being destroyed or given to outsiders because of their unfaithfulness, and so the Lord says, in essence, 'Get some perspective!'

As I contemplate this passage today, I believe that the Lord is saying this to me. I groan over the state of our union – the mass murders, the millions of abortions, the disrespect of people for their fellow human beings, the greed of corporate America, and the corruption and disconnection of many of our government leaders. It seems to me that we are headed for a revolution if things can't be turned around. And if not a revolution, then surely the Lord will step in and do to us what He did to Israel and Judah.

Given the state of the world, I wouldn't be surprised to see this happen before the end of my natural life. I turned fifty this year and would normally expect to see thirty-five more. I believe He's giving me a directive: "Pray for American leaders, the nations of the world, and for a revival in the global church and in America. Get some perspective: The whole world is at stake. Do what you can: pray today for those who need me and spread peace everywhere you can." Yes, Lord, I will.

Lord Jesus: Help me get perspective on the state of the world as you see it to help me pray as I should.

July 2

"Woe to you, scribes and Pharisees, you hypocrites. You pay tithes of mint and dill and cumin, and have neglected the weightier things of the law: judgment and mercy and fidelity. These things you should have done without neglecting the others." Matthew 23:23

The scribes and Pharisees were the teachers of the community – they were supposed to teach the people how to be good children of God. And while they were teaching the people the whole obligation of a life under God, Jesus said they weren't practicing what they were preaching (Matthew 23:3), nor were they helping the people to fulfill the burdens that they were taught that they owed. (Matthew 23:4) The priests were focusing on the small things of one facet of their own obligation and ignoring the larger, more interactive obligations. These obligations were obviously important in the Lord's eyes, so they were, in effect, useless priests.

Tithing is important to the Lord, but it isn't the only thing He wants us to do. He expects us to abide by His laws every moment in our everyday lives. The leaders in the temple were only doing what dealt with them and their one-on-one relationship with God – giving their own tithes. This is interesting to me since everything they had would have come from the tithes of others. That was the source of their income as employees of the temple. They were focusing on the minutiae (and serving themselves) and ignoring their more important and far-reaching duties (not serving the people in any way). It was straining out a gnat and swallowing a camel! (Matthew 23:24)

Lord Jesus: Am I fulfilling all of my obligations?

July 3

These then are the things you should do: Speak the
truth to one another; let there be honesty and peace in
the judgments at your gates, and let none of you plot evil
against another in his heart, nor love a false oath. For all
these things I hate, says the LORD. Zechariah 8:16, 17

Hate is a strong word. I teach my kids not to use it, even though I
occasionally catch myself using it. (I hate it when that happens....)
I don't subscribe to the do-as-I-say-not-as-I-do principle. I believe
in living out what I teach while recognizing that I'm not perfect.
Nevertheless, I have to be very careful since I have a position of great
trust in teaching young minds to live uprightly. And in that course of
instruction, I teach them the things that the Lord especially *doesn't*
want us to do.

He obviously feels very strongly about these things to list them under the
topic of 'things that I hate': lying, misrepresentation, instigation, unfair
judgments, and plotting evil against others. These are the specifics, but
the list of the potential activities that could be covered (which would
include basically any negative behavior) is quite long. And knowing
what we know of God, that should be a no-brainer. If you plan it and it
hurts anyone else, it isn't acceptable behavior.

*Lord Jesus: Stop me before I fall into bad behaviors that you
hate.*

July 4

And if the root is holy, so are the branches. Romans 11:16b

Jesus said that He is the vine, and we are the branches. We are the
part that is supposed to bear fruit. And unless we remain attached to
the vine, we can't do that. If you know anything about plants, you know
that they can't survive without their roots. Even hydroponic systems that

don't use soil promote some root growth. It is a sign of healthy plants that they grow roots – more health, more roots. It's how they are fed and where they store their extra energy and nutrition. Whatever is in the root zone is what gets fed to the plants.

Here Paul says that if the root is holy, then so are the branches. So if Jesus is your root, then your fruit will be reflective of Him because He feeds you. If Jesus isn't your root, that too will be reflected in your fruit. So what kind of fruit are you growing – does it give glory to God or to yourself?

Lord Jesus: Feed my branch and make me holy.

July 5
The LORD is a stronghold for the oppressed, a
stronghold in times of trouble. Psalm 9:10

Before I was a Christian, I had no one to lean on, no one to tell my troubles to. I had no friends who were willing to help me sort out my issues and find solutions to the problems that I faced. Consequently, I would have a mini emotional breakdown every six months – like clockwork – which would be attended by an increase in self-destructive behaviors. It scared me when I realized that there was a pattern to my emotional upheaval, but it was also the kick I needed to wake me up and start asking, "Why am I like this, and how can I get better?"

Many people are broken and in need of healing, but they just don't realize how bad off they are. Only with the leading of the holy Spirit can our eyes be opened to the shortcomings that need repaired. I'm so glad that He was there waiting for me when I asked those hard and painful questions. He is my stronghold now, one that is never absent, always free to listen, and available when I call. No voicemail here! He has earned my trust and my love, something few people have managed.

Who do you turn to when the going gets tough? How do you handle hard times? Your response to your difficulties will show where you place your faith.

Lord Jesus: Thank you for being there for me every time I need you.

July 6

Beloved, do not imitate evil but imitate good.
Whoever does what is good is of God; whoever does
what is evil has never seen God. 3 John 11

I've heard it said that imitation is the highest form of flattery. It's everywhere you look today. Unfortunately, 'life imitating art' is rarely the good kind like you might see in a movie such as *Sleepless in Seattle*. Instead, it looks more like the video game *Grand Theft Auto*. When I was married, my step-son wanted that game. I had no idea what it was, not being a gamer by even the longest stretch of imagination. His dad said it was okay but he had to use his own money, and so it came home with us. I was appalled to say the least: shooting people to steal their car or for no good reason, prostitutes, and drugs. Is it life-like, or did life come to look like it instead? It's the old question: Which came first – the chicken or the egg?

Proverbs 4:23 says, "Above all else, guard your heart, for everything you do flows from it." And in *Star Wars: Episode 1*, Jedi Master Qui-Gon Jinn says, "Your focus determines your reality." Whatever you spend your time on is where your heart will live. If you feed it lies and hatred and evil practices, that's what will flow out from it. Some people can't separate TV, movies, or games from reality. It seems that since it's there for them to see, it's perfectly acceptable to do it as well.

I feel like I'm beating a dead horse, but it still goes back to what children are taught. I myself like the *Harry Potter* series of books and movies, but I recognize that magic as portrayed in them is not realistic. I think that if a spell is cast on someone, then the spell itself is not the physical work of the caster but of an unclean spirit that they have forced on the victim. (My opinion.) I understand that many children have turned to witchcraft as a result of these stories, and I can understand why they would. As is stated by the evil forces in the story, 'Magic is Might.' If a child is being bullied, gets no support from adults, and needs recourse, magic would seem like a great equalizer. What I can't understand is why any adult would allow their child to start down this road. It's not harmless as many people seem to think. It is connected to the spirit world, and dabbling in something that you don't truly understand is simply dangerous.

Lord Jesus: Help me to discern the evil from the good.

July 7
Woe to the complacent in Zion, to the overconfident
on the mount of Samaria…. Amos 6:1

For as long as I have been studying the Word and striving to gain wisdom and knowledge, the Lord has been asking me to focus on this verse. Complacency will destroy any relationship. It has cost more than one person their spouse or their business. And despite my first husband's assurance that he would never take me for granted, in the end he did. It came to the point where I just didn't care anymore.

I think the Lord feels the same way. I think He looks down at His children making their way in the world without consulting Him to find out what He has in store for them and thinks, "Why do I even bother to speak to them? They don't ever listen to my voice!" If people only knew that what He has for us is unbelievably better than we could ever dream of for ourselves, they would reconsider. But I think most people don't realize that many of the dreams we have come from Him. What we try to create out of those dreams is a mere shadow of what He wants to give us. We simply take it for granted that what we've built for ourselves is what He wants for us without ever seeking His direction or permission.

Someday the Lord Jesus will return. When that day comes, will you know his voice? More importantly, will He know you? Have you spent time with him building a relationship, falling in love over and over again, or do you just assume He's there because you married Him one day a long time ago? We all know what happens when you assume. Never assume you're safe from destruction – Jesus might just prove that complacent theory wrong in order to get your attention back.

Lord Jesus: Wake me up from my complacency!

July 8

For God did not give us a spirit of cowardice but rather
of power and love and self-control. 2 Timothy 1:7

Of all the blessings that God wants to give us, I think the one that is least sought after is the gift of power. There are so many more things that we could do in life if we would step up and grab the power of God and make it our own. He would like for us to lay hands on people and heal them, speak the word of God boldly, and show the world a good example of the Christian faith in action.

I think the thing that stops most people is fear: fear of being ostracized from a group for our zeal; fear of being thought a nut-case; fear of death; and fear of persecution in light of changing societal norms where Evangelical Christians are now considered to be as dangerous as al-Quaeda, Hamas, and the KKK[11]. The day may come in our lifetime when we have to make the decision: give up our life for our faith (like Joan of Arc) or deny Christ and live the rest of our lives in shame. Which would you choose today?

What fears drive you? Remember: Fear does not come from God.

Lord Jesus: Take away the spirit of fear that hinders me and fill me with your power.

July 9

You dishonor me before my people with handfuls of
barley and crumbs of bread, killing those who should not
die and keeping alive those who should not live, lying to
my people who willingly hear lies. Ezekiel 13:19

There wasn't much about the Jews of the Babylonian exile era that God
liked, because there wasn't much in the way of faithfulness to Him
amongst the people. There were a few, but they were the minority. In
this particular passage He is railing at the diviners who took people's
money and gave them false hope by lying to them about the future of
the nation. The fault of their messages was in refusing to tell wicked
people to turn from their sins, and to continue on in their wicked ways.
And to the upright, they were delivering messages that were untrue and
causing those persons to grieve. Either way, both groups were given
false hope by these sorceresses. And we know that God didn't want
divination practiced among the Jews anyway. It was banned by the law
and restated to the people during the reign of King Saul.

I can't help but think of our nation today when I read this. There are
so many people out there saying that they can tell you your future by a
phone call and for a fee. False hope that never manifests or unplanned-
for hardships or disasters can drive some with a weak conscience to the
brink of death and sometimes even suicide. It's cruelty of the highest
sort to abuse a relationship of trust, whether it be from a fortune-teller
or a friend.

*Lord Jesus: Help me break any ties with the forces of divination
and the influence of those who lie for their own gain.*

July 10

For the wisdom of this world is foolishness in the eyes
of God, for it is written (Job 5:13): "He catches the
wise in their own ruses." 1 Corinthians 3:19

Have you ever known someone who was always weaving webs of deceit
around everything they did? How about someone like Bernie Madoff? It
was good to see him brought down, but it was sad that it took his sons so
long to out him. So many people lost everything they had to his greed.
You have to wonder, "How did he live with himself?" and "Why did
God allow it go on for so long?" I don't have answers to these questions
except to say that God had his reasons for allowing it to continue.

When we strive to find sense in earthly things, we will most often be
confounded. And we can never comprehend the things and mind of
God. Many things that we think would be so perfect are just stupid
in his eyes. What we can see from our vantage point is less than a
pinpoint in God's view. He sees all of time, and one of our lifetimes is
but a blink of his eye. So when we try to figure out why things go the
way they do, we'll have to ask if He is willing to explain. Our wisdom
is nothing to Him. And when you think you can do whatever you want
and get away with it, remember this verse. He sees everything, and you
will be exposed eventually.

Lord Jesus: Stop me before I become wise in my own eyes.

July 11

Only the one who sins shall die. The son shall not be charged
with the guilt of his father, nor shall the father be charged with
the guilt of his son. The virtuous man's virtue shall be his own,
as the wicked man's wickedness shall be his. Ezekiel 18:20

Back in the days of Moses, the Lord held the sins of a man against his
family to the third and fourth generation (Exodus 34:7). With the fall

of Jerusalem, He stopped that practice. Each person has since been responsible for their own sins. Each person will stand alone in front of God and answer for their life.

I try to make sure that I confess my sin as soon as it happens, and ask forgiveness and help to do better the next time. I don't want unforgiven sins hanging over my head when I arrive at the throne. And sometimes I wonder: what if someone is saved and led a pretty good life, but didn't ask forgiveness along the way? What happens to those unconfessed sins in the end? Does it depend on whether or not they recognized that they were sins?

I used to work in a CPA office. It amazed me how many 'Christians' wanted us to lie about things on their taxes because they didn't want to pay what they legitimately owed. If they had just done more giving to charity, they wouldn't have owed so much tax. But in the end, it would still have come out of their pocket, and therein lies the problem: greed, the greatest sin that leads to all others – the lust of our hearts and the lust of our eyes.

I'm glad I don't have to suffer for the sins of others when I get to heaven – I've done enough of that over here.

Lord Jesus: Forgive me when I am remiss.

July 12
"Amen, amen, I say to you, unless a grain of wheat falls
to the ground and dies, it remains just a grain of wheat;
but if it dies, it produces much fruit." John 12:24

This is the hardest thing for me to do: live and yet die. I can talk all day about how a Christian life is supposed to be lived, but until I actually do it, I'm just a 'resounding gong or a clanging cymbal'. (1 Corinthians 13:1) Paul was talking about love in that passage – so am I. Everything that Jesus wants us to do comes from our love for man as a result of our love for Him. We are to die to our selfish desires and live for Him. I'm still working on this, along with all the other things that we're supposed to do. If I ever get it 100% right, He'll probably take me home right away since there won't be anything else to learn.

I've read biographies of several of the Saints. One thing that I've noticed about the ones that I chose to study was that they gave their lives over to Christ early and also died in their 20's or 30's. They were so amazing! I wish I had the faith and conviction that they had in order to accomplish their works.

One thing I know for certain – you have to die (like a grain of wheat) for fruit to come out of you. You have to die every time He asks you to do something in order to be truly faithful. And the number of times a day He might ask depends on your willingness to follow His lead. This book has been an occasion of dying for me. A great many hours have gone into this book, and I hope it produces at least as much fruit for you as it has for me.

Lord Jesus: May I be willing to die to myself and serve you as often as you want me to.

July 13

I will tear down the wall you have whitewashed and
level it to the ground, laying bare its foundations.
When it falls, you shall be crushed beneath it; thus you
shall know that I am the LORD. Ezekiel 13:14

God doesn't like hypocrites. In this passage, He calls it whitewashing. It is the principle of a fresh coat of paint, but only for the purpose of covering up filth and deterioration. It's like a marriage that has fallen apart, but the two parties are putting up appearances to make everyone think things are okay. It's a lie.

God told the Jews that He was going to destroy them and their whitewashed walls and expose their evil deeds to the world. Similarly, Jesus said that everything we've spoken in the darkness and in secret will be proclaimed in the daylight (Luke 12:3). He will tear down our walls and expose our filthy foundations. Think about that the next time you're about to spread gossip about someone or perform a dastardly deed.

Lord Jesus: Lead me to a clean heart and a purified foundation.

July 14

The people stood by and watched; the rulers, meanwhile, sneered at him and said, "He saved others, let him save himself if he is the chosen one, the Messiah of God." Luke 23:35

How sad is it that the rulers and teachers of the people who are supposed to know the sacred scriptures and the prophecies can't see the fact that they just fulfilled every prophecy contained in the Old Testament related to the Messiah's death? Even they were blind to the nature of the Messiah, thinking that He would be someone who would live the law, not change it.

One of the most interesting things to me about Jesus' trial before the Sanhedrin is that they ask Him if He is Messiah. If He says no, He lies. If He says yes, He tells the truth and yet is guilty of blasphemy according to the law given by God to Moses. It isn't blasphemy if it's the truth, but only if the person listening believes that He is the true Messiah. It's a no-win for Him, since they already have their minds made up as to His fate: death. And for what? Outing them for their hypocrisy and selfishness. Pretty drastic measures, I'd say, but it shows the level of their greed in feeling justified to going to such lengths.

It was the condition of their hearts that allowed them to think that murder was justified in this circumstance. He was stealing away their followers and teaching new ways to live that would reduce their livelihood. And to make matters worse, He was a man of peace. Maybe that was part of the problem – the old kings of the Jews were always murdering each other in order to take over the throne. Perhaps they thought the Messiah would be a warrior king, not a peaceful one.

What do we believe about Jesus? Is he a lion, or a lamb? I would say that, when he walked the earth, he was the Lamb of God promoting peace and love and harmony. When He returns, He will be the Lion of the tribe of Judah who will judge the world by the Word of God, the double-edged sword that comes out of His mouth. (Revelation 1:16) If you're saved, you'll be spared this judgment. If not, your life as gauged to the word of God will convict you.

Lord Jesus: You are the Chosen One of God!

July 15
Weeds shall overgrow their silver treasures, and
thorns invade their tents. Hosea 9:6b

I can't tell you how many times I've read the book of Hosea. It is a book of judgment against the Israelites and a call to repentance and return to the LORD. But in my reading this year, I've been asking the Lord to open my heart to His word rather than to open His word to me – a fine line of diction, but a chasm of perception. In my reading, I stumbled on this verse. One of the things that I do when I study is try to imagine what the pictures of the words in scripture might look like in the time it was written, in the present, and in the future of things to come. When I was reading this verse recently, the image of homes turned into rubble and abandoned cars popped into my mind.

'Weeds shall overgrow their silver treasures' looks like cars sitting abandoned everywhere with weeds growing up all around them or having gardens in the trunk. And if the crisis in the Middle East doesn't end soon, we could see that reality within in a few short years. Idle cars could be the result of no oil imports, a huge solar flare (increasing activity in 2013) or an EMP burst (nuclear blast over the atmosphere) that would knock out all electronic components.

'Thorns shall invade their tents.' One thing I know from growing up in the countryside is that, if you turn the soil and don't seed it, something *will* grow there. Whatever seeds blow in on the wind take up residence, and those seeds are frequently thistles of some sort – thistles with needle-like stickers all over them. Needles are kind of like thorns – they hurt when you get against them. And if homes are rubble, they're like untended soil, sprouting whatever seed blows in on the wind.

It's amazing what you can find when you open your heart and mind to be receptive to something you thought you had a handle on. It just goes to show – we're never as smart as we really think we are.

Lord Jesus: Continue to open your Word to my heart that I might learn even more.

July 16
"You disregard God's commandment but
cling to human tradition." Mark 7:8

Sometimes I worry because the Church has been split so many times. There used to be just 'The Church' – what we know most often today as the Catholic Church. Nowadays there are nearly 100 different groups that have been started as separatist movements, some being three, four, or five levels removed from the original church started by the disciples. Every time there's a split there is a change in philosophy and interpretation of the scriptures. Some are more social group than worship group; some are heavily laden with bureaucracy; some focus more on the spiritual gifts than the One who bestows them; some change the scriptures altogether and say that they have received new revelations.

The Bible warns us not to add or subtract from the words we've been given. (Deut 4:2; Prov 30:5, 6; Rev 22:18) It concerns me that there are young people who have been brought up in churches that aren't teaching Biblical truth. I can't say which ones these might be since I haven't been to all of them. And most of the people that I've met from other denominations have never been so offensive to me that I couldn't stand to be around them. I simply disagreed with some part of their interpretation of the Bible. The bottom line is this: Are you finding Jesus Christ and his sacrifice in your church and its teaching? If the answer is yes, then I think you're okay. Everything else is preference.

I said to you before that I never expected that I would ever want to be Catholic, but here I am a member. What I find interesting today, and have seen repeatedly over the past six years, is that the people who are coming back to church after being away for many years are coming into the Catholic Church. (I'm not suggesting that you run out and do it yourself, this is just my personal observation.)

The primary reason that I'm hearing from others for their desire to return is that they want their kids to find Christ, and they themselves are looking for Him too. They are finding Him in the Sacraments of the Roman Catholic Church, Sacraments that are mostly missing from the other denominations (the ones I went to). And there is a holiness to the Mass that is often lacking elsewhere. Granted, not all Catholic churches are the same – music and some practices will vary, along with the personality of the priest. And I admit that when I first started there, I was concerned about the Catholic 'Traditions' because of this very rebuke cited today that Jesus gave to the Pharisees. But I haven't found anything that I can't live with.

Do you know Jesus? Is He in your church? Is He your commandment, or just a tradition?

Lord Jesus: Be my commandment.

July 17

Trust in the LORD and do good that you may dwell in
the land and live secure. Find your delight in the LORD
who will give you your heart's desire. Commit your way
to the LORD; trust that God will act. Psalm 37:3-5

Trust, delight, and commit. You'd think it would be easy to do this, but it never seems to work out that way. I think it has to do with the seen, the unseen, and the quality of the relationship. If you've ever been in love, you know how it feels when you're separated from the subject of your adoration. The more time you spend with that person, the more attached you become. You begin to trust them. You can't trust someone you don't know, nor can you find delight in their company; and you certainly wouldn't commit your life to them.

The only way that you can successfully trust in, delight in, and commit your way to the Lord is to nurture your relationship with Jesus the same as you would with your human beloved: you must spend time with Him. I'm not talking about one Sunday morning per week, but real time together, the two of you alone. Start with one day per week and then add another, and another. I hope that you find very quickly that you begin to anticipate your time together just like that other special someone you're sure you can't live without.

There are several places that you can go to be alone with him, but the most critical things you need to have with you when you go are your Bible, a notebook, and a pen. I like to go to the chapel during the day when people are at work so that there are fewer interruptions and distractions. You can stay at home and commune there, but you have to turn off the TV and your phones.

Pray first. Thank Him for His blessings and for listening to your prayers. Ask Him to share Himself with you. Tell Him what's bothering you or what you need help with. He already knows, but He loves it when we acknowledge that we're aware of our shortfalls and ask for His help.

Ask Him to open his word to you, then open your Bible and read. If it works for you as it does for me, the words will practically leap from the page to answer questions and concerns that you have. Keep a log in your notebook of what you asked for and the scripture He gives you. I hope you find that your time together produces great peace and a new sense of understanding.

I started this practice ten years ago and still read at home every day. I wish I could do more chapel time, but work and life seem to interfere. My time is at the end of the day when I have sins to confess and questions that have arisen that need answering. Sometimes I have people that are on my heart that need prayer, and He will occasionally tell me what that person is up to in our time together. Keep quiet and let Him do most of the talking. You talk all day – give Him His time to share.

Lord Jesus: Help me build our relationship so that I can trust, delight in, and commit to you.

July 18
Do nothing out of selfishness or out of vainglory; rather,
humbly regard others as more important than yourselves.
Philippians 2:3

In a world where power, fame, and money are heavily desired and admired, some would never consider living at a level that Paul speaks of in today's verse. How many people do you know that aren't selfish? I don't know one – not even me. We need to take care of our business because we have others who depend on us for sustenance; beyond that, we should also be taking care of those who need help through acts of charity or simple kindness. A person may not be a direct dependent of ours, but being a child of the Living God makes them our responsibility. We should be serving our brothers and sisters in Christ through giving of our time, talent, or treasure.

With Jesus as our role model, we should be striving to become more like Him: humble, not seeking glory for our works, but working due to our love for Him and willing to give our own possessions or funds to help others. Paul says Jesus made himself nothing. So far, I can't say that about myself. He gave up everything for me – His place in heaven, His glory and praise – and died an excruciating death in shame on the cross so that I can be reconciled to God for eternity. I have accepted His terms for salvation by believing in Him and His works that were done for me. What I have to do now is become as he was – a servant. It takes the focus off of me and puts it where it belongs – on Him.

I try to have the heart of a servant as He did, and sometimes I succeed in serving others well. Other times I fail miserably. I've spent most of my life to this point trying to be somebody. It takes a true change of heart to want to be nobody.

Lord Jesus: *Open my heart and my eyes so that I can see the path to service and humility.*

July 19

May the LORD, our God, be with us as he was with our
fathers and may he not forsake us nor cast us off. May
he draw our hearts to himself that we may follow him in
everything and keep the commands, statutes, and ordinances
which he enjoined on our fathers. 1 Kings 8:57, 58

I have seen a billboard that says, "Feel far from God? He hasn't moved." It was a poke at me when I saw it, because I had let my work and other distractions draw me away from Him. I knew immediately that what the billboard said was true. He was right where He had always been – it was me who had wandered off and created the distance in our relationship. I know that I am prone to getting distracted and not thinking about Him during the day, so my prayer is for Him to draw my heart throughout the day, to send me little notes through people, emails, or whatever medium that will bring Him to mind. I'm afraid that if He left it to me, I might just forget about Him completely.

Isn't it amazing how we start out with the greatest of intentions and end up flat on our face with no one to lift us up? And it's no one's fault but our own. We allow things and people and work and boredom to get us off target and keep us there. One lesson that I have learned is that if I want to be focused on anything, I have to be intentional in my pursuit of it. I learned long ago that if you want to be remembered by someone, you have to be intentional in your dress, your words, and your actions. Now I apply that principle to my relationship with the Blessed Trinity as well. It's the only way to keep them in the forefront where they belong.

Lord Jesus: Draw my heart close to you.

July 20

The centurion and the men with him who were keeping watch over Jesus feared greatly when they saw the earthquake and all that was happening, and they said, "Truly this was the Son of God!" Matthew 27:54

These are strictly my thoughts. Nowhere in Scripture does it say anything that supports why I perceive the following things.

As Jesus hung dying on the cross, I think that God was standing with His back turned to him, tears running down His cheeks. I think He could not bear to see the pain His Son was suffering. I also think that as the moment of His death arrived, the angels, the devil, and all of creation were holding their collective breath: the angels watching in wonder as Jesus completed his mission and anticipating His return to their midst; the devil wondering if God was really going to let His Son die there, anticipating a free reign on earth; creation awaiting the event that would ensure the eventual moment when it will be released from its bondage under the realm of sin.

When I think about the response of the devil to Jesus' death I am reminded of the creature Gollum in the third *The Lord of the Rings* movie when he finally gets the ring back from Frodo and he's dancing around in elation. A moment later he's sinking into the lava never to be seen again, and both he and the ring are destroyed. I'm sure the devil danced and cheered as Jesus let go of his hold to life on this earth, as once again the fallen angel showed his lack of understanding of the things of God. He isn't dancing and cheering now, though. He has finally realized that time is growing short. Evil is growing around us at an alarming rate. The devil and his minions are working overtime to try to get as many people to fall into disbelief as they can before time runs out.

Scripture does say that there was a great earthquake after Jesus' moment of death (reaction of creation?); the veil was torn in the Temple (angels opening the way for the masses to pray in God's personal presence?); the tombs of the saints were opened and their bodies raised (release from the old afterlife to be taken into the heavenlies?). It also says that the centurion and the other Roman soldiers saw these things (the darkness, the earthquake, and maybe some dead people) and were greatly afraid, saying, "Truly, this was the Son of God!"

For some people it takes an earthquake, an eclipse, and some dead people, all at once, to believe in Christ. I hope that this is not you. There are so many blessings that can be had once you've given in to His leading. And even though life doesn't become completely easy, it's good to know that there is a Light at the end of the tunnel.

God bless. Be safe. Watch out for minions.

Lord Jesus: Thank You!

July 21

Keep my commands and live, my teaching as the apple
of your eye; bind them on your fingers, write them on the
tablet of your heart. Say to wisdom, "You are my sister!"
call Understanding, "Friend!" Proverbs 7:2-4

I wonder if this is where someone got the idea that the fruit from the garden that Eve ate was an apple. 'She saw that the fruit of the tree was pleasing to the eye and also good for eating.' There are three other verses in the Bible that refer to the apple of one's eye. Apples and apple trees are mentioned four times in the Song of Songs, but they were not one of the fruits carved into the temple's furnishings and embellishments.

The old saying goes that 'an apple a day keeps the doctor away', and it is now known that apples cleanse the colon where it is believed that many cancers begin due to toxin buildup. So apples are good for the body, and are highly desirable for cleansing and overall health. Perhaps this is why the Lord led Solomon to create this verse when he was writing the book of Proverbs. Maybe He wanted to place His wisdom alongside a part of his creation that would also lead to health and well-being.

Perhaps He's saying that for spiritual health we should not only follow the law of the Lord (Ten Commandments) but also study them so that they become ingrained on our hearts. Then we will be able to gain understanding in many areas. And what is wisdom after all except the application of knowledge, gained through understanding, to the events in our lives.

Lord Jesus: Grant me the grace of understanding that I may grow in wisdom.

July 22

They are filled with every form of wickedness, evil, greed and
malice; full of envy, murder, rivalry, treachery and spite. They
are gossips and scandalmongers and they hate God. They are
insolent, haughty, boastful, ingenious in their wickedness, and
rebellious toward their parents. They are senseless, faithless,
heartless, ruthless. Although they know the just decree of God
that all who practice such things deserve death, they not only
do them but give approval to those who practice them.
Romans 1:29-32

Sound like anybody you know? If so, you might want to distance yourself
from them before they wear off on you. I used to run with these types,
but PRAISE THE LORD!!!! He rescued me from their clutches. Life
with them was a dead-end street, nowhere to go but down. The sad part
about these people to me is that those among us who are struggling
to find a place to fit in will stumble across them, fall prey to their
wickedness, and stay with them because of their approval. There are so
many young people today who have no home life to speak of that they
oftentimes end up as one of these unfortunate souls. They didn't receive
love and kindness at home, so they have no idea what it is or the ability
to share it. They only know that they want something to fill that void in
their heart, and someone with evil intent will often find them and offer
them something that seems like love.

Knowing that there are people out there who want nothing more than
to steal away your kids for their indecent purposes is one reason that
I teach kids. It's also why I support programs that bring the Lord to
the dangerous neighborhoods and work to teach boys and girls what a
life of responsibility and love looks like. It's not drugs, alcohol, sex, or
gangs – it's love, kindness, and friendship with God. It's living life on
purpose and for a purpose. It is also a life where you think for yourself
and take responsibility for your actions. And as I teach my kids, 'I
wasn't raised right' is no excuse for bad behavior from an adult. Grow
up and be a good example! Practice the virtues and the fruits of the

spirit, and you may find that you don't have the time or the inclination to practice your old wicked ways.

Lord Jesus: Surround me with people who will lift me up, not break me down.

July 23

I will bring upon Judah and all the citizens of Jerusalem every
evil that I threatened; because when I spoke they did not
obey, when I called they did not answer. Jeremiah 35:17b

The only thing that the devil can take from God is His children. So if you hear a little voice calling to you, find out who it's from before you go wandering off after it. The source will be easy to ascertain; just look to where it will lead you. If it requires you to compromise your values, lie or misrepresent your intentions, or step on someone else to do it, then it isn't from God.

Every situation is an opportunity. Choose wisely which way to turn and which voice you will listen to. If it's God calling, don't delay in responding – even if you have to say, "Lord, I'm not ready! Help me!" just so He knows that you're hearing Him. After all, we don't want Him to get tired of calling, just like the owner of the vineyard that kept looking for fruit from the tree that wasn't producing.

Lord Jesus: Help me to hear your voice more clearly.

July 24

Consider this: whoever sows sparingly will also reap sparingly,
and whoever sows bountifully will also reap bountifully.
2 Corinthians 9:6

I know you've heard 'You reap what you sow,' but did you stop to think that the amount of seed is just as important as the seed itself? The fact that a person sows the seed of the Lord is a statement of faith. But the greater statement is made by the amount of seed offered for planting. It's like the woman putting her two coins worth only a few cents into the temple treasury (Mark 12:42): it was only a few cents to the accountant, but it was everything she had – 100% of her funds. She would have no money for food or shelter after giving it away. Alternatively, those who have much money (or time) and give only a small percentage will reap heavenly rewards in the same percentage.

I remember my grandma telling me that she had made a pledge to give money to a fundraising event. When the post came requesting her payment, she was short on funds. If she paid it, she wouldn't have money for food or prescriptions for the rest of the month. It was a short time (a week or so) until her next pension payment, but it meant she would have no money until it arrived. She was quite apprehensive about that prospect, as we all would be. Nevertheless, she told me that she had told the Lord that she would make good on her commitment and rely on His goodness for the rest of the month. She sent the pledge. The next day she received a refund check from a doctor's office for an overpayment she had sent to them. Remember when I talked about trust, delight, and commit? She is the one who modeled those principles for me. I thank God every day for her faithfulness – that she showed me the way, even though I chose not to follow it for a time.

"Give, and it will be given to you. A good measure, pressed down, shaken together, and running over will be poured into your lap. For with the measure you use, it will be measured to you." Luke 6:38

Lord Jesus: Grant me the grace and trust to be a generous and cheerful giver.

July 25

He would have decreed their destruction had not
Moses, the chosen leader, withstood him in the breach
to turn back his destroying anger. Psalm 106:23

I want to tell you some more about my grandma today. She was the queen of intercessory prayer. She was *always* praying for someone – usually one of us grandkids. She was the one who always said, and meant, 'Hate the sin, love the sinner.' Sometimes I think her prayers were the only thing that kept me from getting killed in my youthful stupidity.

There was more than one time that Moses stepped up before God and begged for his mercy when the Lord was planning to destroy the Israelites, despite the fact that they didn't seem to trust him – or God for that matter. You'd think that ten plagues, the washing away of Pharaoh's army, a fiery pillar by night, and a cloud by day would have been enough to build some faith in those people, but evidently not. They were always grumbling against Moses and God, and yet Moses interceded with God about them for their welfare. I think some people are just born to be prayer warriors, and Moses and my gran were two of those people.

How about you? Who do you pray for? Is there someone out there that is alive today because you stepped into the breach for them? I look at America today, and I see a nation in need of intercessory prayer. It's like God said to Jonah about the plant He provided and the sinful Ninevites: "You have been concerned about this plant, though you did not tend it or make it grow. It sprang up overnight and died overnight. And should I not have concern for the great city of Nineveh, in which there are more than a hundred and twenty thousand people who cannot tell their right hand from their left—and also many animals?" Jonah didn't want to go to the Ninevites and tell them to repent, because he knew that if they did, God would show them mercy. How cold-hearted he was! He cared more about one plant than he did for over 120,000 people.

We all want mercy even when we aren't aware that we need it, and America needs prayer. Pray that hearts will be opened to the need for God. Pray for a revival to sweep the nation. Pray that our leaders will have changed hearts that will serve the people, not their own pockets, corporate lobbyists, or PACs. And pray also that you will remain faithful whatever comes.

Lord Jesus: Have mercy upon our nation; open our hearts to receive you.

July 26

If your hand or foot causes you to sin, cut it off and throw it away.
It is better for you to enter into life maimed or crippled than with
two hands or two feet to be thrown into eternal fire. Matthew 18:8

Is heaven the place where you want to spend eternity? If so, what would you be willing to give up to get there? Cigarettes? Beer? Porn? What about an arm or a leg or an eye?

If you don't have a good understanding of how God feels about sin, look closely at today's verse. All sin is offensive to Him. And while He forgives sins, His preference would be that there wasn't a need for it. Jesus said to cut off the body part that causes you to sin if you can't control it. I don't think He really wants you to dispatch it from yourself, but rather to find a way to distance yourself from the things that the eyes, hands or feet lust after. If your feet cause you to run to places you shouldn't be, you have to find a way to prevent them from going to that place. Your eyes may lust for porn – give them something else to do. And pray for deliverance.

But what if the real problem is your heart? Would you cut it out to stop the sinning? In the book of Ezekiel, God says that He will take away the heart of stone of His people and give them a heart of flesh, a heart that is tender, loving, and forgiving like His. You don't have to cut out your heart, just ask God to change it to be the one He wants you to have.

There isn't anything that God *can't* do. The thing to remember is that He will give you anything good (good for the kingdom) that you ask for. The key is that you have to ask and truly desire that which you ask for. If you want that foot, hand, eye, or heart to stop sinning, you have to ask for help to get it done. A fight against the devil is one that we cannot win on our own. We need Jesus to help us fight that battle.

Lord Jesus: *Help me change my heart and stop sinning.*

July 27
What has been, that will be; what has been done, that will be done. Nothing is new under the sun. Ecclesiastes 1:9

There's nothing new under the sun.... People like to think that they are original, but the truth is that they aren't. The sins are all the same, they just may look a little different to some. And God has seen it all before. I don't think He can be shocked by anything that we can dream up. The rest of us who aren't prone to hate and violence, however, never cease to be horrified by the escalation of violent deaths in the world and the manner in which those deaths take place: terrorist beheadings, bombs, guns, chemical weapons, and man-made viruses. Is there no end to the viciousness which mankind will inflict upon its own and the earth?

Paul said that all creation has been groaning as it awaits the redemption of the world (Romans 8:22), and that was almost two thousand years ago. Think of all the wars this planet has seen since that time, of all the evil that has crawled across the face of the earth. Just because a sin isn't new doesn't mean you should keep looking for one that is. And it's like I tell the kids: Just because you can doesn't mean you should.

Lord Jesus: Stop me from looking for something new that isn't You.

July 28

"Take what is yours and go. What if I wish to give this last
one the same as you? Am I not free to do as I wish with my
own money? Are you envious because I am generous?"
Matthew 20:14, 15

How many of you have worked at a job where you discovered that
someone else there used to do it, but they made more money at it? How
did you feel? I confess that this happened to me one time, and I reacted
to the situation the same as the workers in the vineyard who had worked
all day: I perceived that the situation was unfair, despite the fact that I
had taken the job knowing what the pay was beforehand.

Jesus' parable today shows us the Father's generosity toward those who
come to salvation late in life. I have heard some people say that those
on their death-bed shouldn't be allowed into heaven. How arrogant!
Every Christian should rejoice when a soul is saved – the angels do – no
matter what stage of life they are in. Thankfully God doesn't have the
same merit system that we do, otherwise nobody would be allowed in.

I used to know a woman who was constantly comparing other Christians
to herself to see if they were living up to her standards. She was quite
puffed up in her self-righteousness. (She would have made a good
Pharisee!) I heard her more than once criticizing others for their
behaviors (without them being present to defend themselves) in front
of people who knew them. I would jump in to defend them whether I
disagreed with her assessment or not. She had no right to compare
anyone to someone else. Or judge them by her evaluation.

God's grace and mercy are boundless. Hallelujah! We can all get in
just by believing in and serving His Son, whether at an early age or a
late one. If you accepted His call at an early age, you should be the
one bringing other souls into the kingdom along your way. It's called
storing up treasure in heaven. And don't compare yourself to others, in
any way, ever. Their path is not yours, and vice versa. It's not our job to

determine if someone else is doing their job or receiving equitable pay for their deeds. That will come to all on judgment day. Fair and unfair reside only in our minds. Let's get rid of this notion, and life will be much easier to tolerate.

Lord Jesus: Thank you for not using our ideas of fairness.

July 29

For you love all things that are and loathe nothing that you have made, for what you hated, you would not have fashioned.
Wisdom 11:24

If you had ever received an email from me, you'd have seen that my electronic signature reads as follows: "God doesn't care where you were born, how you were raised, what language you speak, or what color your skin is. He loves everybody the same. The only difference between people is how much each one loves Him back."

Believe it or not, I used to say that before I ever read this verse. It gave me reason to smile when I came across it. One of the things I tell people when they say hateful things about others is that they aren't allowed to do so because God loves that person, otherwise He would not have allowed them to exist. And if God loves them, then we also need to learn how to do so – even if we have to do it from afar because we can't stand to be in the same room with them. If they choose to not love him back, that's on their head. We should pray for them to have a change of heart. It isn't God who makes junk, it's the people of this earth that take what He creates and destroy that creation and the purpose for which He created it.

Lord Jesus: Help me to love those who are unpleasant.

July 30

If we acknowledge our sins, he is faithful and just and will
forgive our sins and cleanse us from every wrongdoing.
1 John 1:9

The hardest part of being a Christian is having to recognize that we
are not perfect. When I was young, I thought that I could be perfect,
and I worked hard to get there. Then I realized that perfection is a
moving target, always being revised by myself or the one that I sought
to please. And the stupidest thing about that process was that the one
I was aiming to please wasn't the Lord.

Even though He loves me as I am (else He would not have rescued me),
He still expects me to work to clean up my act (sanctification). This is
not the same as striving for perfection. Only Jesus was perfect, and He
had to be divine to make that happen. We simply can't get there. And
even when we might be close, there is always a minion breathing hatred
in our ear telling us that we have become proud in our sanctity. The
most pious of the Saints believed themselves to be the worst of sinners,
and they flagellated themselves (struck their flesh with a strap or belt)
for their iniquity. Even Pope John Paul II did this.

So long as we strive to grow our faith and recognize that we are sinful
and need God's mercy, He will forgive us and help us to improve our
condition.

Lord Jesus: Cleanse me and make me whole.

July 31

In the visions of the night I saw the fourth beast, different from all
the others, terrifying, horrible, and of extraordinary strength; it
had great iron teeth with which it devoured and crushed, and what
was left it trampled with its feet. I was considering the ten horns it
had, when suddenly another, a little horn, sprang out of their midst,
and three of the previous horns were torn away to make room for it.
This horn had eyes like a man and a mouth that spoke arrogantly.

Daniel 7:7, 8

Ha! You thought that came from Revelation, didn't you? It's a precursor
for the person we will see come to lead us in the end times. Somewhere
along the way, he will usurp three of the ten heads of state in his bid
for control. I find this one fascinating trying to figure out how Daniel
saw it and was led to describe it this way. It's a man as well as a nation,
exceedingly destructive and arrogant. He will chew up peoples and
spit them out. And the ones he can't get his hands on, he will trample
underfoot. He will be evil and unkind and hide it by deception. People
who vote him into power will be swayed by his charm until he takes
control and reveals his true nature – just like Hitler.

I saw a program many years ago that said Nostradamus had predicted
that the antichrist would be born in 1962, but I can't find that tidbit
anywhere. I don't know where that piece of info came from, and I can't
remember what show it was. Regardless, we won't know who he is until
it's too late to stop him. Then, only prayer and the hand of God will
save us from his clutches.

Lord Jesus: Open our eyes to see the evil one when he appears.

August

August 1

To me, the very least of all the holy ones, this grace was given, to preach to the Gentiles the inscrutable riches of Christ. Ephesians 3:8

I've heard it said that 'God doesn't call the equipped – He equips the called.' I was very enamored by this statement when I first heard it, and I agree with it greatly up to a certain point. As I've gotten older (and a little wiser) I've recognized a certain pattern that shows that there are people who are selected for jobs that have the skill sets already in place. They simply need a push to get started.

Such was Paul. He already knew the law inside and out. Who better to refute its limits and constraints and understand the freedom of life in Christ than him? He was uniquely qualified to understand the mysteries revealed to him by the holy Spirit about the nature of salvation, the members of the body in unity, the need for all of the gifts to be represented and used, and the willingness to suffer for the only One who could reward him properly.

As I have traveled my journey I've discovered much about myself and others. One of the most important things I've learned is that it usually isn't a matter of can't; it's a matter of won't. Sometimes a person lacks self-confidence and fails to believe in the ability of God to bring them up from where they are: they *won't* believe. Other times people simply refuse to do a work because they don't see anything in it for themselves, because it's all give and no get: they *won't* share their time, talents, or treasure.

Time is one of the most important things that we need to be better stewards of. It is also one of the best gifts that we can give to others.

Sharing our time says that someone is more important than whatever else we could be doing. Most services to God don't require special talents or lots of money – they just take time. Try to touch at least one person in a special way every day by sharing a bit of your time.

Lord Jesus: ***Teach me to be a better steward of my time.***

August 2

You were renowned among the nations for your beauty,
perfect as it was, because of my splendor which I had
bestowed on you, says the Lord GOD. Ezekiel 16:14

Beauty comes from within despite what is on the outside. I watched the movie ***Shallow Hal*** one time, a movie which takes an interesting look at the perception of true beauty. Hal had been hypnotized to disregard appearances and perceive only people's inner beauty. The reality of his situation didn't register with me the first time I saw the nurse from the children's ward at the hospital. I had to see the shots flip from Hal's view to the other guy's view of this woman a couple of times for me catch on. In actuality she was a ravishing beauty, but to Hal she looked like a hag. She may have had a pretty package, but inside she was cold, dark, and selfish.

Ancient Israel was known for its blessings which came from the Lord. But because they were falling away from Him and following pagan gods, they began to look like a hag to the Lord. Their beauty came as a blessing from God, but when they turned away from Him, that beauty also fell away. They were cold, dark, and ugly; murderers and adulterers; unfaithful to Him and to each other. Repeated calls to return to God and holiness went unheeded, and so they had to be brought low in order for their beauty to be restored. They had to hit rock bottom to find that the Rock at the bottom is God.

Lord Jesus: You make me beautiful!

August 3

"I know your works; I know that you are neither cold nor hot. I wish you were either cold or hot. So, because you are lukewarm, neither hot nor cold, I will vomit you out of my mouth." Revelation 3:15, 16

One of the reasons that many people don't want to be Christians is the outward appearance that many so-called Christians show to the world. (Ghandi felt this way too.) The faith they profess is a treatise they claim but don't work to enact or support.

Jesus wants to see a 'go big or go home' kind of person; one that is all in or all out. For those that don't share their faith or serve others, He has no time. They are an embarrassment to those who are true to their faith and their God. The ultimate fate of these is that they will be vomited out of his mouth. He will spew them away from Himself on the judgment day and assign them a place with the evildoers, because **not** doing good is the same as doing bad in His view. Other words for these folks are apathetic or complacent, and they are unaware of the danger of their condition.

Lord Jesus: Rescue me from apathy and complacency!

August 4

Our eyes ever wasted away, looking in vain for
aid; from our watchtower we watched for a nation
that could not save us. Lamentations 4:17

Herein lies the heart of the problem of the Israelites: that they relied on the strength of man rather than the strength of God....

I look at the nation of America today, and I see ancient Israel. We have turned our backs not our faces to God and removed Him from our schools and our government buildings; we have murdered and stolen and corrupted the system of government; we have harmed the children at every turn and in every unthinkable manner; and we have not sought His wisdom and intercession in great enough numbers to be effective. We have spent money we didn't have and printed more to pay our bills; we've poisoned the soil and the people with chemicals; and we've lost our sense of decency, modesty, respect, and propriety.

The Chinese government owns so much of our debt that they basically own our nation. Amos 6:14 says, For the LORD God Almighty declares, "I will stir up a nation against you, Israel, that will oppress you all the way from Lebo Hamath to the valley of Arabah." I fear this is China coming to collect its payment from the American people for the debts our government has incurred in our name, hence the verse for today.

No matter how many people you put on the watchtower, what they see doesn't matter if you have no weapons to fight with and those weapons are what you rely on for deliverance. Only the Lord can save this nation, but the nation doesn't seek His face and His mercy and ask for deliverance.

Lord Jesus: Be our strength and our defense.

August 5

"Are not his sisters all with us? Where did this man get all this?" And they took offense at him. But Jesus said to them, "A prophet is not without honor except in his native place and in his own house." And he did not work many mighty deeds there because of their lack of faith. Matthew 13:56-58

How many of you are the same person you were when you were growing up? When you were in college? As you were five years ago? It is a normal thing to grow, learn, and to be changed into something better than what we used to be, and prayer and meditation can change even the hardest of hearts.

Donna Noble

In today's passage, Jesus has been teaching in the synagogue in Nazareth. He speaks of heavenly topics as from knowledge or great teaching. But the people there know Him from when He was growing up in their community. He is the son of Joseph and Mary; His family still lives there. To them, He is still the carpenter's son – no one of importance. They can only see Him for what human appearances he has. They barely see Him even as gifted, much less as the Son of God. They seem to say, "He is the son of Joseph – He can't be the Son of God. We know who His father is, and He's not God." To use a phrase that my grandma used to say, they thought He was being 'too big for His britches,' trying to be something that He really wasn't. But Jesus wasn't just the Son of Man; He was and is the Son of God. The people of His hometown weren't open-minded enough to see Him for who He was and be saved.

Many people today have the same problem – they can't see beyond the physical they know to the spiritual behind it. They are too busy seeing the human person we used to be to allow for growth and a change in life. I can understand this situation. Before I became Catholic, I was in ministry. I used to visit people in their homes and at the hospital. I also spent a year preaching. None of my family has ever heard me preach. My siblings have good reason – they lived far away. My parents, however, did not. I lived with one, and the other lived less than one mile from the church. To them, I was still their child, not a grown woman who had spent much time reading, learning, and praying for wisdom and guidance.

I am not holding a grudge – my point is simply this: please don't restrict someone to who or what they used to be. Allow them the freedom to be who the Lord has created them to be. Allow them to keep growing, and you do the same. The Jews of Jesus' day missed out because they were stuck on what used to be. Don't miss out! Receive His blessings no matter who they come through.

Lord Jesus: Allow us to see your wisdom in each other.

August 6

Then they who fear the LORD spoke with one another, and the
LORD listened attentively; And a record book was written before
him of those who fear the LORD and trust in his name.
Malachi 3:16

I was told that your name gets written in the book of life when you get
baptized. In the Catholic Church, most people believe that the babies
who are stillborn or are very sick and die before a priest can christen
them don't get to go to heaven. I disagree. I believe that babies and
very young children are innocent and could not possibly go anywhere
but heaven if they should die. They get special considerations I guess
you could say.

What does it mean to you to fear the Lord? Is it fear of punishment
or discipline? Fear of hell? Fear that you'll never understand Him? A
preacher once told me that the fear I should have for God is really awe
and wonder. I think it's actually a bit of all three. You have to be in awe
of his amazing power and mercy, stand in wonder at how everything He
created in the universe works so perfectly, and fear that you could fall
so far from Him that he would finally drop you out of his hand and let
you go forever. That's the only thing that I would fear.

I trust that He tells me when I'm out of line, and I get my house back in
order. I don't put things like that off as I used to. Keeping my salvation
passport up to date is the most important thing in the universe for me.
I don't want to miss that ride.

Lord Jesus: You are AWESOME!

August 7

Rejoice always. Pray without ceasing. In all circumstances give
thanks, for this is the will of God for you in Christ Jesus.
1 Thessalonians 5:16-18

Faith 101. Here it is: the perfect synopsis for how to live the life of
faith. I've heard a lot of people say that God wants us to be happy. I
say, maybe. He never promised that we would be happy. And Jesus said
that we would be happy if we were poor and merciful, if we mourned,
were peacemakers, and hungered for righteousness. Poor, hungry,
and mournful doesn't sound like happiness to most people. But the
beatitudes (which is what that list is) reflect a state of the heart, not
a state of the mind. Being happy and rejoicing because I'm poor in
things of the spirit is a positive thing because I get to pray for blessings
which I then receive. I can rejoice in my mourning over my sinfulness
because I can ask for forgiveness and receive it. I rejoice in my hunger
for righteousness because He is faithful to fill me full when I ask for it.

This is a prescription for joy in the heart – a heart filled with the love
and mercy of God. And knowing that every moment is a challenge to
maintaining my holiness, I pray in every moment to receive that which
I need at that time. And all of these blessings are mine because of the
sacrifice of Jesus Christ, so I give thanks that I was found worthy to be
saved and kept by Him. God didn't have to promise us happiness. He
gave us His Son, and that brings all the happiness I need.

Lord God: Thank you for the joy of receiving your Son – my
happiness.

August 8
My being thirsts for God, the living God. When can
I go and see the face of God? Psalm 42:3

Some days I don't take being alive and human very well. I get tired and frustrated with the world, with the government, with people who walk around with their head in the clouds denying that the world is a cesspool. It's a terrible time to be alive, and yet it's a great time to be alive. I take small comfort from the fact that the world is so bad that the Lord can't leave it go much longer, so I expect to see Him come back soon.

This might be a good time to talk about emergency preparedness. There are things going on in the world that I don't see being rectified peacefully. There are more than a few governments on the verge of collapse, and some American cities have filed for bankruptcy.

It isn't uncommon these days to hear the newscasters and weather people talking about events of Biblical proportion. There are strange things going on with the sun and in the earth's weather patterns, and there are lots of earthquakes and volcanic eruptions. Maybe it means something, and maybe it doesn't.

I choose to believe that they are signs of judgment upon mankind. And because I believe this, I have a small store of food, water, candles, and first aid supplies – just in case. You can't rely on the electrical grid to sustain a direct hit from a terrorist, and a massive solar flare could knock out power as well. The power lines to my house aren't buried, so being without electricity is something that happens here about once a year. Even if nothing happens, I still have supplies ready in case I get snowed in. Jesus doesn't have to come back for that to happen.

If you want to start preparing yourself, just start picking up a few extra things on your regular trips to the store. Before you know it you'll have a nice little stockpile. Other things to think about are wood, gasoline, a generator, matches, and camping gear. If you think you need help, there are plenty of books out there to guide you. Better yet, just ask God to tell you what you need to do.

Me, I'm ready to go and see God; but I don't feel like my mission is complete yet, so I expect to be here a while longer. Nevertheless, I can still long for His company and desire to be in the peace of His presence.

Lord God: I want to see you soon and be free from this human bondage.

August 9

So turn from youthful desires and pursue righteousness,
faith, love, and peace, along with those who call on
the Lord with purity of heart. 2 Timothy 2:22

Who is teaching your children how to behave? Is it you? Are you relying on their school teachers? Are they learning from TV, video games, and YouTube? The desires of youth are hard enough to overcome when a child grows up learning morality and propriety in the home. If their views are skewed by the amorality of the world, they are not in a favorable position to rise above that – especially when they see many others living that lifestyle. And what would be their motivation to turn from such a life?

Studies suggest that the human personality is fully developed by age 8. After that time, it might take a traumatic event to cause someone to want to change their beliefs and behaviors. I know from teaching religious education that some people have not created self-sustaining, moral, mindful children. I had two kids in my class of sixth-graders that said they never came to church. I asked why they were there, and they replied, "Because my parents make me." I thought sometimes that I was their babysitter. Those were the ones that caused the most disruptions, and they weren't ever able to answer any questions about the Bible. One said he didn't think they even had one at his house, because he didn't remember having seen one.

I understand the rambunctiousness of children, but that doesn't excuse failing to teach them proper behavior whether you teach them about Jesus or not. And think about this (if it applies): How will you answer God when He asks you why you didn't teach your children about Him and how to behave in a righteous manner? (Deuteronomy 11:19)

Lord Jesus: Help me to teach my children to be good citizens and Christians.

August 10
Seek good and not evil, that you may live; then truly the LORD, the God of hosts, will be with you as you claim! Amos 5:14

Amos was a really unpopular guy in Israel. First of all, he was from Judah. Second, he brought a very unwelcome message from the Lord: Repent, or be destroyed! We know that the Ninevites listened when Jonah said it, but the Israelites were so blinded by their pride in being the chosen race that they didn't believe the Lord would ever do such a thing. Never mind the fact that they didn't worship the Lord but rather a golden calf in the temple in Samaria. They substituted an idol for God thus breaking the first commandment He ever gave them – the greatest of evils in the eyes of the Lord.

The activity some of us engaged in as children comes to mind; you know, the one where you say, "My dad blah blah blah...." And I respond, "Well, *my* dad...." It's a one-upper thing, always trying to top someone else with ours which is better (in this case a god). The Samaritans strayed from the true path to freedom, security, and blessing when they separated themselves from the temple in Jerusalem and sought other gods; their pride then kept them away. They did not have a book of the law to teach the people the ways of God (it was in the temple in Jerusalem), and so they raised their children to serve a false god. And generation after generation took them ever farther away from their Redeemer.

Sometimes I think that we, too, claim that the Lord is with us despite all evidence to the contrary. Some people just can't seem to get anything to go right, and it makes me wonder what they are harboring in their heart that keeps God from blessing them with abundance. And while it may be a time of testing, our response to that testing will determine whether God chooses to continue to bless us.

I have a friend who lost his job and remained faithful for a time. But when he couldn't get another job, he blamed God for not blessing him – despite the fact that their bills still got paid. They weren't suffering greatly, but they weren't as comfortable as they had been before. God doesn't promise comfort at all times. He promises to stay with us so long as we stay with Him. Mother Teresa is reported to have said that she never felt close to Jesus after He gave her the assignment in Calcutta, and yet she still remained faithful to both.[12]

Lord Jesus: I want to always be close to you – no matter what comes.

August 11

The aim of this instruction is love from a pure heart, a
good conscience, and a sincere faith. 1 Timothy 1:5

"If God is love, then why do bad things happen? A truly loving God would never allow these things." So goes the argument from some who would say that there is no God because bad things happen in the world. What this argument fails to consider is that a loving God and Father will not force us to acknowledge or serve Him. He wants us to come to Him willingly. Nor will He stop all bad things from happening since they come from our ability to choose right or wrong.

I submit that for each large bad thing that transpires in the world, there are many smaller ones that are stopped. Remember yesterday's reading from Amos? The people said that they knew God, but what they really knew was a story about a being who had saved their forefathers but whom they did not know, serve, or love. How can you love that which you do not know?

True love comes from purity, faith, and a clear conscience. You cannot have a clean conscience with sin in your heart. And those big, bad things that happen are allowed in order to awaken us to the presence of sin in the world and our hearts, and to show us the need for God. We should be careful when pointing fingers at those who act out their sins until we have cleansed ourselves from our own iniquities. And until we do, we cannot claim that we have love. Anything that we think is love is just a false shadow of the truth.

Lord Jesus: Teach me how to love.

August 12

Catch us the foxes, the little foxes that damage the vineyards;
for our vineyards are in bloom! Song of Songs 2:15

Think of this as a metaphor.... As we travel though our life and do whatever it is that each of us does, we sometimes do things that aren't quite kosher: an off-color remark, an untimely smirk, or a brief outburst of angry profanity. Our failings may be habitual, intentional, or accidental. As a spokesperson for Jesus, I try to keep my sins out of public view and only show my positive and uplifting side to the world. I don't want to share my selfish, occasionally negative or tired self any more than I have to. I have made it my goal to produce an excellent vintage from my area of the vineyard and leave a trail of smiles behind me. To do that I must catch these little sins, these little foxes, before they take over and ruin my vines.

If people know you are a Christian, they hold you to a higher standard of performance and behavior. I haven't always behaved like a Christian, and I regret that I gave our faith a black eye. I have learned that those outside the church will not only judge you but also your faith group by the activities they see you do. Is that fair? Of course not, but they aren't the ones that are supposed to refrain from judging others, are they?

Lord Jesus: Help me to be under control.

August 13
Strive for peace with everyone, and for that holiness without which no one will see the Lord. Hebrews 12:14

If we could get everyone on the planet to subscribe to just this one verse, the world would be like heaven. Imagine: No one blowing your doors off and then cutting you off in traffic; people rushing to open doors for others; no one blaming someone else, but each admitting when they messed up and caused the problem; everyone picking up their socks and putting them in the laundry and keeping their shoes by the door, ready to go; Please and Thank you and My pleasure!

Wow! Wouldn't that be great? Peace, harmony, and brotherly love at every turn; what could be better? Only this: Knowing that peace leads to holiness and holiness leads to God. It doesn't seem natural any more for people to behave this way, so here is my challenge: Go through today and tomorrow and the day after that and the day after that and so on, and only say kind things; open every door for someone else that you can; when someone on the road mistreats you, say out loud, "I LOVE YOU!" You can't hate someone when you're saying I Love You. Thrive on the strange looks that you get from people you don't know and the even stranger ones from those you do know. See how much better you feel in a week, and then see how long you can keep it going. Revel in the love of the Lord which has enabled you to make this change, because that's what it is – a change of heart. Feel free to teach it to others, especially the ones who give you the looks of mistrust.

Lord Jesus: Help me practice peace and holiness today – no matter what.

August 14

If you do not stand firm in your faith, you will
not stand at all. Isaiah 7:9b (NIV)

Throughout our lives the Lord has been bringing us new to every moment: testing us, stretching our faith and making it grow, teaching us about love and kindness and mercy, and giving us the opportunity to grow closer to Him. Every moment is a test to see if everything from the past will fall away to make room for the new life in Christ. Every second is a choice to continue to love and serve or to turn and fall back into degradation. I've told you to be intentional; I've asked you to grow and change. I want you to love God and your neighbor, and be kind to everyone. But I am simply the messenger. God is wanting and telling and asking. He sent me to you to deliver these messages. He wants you to be prepared for whatever comes whenever it arrives, because … unless your faith is firm, you will not stand.

Any heartbeat could be your last. How do you want your life to end? In faith and trust, or in fear and insecurity? Every breath is a conscious decision to live in faith or to fall. Choose wisely.

Lord Jesus: I choose faith and life!

August 15

Anyone destined for captivity goes into captivity. Anyone destined to
be slain by the sword shall be slain by the sword. Revelation 13:10

When this verse was written in the book of Revelation, the speaker wasn't talking about the wicked. He was referring to the elect who are alive at that time under the dictatorship of the antichrist. Some will be allowed to be found out and murdered so that they can be examples of faith to others. Remember yesterday's verse about standing firm in your faith? This is the ultimate trial. You can stand firm and be slaughtered, or you can recant and give up your salvation and eternity in heaven. Which would you choose today? The good news is, many will die in the earthquake that will be so large as to displace mountains; and if your faith is weak, maybe that's your best way out. Still none too pleasant, though.

Just remember to breathe and pray for the strength you need to get through each moment as it comes. And if you have to die for Jesus, well, it's only fair since He died for you. And His death on the cross was strung out over an estimated six hours. Maybe we won't have to suffer that long.

Lord Jesus: Thank you for dying for me.

August 16

If I tell a righteous person that they will surely live, but then they trust in their righteousness and do evil, none of the righteous things that person has done will be remembered; they will die for the evil they have done. Ezekiel 33:13 (NIV)

A lot of people are fond of saying, "Once saved, always saved." This verse is the reason that I disagree with that position. Now, I have to say that I don't know exactly what qualifies for evil that will disqualify someone for the prize. It certainly would be full-blown apostasy, where someone walks away from God and belief in Him. I have no idea what else might be considered sufficiently evil in the eyes of the Lord to cost someone their salvation, but a good guess might be the list we had from Paul in his letter to the Romans last month:

> They are filled with every form of wickedness, evil, greed and malice; full of envy, murder, rivalry, treachery and spite. They are gossips and scandalmongers and they hate God. They are insolent, haughty, boastful, ingenious in their wickedness, and rebellious toward their parents. They are senseless, faithless, heartless, ruthless. Although they know the just decree of God that all who practice such things deserve death, they not

only do them but give approval to those who practice them. (Romans 1:29-32)

You would think that these people would never have known God, but earlier in the letter he wrote this:

> For although *they knew* God, they neither glorified him as God nor gave thanks to him; but their thinking became futile, and their foolish hearts were darkened. Although they claimed to be wise, they became fools and exchanged the glory of the immortal God for images made to look like a mortal human being and birds and animals and reptiles. (Romans 1:21-23, italics added)

It clearly says here that they knew Him and yet left Him for a life of indulgence and the worshiping of created things. This is what happens, then, to those who know of God and continue to ignore His existence – He gives them over to their selfishness and does to them exactly what they do to Him: He leaves them alone – for all eternity.

I've said it before, and I'll say it again and again and again: Don't ignore or walk away from God and think that there will always be time to go back later. Don't take that chance. Return, repent, and be reunited to Him.

Lord Jesus: Forgive me for my waywardness!

August 17

First of all, then, I ask that supplications, prayers, petitions, and thanksgivings be offered for everyone, for kings and for all in authority, that we may lead a quiet and tranquil life in all devotion and dignity. 1 Timothy 2:1, 2

I've noticed over the past few years that the people of America are becoming polarized in their view; at least that's the way it appears when you look at TV and facebook. I have friends that are all over the board when it comes to beliefs and practices, but there seems to be a clear distinction in the way they think the country should be run and a widening in the gap between what the two sides are willing to support. You see it on news programs also: the liberals and conservatives are duking it out on live TV, and no one wants to give in to the other's position. Everyone thinks they're right, and they are unwilling to consider that there is value in others' proposals.

It seems as though there is no way out of the political gridlock that is the new normal. In today's verse, Paul instructs Timothy to teach his flock to pray for the leaders of their nation. I think this needs to be stressed amongst the Christians of America (and the world) more than ever. If there is to be any hope of peace and community in the future, we need to learn to find common ground and compromise (in some areas) once again. And then maybe we can have some devotion and dignity restored to our nation, at home and abroad.

Lord Jesus: Please bless our leaders with open hearts and minds to serve your people with dignity and devotion.

August 18
He turned to God with his whole heart and, though times were evil, he practiced virtue. Sirach 49:3

The writer of the book of Sirach was referring to King Joash in this verse. He took over as the ruler in Judah after his father who had also served the Lord. The problem with these two was that they did not finish the work set before them by the Lord. They failed to destroy all of the 'high places' (pagan temples) in the country, and so allowed the people to continue to worship other gods as an option to the Temple of God.

Similar things happen with us today. We find God, get saved, and try to move forward with Him while still dragging our old pagan ways with us.

The two are not compatible. We are called to set aside the things of our old life when we come to God – clean out that sin closet, and get rid of the dirt. That was my problem when I was baptized: I had no one to be accountable to, no one to make sure that I was putting off the old self in favor of the new. A sinful life after salvation should not be an option but rather a hindrance that we are continually trying to cast aside.

Sometimes we have to step up and speak against practices that we think are wrong in our homes, our churches, our cities, our nation, and our world. As a nation with a heart, we need to support those who cannot do it themselves. We must turn to God with our whole heart, pray for our people and the also those of other lands, and practice the virtues for which Christians are supposed to be known: Charity, Chastity, Self-Control, Patience, Kindness, Humility, and Diligence.

Lord Jesus: Remind me to practice virtue.

August 19
Follow the way of love and eagerly desire gifts of the
Spirit, especially prophecy. 1 Corinthians 14:1 (NIV)

When you were born you were given certain, specific talents to work with, and when you were baptized you got something else – the fruit of the holy Spirit. (See Galatians 5:22, 23.) After baptism, the holy Spirit starts to work on you to develop these traits and talents. Sometimes He also gives you something else, one or more of the gifts of the spirit: a message of wisdom, a message of knowledge, faith, healing, miraculous powers, prophecy, distinguishing between spirits, speaking in tongues, and interpretation of tongues. (1 Corinthians 12:7-10) Sometimes these are referred to as 'manifestations' of the Spirit. It's how He makes himself known to the world through the children of God.

Many times we have these abilities and are unaware of their presence. It is perfectly acceptable to ask for one or more of these gifts or to have the Spirit make you aware of the one(s) you already have and to help you develop them. Paul says that the most desirable of these gifts is prophecy. So what is it? Prophecy is a prediction of something to come and can be positive or negative in nature. It may relate to a person, a place, or an event. Much of the Bible is prophecy in one of several forms, with the balance often being the fulfillment of those prophecies. The predictions of the Messiah from the Old Testament are all fulfilled by Jesus in the New Testament. Many of the prophecies from the book of Daniel were fulfilled by the Greeks that destroyed Jerusalem in the 70's a.d. and are expected to be fulfilled yet again when the time nears for the *parousia* (Second Coming of Christ) and we meet the antichrist.

There are still prophets today. If you want to check out some of their information, here are a few websites to check out.

http://www.hopeoftheworld.org/
http://www.bobbyconner.org/
http://www.streamsministries.com/

Even you can be a prophet. When I ask the Lord to speak to me at night, I sometimes ask Him to tell me what's coming. He told me about the tsunami in 2004 the day before it happened; He also told it to a thirteen year-old girl in my Bible study group. It was related to some of the people on the beach in India who were worshiping the moon when the tsunami came in and washed them and their children out to sea. He gave us both the same passage:

> "Stop bringing meaningless offerings! Your incense is detestable to me. New Moons, Sabbaths and convocations — I cannot bear your worthless assemblies. Your New Moon feasts and your appointed festivals I hate with all my being. They have become a burden to me; I am weary of bearing them." (Isaiah 1:13, 14 NIV)

He also kept telling me about an island that was going to be destroyed. I thought it was Manhattan, but it turned out to be Japan's earthquake and tsunami. It had been quiet since the last election in Egypt, but he told me there was more coming. He's been telling me for over a year about problems in Egypt; now the county is in revolt since the military removed the Muslim Brotherhood president from office.

Pray for wisdom, pray for knowledge, and pray for understanding; but most of all, pray for the gift of prophecy. It will prepare you for what is to come. And please share the messages that the Lord sends you with others.

Lord Jesus: Grant me the gift of prophecy.

August 20
Because all Israel transgressed your law and went astray, not heeding your voice, the sworn malediction recorded in the law of Moses, the servant of God, was poured out over us for our sins. Daniel 9:11

One thing that people never want to hear is that they have been bad and deserve to be punished. Nevertheless, God told the people through Moses that if they did certain things that were heinous to Him, He would withhold His blessings and pour out curses upon them. The Lord did, in fact, destroy the entire nation of Israel. They had split into two kingdoms, Israel in the north and Judah in the south, and each was living sinfully and worshiping pagan gods. This is the one thing that God absolutely will not stand for, and He brought down upon the Hebrews the curses that He promised through Moses. The northern kingdom was defeated and sent into bondage by Assyria in the 700's b.c., and the southern kingdom was sent into slavery in the 500's b.c. by Babylon (modern-day Iraq).

This verse is Daniel praying to God from Babylon for mercy for himself and his fellow Judeans who were living in bondage. He was stepping into the breach, interceding with God for a change in their hearts so that they could return home to Jerusalem.

When George Washington was sworn in as our first president, he likewise prayed over the nation, dedicated it to God, and said, in effect, that those same curses would come upon the people of America if they would ever forsake the Lord God. (View a YouTube video of Rabbi Jonathan Cahn on the Sid Roth Show talking about the judgment on America for falling away from God at this link: http://youtu.be/hHSs73IAoPs).

We have become a nation of God-haters and complacent Christians. The judgments on our nation have begun, and there are more to come. It's time to get off the fence and choose a side. I would also like to point out the citation of this verse, 9:11. Uncanny, isn't it?

Lord Jesus: We have ignored you and turned our backs to you. Have mercy on us!

August 21

Grace to you and peace from God our Father and the
Lord Jesus Christ, who gave himself for our sins that he
might rescue us from the present evil age in accord with
the will of our God and Father. Galatians 1:3, 4

When Paul wrote the opening to a letter, he didn't just say Hi from himself; he always included greetings from God and Jesus as well. I think he was extremely aware of their presence and wanted his flock to know that they were with him and available to them as well. In this particular greeting he expounds a bit on the nature of Jesus reminding the Galatians that he gave up his life to redeem ours. The purpose of Jesus' life was to become the perfect sacrifice so that by believing in Him we can be rescued, not just from the evil age around us, but from our own evil nature as well.

There is no age that has passed that was not evil, although some were markedly worse than others. Every so often I take time to review the crimes I see in the world, see who is doing them, and ponder their motives for doing such things. I have always tried to put myself in someone else's place and try to understand what makes them do the things they do. More often than not I am confounded by the depravity of some. The hardest thing for me is to see someone who destroys a child. How can you look into those beautiful, trusting eyes and still be able to beat or demean one so innocent? Defenseless children and puppies: they only know how to love, and yet we beat fear and hatred into them as if they deserve it. They're just trying to learn and understand. That kind of evil behavior I will never understand.

Lord Jesus: Please protect the children and the puppies from us.

August 22

For the vision still has its time, presses on to fulfillment,
and will not disappoint; if it delays, wait for it; it will
surely come, it will not be late. Habakkuk 2:3

As I have read and learned about the ways of the Lord, I sometimes have to smile because He truly does have a sense of humor. If you ask for something and don't specify how you want it, He will give it to you in a manner that you will never forget. That's why I know that the things He keeps telling me over and over will come to pass. I may not like the visions that He shows me, but that only makes it more important for me to write these things down for you to read.

Bad things are coming to America – worse than this country has ever seen – much worse than the Great Depression of the 1920's and 30's: famine; oppression by our own government; diseases that will kill thousands; roving gangs that will ransack homes, kill the occupants and take whatever they want; and some will engage in cannibalism.

Frightened yet? You should be. Get your plan together now. I can't say when it will come, but I know beyond any doubt that it will.

As I mentioned before, September 2014 begins the next Sabbath year on the Jewish calendar. It is the seventh year designated by God for the land to rest and for the wiping away of debts. The last one started in September 2007 and ended in September 2008. Ring any bells? That was the time frame when the mortgage system collapsed and started this recession that we still haven't crawled out of. I suspect we will not be completely free of it since the next cycle starts so soon. The one before that ended in September 2001. The collapse of the economy may not happen with this *Shemitah*, but it will eventually come. And if I'm right, bartering will become the transaction method. Make sure you have something to barter with – food, guns, water, and fuel.

Lord Jesus: I trust you – help me to prepare for whatever comes each day.

August 23

For you yourselves know very well that the day of the Lord will come like a thief at night. When people are saying, "Peace and security," then sudden disaster comes upon them, like labor pains upon a pregnant woman, and they will not escape.
1 Thessalonians 5:2,3

Are you in a situation that you believe to be ideal? Maybe it's a marriage or a job where you have full faith in your partner or employer, and you're sure that tomorrow's sun will rise and bring you a day filled with all of the security and happiness of today. If this is you, Congratulations! If this is not you, know that there is always hope for better. Remain faithful to God, and He will be faithful to you.

I used to be in that place, and it felt really wonderful until the day that my husband told me that my feelings didn't matter – he was going to do what he wanted whether I liked it or not. That was the beginning of the end. It doesn't matter what the subject was; what mattered was that he chose to be selfish and disregard me completely in his decision. This is not the way a relationship should go. By the way, God doesn't like it when we do this to Him, either – totally disregarding His feelings and doing whatever we want. I understand how He feels, because I did it to Him just as my ex did it to me.

My point is this: the rug can be pulled out from under your feet at any time if you aren't paying attention to everything around you. It takes diligence to always be aware of the condition of our surroundings. Rarely does a situation disintegrate on the spot; there are usually signs along the way if we are paying attention. There aren't many people who can pull off a change of heart and not show any signs of their infidelity.

It is the same in the world. We should be diligent about paying attention to the things going on around the earth since we now live in a global community. There is always someone trying to create peace between Israel and her neighbors, but that will only happen toward the end of time. That will be the sign. When people are celebrating 'peace and security,' then will come the greatest time of trial and testing ever thrust upon humanity. Don't get caught off guard – pay attention to the news, and Jesus' return will not catch you unaware. Only those who do not know or serve Him should be caught off guard, because the rest of us are watching for Him.

Lord Jesus: Open my eyes to see and my ears to hear.

August 24
A little sleep, a little slumber, a little folding of the arms to
rest – then will poverty come upon you like a highwayman,
and want like an armed man. Proverbs 6:10, 11

Complacency is a very sad state that causes people to take others for granted and be overconfident in their irreplaceability. This particular verse is connected to the discussion of the ant – 'consider its ways and be wise! It has no commander, no overseer or ruler, yet it stores its provisions in summer and gathers its food at harvest.' (vv.6-8)

This verse is intended to motivate us to be diligent in handling our business and not be a procrastinator. We should always be putting something back for a rainy day – just in case. This makes it sound like you should be working all the time and never take a day off. I don't know about you, but I can't work sun-up to sundown every day. Maybe when I was younger, but not anymore. That's why you work at putting a little something back – because the rainy days come when no one can work.

And it isn't a law that you have to work all the time. Even the disciples were told by Jesus to 'Come away by yourselves to a quiet place and get some rest.' (Mark 6:31) Of course a few verses later He's feeding a crowd of 5000+ persons. Just remember that this is against laziness which is one of the seven deadly sins. All of the time that I fritter away each day playing games or watching videos is wasted in the big picture. It brings no edification to me, nor does it give any glory to God or serve my neighbor. Vacation is one thing – laziness and avoidance theory are quite another.

Lord Jesus: Help me to be motivated and accomplish my tasks that you have assigned to me.

August 25

Whoever serves me must follow me, and where I am, there also will my servant be. The Father will honor whoever serves me. John 12:26

I've occasionally wondered why people have chosen to not follow Jesus. I think some of it is because they don't really know what being a Christian is about. Perhaps they think that Christianity is a long list of things you can't do, a life of restrictions: "Thou shalt not." No smoking, no drinking, no sex. It doesn't say that in the Bible. It doesn't say all things in moderation, either, although most people think it does. Sex outside of marriage is, of course, against the rules, but you and I both know that it goes on. My mom told me once that when it comes to religion and sex, religion always loses. I think this is not totally true, but it is frequently true. That's why there's repentance and mercy.

I think another reason some don't follow Him is because the ones they know who do are not perfect models of humanity. They think of Jesus as perfect and believe that His followers should be too. They also believe that they can't (or won't) strive to reach that level. Maybe it's laziness; maybe it's fear — maybe they're afraid they'll like it, and their friends will drop them; or maybe the devil is whispering in their ear that they aren't good enough for that life. I'd place my bet on that last one. And if this is you, know this: No one is good enough for Jesus — ever — because He *is* perfect. And despite this fact, He still chooses to call us and live in our hearts, and encourage us to get better at loving our brethren and following Him.

Why should we follow Him? Because where He is, we will be also. I know that someday I will leave this world, and when I do, I want my trip to His side in heaven to be as short as possible. That will be the only honor I want — to be found worthy of making it into heaven when my time here is done.

Lord Jesus: *Where you lead, I will follow.*

August 26
Though my flesh and my heart fail, God is the rock
of my heart, my portion forever. Psalm 73:26

Some days I just don't want to get out of bed. On mornings like that I seem under the delusion that no matter what I do, it doesn't make a difference. I know it isn't true, but somehow that little minion crawls up on my pillow and says, "It's not worth it. Just stay in bed and do nothing, 'cause nobody will notice anyway." God knows. He is the one who rolls my tired, frustrated butt out of the bed and says, "Everything you do matters to someone. Get on with it!'"

They may not tell you. You may never get thanked. You *will* feel like giving up and think that no one notices or cares. Jesus sees; and He cares. You may never get a reward here, but you will be blessed many times over in heaven for carrying on under those circumstances. Simply allow God to fill your heart and keep you moving forward. And don't listen to that negative voice – it's interested in your destruction, not your salvation.

Lord Jesus: Strengthen me to keep moving forward every day.

August 27

Whoever is without love does not know God, for God is love.
1 John 4:8

I don't understand people who hate others without even knowing them. I'm thinking of the radical Islamists who seem to hate everybody but their own; they don't even like other Islamists. They view Americans as corrupt and depraved, and while many are, we're not all that way. And they're not the only people in the world that exhibit hate; they're just the ones that we hear the most about. According to John the math is very simple: more hate, less God.

There's plenty of hate among Americans, as well, and it spills over into the news more and more every day. The media is exhibiting a horrifying trend of showing us almost solely negative news reports. Does anyone besides me think that this only spawns more negative behavior so that crazy people can get their face and name on the news? Just once I'd like to see a news report that is *at least* 50% good news. Do you think that would sell any advertising? Is the majority too consumed with blood and guts to tune in to a newscast like that? I know there are enough feel good stories out there to do it. And I also think that it would truly change the things that people would do to get on TV.

Supposedly, about 32% of the American population is practicing the Christian faith. There are more not-for-profits out there than you can shake a stick at, and more church programs helping others than the government. So how come we can't see those stories more often? It would give people something to support and be happy about instead of all the negative vibes and fear flowing into our homes through the media outlets.

Lord Jesus: Help us to find more positive programs and turn away from viewing hate.

August 28

And in return for their senseless, wicked thoughts, which
misled them into worshiping dumb serpents and worthless
insects, you sent upon them swarms of dumb creatures for
vengeance; that they might recognize that a man is punished
by the very things through which he sins. Wisdom 11:15, 16

Does this make sense to you? Have you seen people that this applies to? I've seen a few. When we spend our time in sin with a specific focus, we are sometimes harmed physically by the fallout from our activities. The writer of Wisdom says that those who worshiped bugs were attacked by bugs, referring to the plagues on the Egyptians before the Hebrews were led to freedom.

In Jesus' time, there was a man lying near the pool at Bethesda who wanted to be healed. It was told that when the waters were stirred, the first person into the pool would be healed. But this man could not walk and so help himself into the pool. Despite the fact that there were evidently many people there, it seems that Jesus only healed this man who had been lame for 38 years. The healing took place on the Sabbath, so the man got in trouble from the Pharisees for carrying his mat after his healing.

When questioned about his healing, he could not identify who had done it. Later on, Jesus went to him and said, "See, you are well again. Stop sinning or something worse may happen to you." We don't know what his sins were – only that Jesus warned that continuing to sin would cause something worse than being lame and unable to walk for 38 years.

I have seen people who cheated on their spouses get reproductive cancers. I'm not saying that their disease was a judgment, but you have to wonder. For some people, food is their sin. For those who don't exercise restraint and healthy guidelines in their eating habits, the food they worship can kill them from a variety of maladies. Picture your sins in your mind. If you were to be made sick by one of them, what kind of torment, disease, or death might you suffer at its hand?

Lord Jesus: Please help me to give up my sins!

August 29

At the time when you hear the seventh angel blow his trumpet, the mysterious plan of God shall be fulfilled, as he promised to his servants the prophets. Revelation 10:7

There is a school of thought that says that the rapture of the Church will take place before the seven years of the Tribulation. There are only a couple of verses that they cite to support their position, and my perception is that they have changed the context. There is *no* clear-cut statement in the Bible – anywhere – that says we won't go into the time of testing. If you read Jesus words regarding the end times in Matthew 24, you notice He doesn't say He will remove us from danger. On the contrary, He tells the disciples what to look for to know that the time is near.

This pre-tribulation rapture teaching is fairly new in comparison to the age of the Church. It started around 1850. When I ask people why they think it took that long for us to figure it out, they say they believe that the scholars of the past just didn't understand the language in order to properly translate it. They are never happy when I try to debunk their position. But the scriptural evidence simply does not support it.

Paul talked repeatedly of the end times in the first person suggesting that he thought that he could be included in the time of testing:

> Listen, I tell you a mystery: We will not all sleep, but we will all be changed—in a flash, in the twinkling of an eye, at the last trumpet. For the trumpet will sound, the dead will be raised imperishable, and we will be changed. (1Corinthians 15:51, 52)

Jesus also spoke of the trumpet call of God as being just before His return and the day of the Lord's wrath (the final seven judgments):

> "Then will appear the sign of the Son of Man in heaven. And then all the peoples of the earth will mourn when they see the Son of Man coming on the clouds of heaven, with power and great glory. And he will send his angels with a loud trumpet call, and they will gather his elect from the four winds, from one end of the heavens to the other. Now learn this lesson from the fig tree: As soon as its twigs get tender and its leaves come out, you know that summer is near. Even so, when you see all these things, you know that it is near, right at the door." (Matthew 24:30-33)

And Paul speaks again of the last trumpet in 1 Thessalonians 4:16.

> For the Lord himself will come down from heaven, with a loud command, with the voice of the archangel and with the trumpet call of God, and the dead in Christ will rise first.

My personal feelings regarding the idea of a pre-Tribulation rapture is that it is a heresy introduced by the devil to give Christians false hope that they won't have to suffer. There is nothing more frightening than pain and suffering to most people, and if the devil can get people to believe this position, when it becomes clear that the times are truly upon us and they are still here, they will become despondent and disbelieve the truth and drop their faith. I believe this is supported by the words of Jesus in Matthew 24:12,13:

> "Because of the increase of wickedness, the love of most will grow cold, but the one who stands firm to the end will be saved."

I could be wrong. I've been wrong before. And in this case, I would *love* to be wrong. But I don't think I am. After all, God didn't stop his only Son from suffering a scourging and a grueling death. What makes you think you're so special as to warrant a free pass? I know I'm not, and I accept that He will give me the ending that has been decreed for me. I only hope that I can remain faithful until it arrives.

Lord Jesus: Show me the truth of your word.

August 30
He has shown you, O mortal, what is good. And what does the Lord requires of you? To act justly and to love mercy and to walk humbly with your God. Micah 6:8 (NIV)

Sometimes I don't want to be nice. Sometimes I just want to be alone. Most of the time, I suck it up and do what I'm supposed to. Why? Because no matter how bad or contrary I feel, I want to please Jesus. He doesn't ask for a lot most of the time. I think He just wants to know how selfish I really am. Am I willing to give up my quiet corner to care for the needs of someone else?

I am very fond of the verse that I've cited for you today. It is a simple reminder for me of what God wants. I used to try too hard to figure out what God wanted me to do. Then I realized that, so long as I live by this verse, I'll do fine. It's the same as living by the two greatest commandments: love God and love your neighbor. If you can remember those two, you don't need a book of laws – everything is covered. There are only three things I need to learn to do well – justice, mercy and humility – and everything else will fall into place.

Lord Jesus: Teach me gently to practice justice, mercy and humility.

August 31

I urge you, brothers, to watch out for those who create dissensions and obstacles, in opposition to the teaching that you learned; avoid them. For such people do not serve our Lord Christ but their own appetites, and by fair and flattering speech they deceive the hearts of the innocent. Romans 16:17, 18

My former mother-in-law liked to get involved in groups that allowed her to get out of the house and be with people in a positive environment. Her husband had to be placed in a nursing home because of the late stages of Alzheimer's disease, and she needed to be busy and away from home for a time every so often. She was working with a group at her church one day when she met a woman who had recently come to their parish. My mother-in-law's first impression of her was not a positive one, but she opted to give the woman another chance. What she discovered was that her first impression was correct – the woman was an instigator and pot-stirrer, and she had been asked to leave another church for these behaviors.

People who exhibit these tendencies are a nuisance – they feed off the energy that they steal from others and the discord that they create.

There should have been some point in her time in the church when a personal awakening could have occurred, but I think she missed it.

So if you have someone like this in your congregation, you may want to think about having an intervention. If they fail to acknowledge their negativity and need for reform, the elders may have to ask them to leave. We each fight our own personal demons enough without having to fight theirs too. Paul says that they feed their own appetites and not the body of Christ. It also isn't a good idea to allow these people access to the young people who might think that such behavior is acceptable in a Christian.

Lord Jesus: Touch the hearts of those who would destroy the Church from the inside.

September

September 1

The eyes of the LORD are upon those who love him; he
is their mighty shield and strong support, a shelter from
the heat, a shade from the noonday sun, a guard against
stumbling, a help against falling. Sirach 35:16

For those who give control of their lives to God, these are the blessings
that await their decision. Many, however, are unwilling to let go. These
are the ones trying to make things happen in their own lives – the ones
who are always looking for the next step up on the ladder. They're not
waiting for anything to come to them, but are trying to force things to
happen without consulting the Lord to see if their goals are on His
agenda.

Repeatedly throughout the Bible we are told not to rely on other humans
to take care of our needs. But the Lord does sometimes use people to
deliver the things we need, so don't turn them away if they bring that
something with no strings attached. They may be an angel, or they
may be fulfilling their own act of faith. If we are His faithful followers,
He will see that we have all that we need. There may not always be
abundance and freedom from bumps in the road, because sometimes
He does have to stretch our faith to make it grow.

Protection at every level is what God's faithful children can expect from
Him. Why not give it a try if you haven't already? Just make up your
mind to let Him have control and take care of you. All you have to do is
keep in touch with Him every day to let Him know that you trust Him,
and that you are waiting patiently and expectantly for His next provision.

Lord Jesus: Grant me the graces of patient waiting, faith and trust.

September 2

Then a cloud appeared and covered them, and a voice came from the cloud: "This is my Son, whom I love. Listen to him!" Mark 9:7 (NIV)

In the days of the exodus, the Lord would speak to Moses and the Israelites from a cloud – first at the mountain, then at the tabernacle. God spoke solely to Moses after the people became afraid at the sound of his booming voice and requested that He not speak to them except through Moses. And at that time the cloud never settled upon any person, but only the mountain or the tabernacle. The cloud hovered over the tent of meeting (tabernacle) until Moses would enter, and then it would block the door so that no one else could enter while the Lord and Moses were speaking. (Exodus 33:9)

During the Transfiguration, the Lord once again spoke to the people from the cloud, but He also covered them with His presence. Moses said that one day the LORD would raise up a new prophet from the Jews' midst to lead them (Deuteronomy 18:15), and here is Jesus, on the mountain, in the cloud, with Moses and Elijah.

I think the cloud covering the disciples is significant. They represent the people – us – signifying that we can also approach God and be spoken to from the cloud. This is the new covenant – God with his people, among his people, upon his people, and speaking to his people without the need for an intercessor to deliver the message. Please do not misunderstand: I am *not* advocating an exodus from the church; the Lord still speaks His words to us in every sermon or homily that is delivered. I am only suggesting that we can go directly to God with our concerns and hear from Him if we choose to do so. And He chose us for this relationship with Him, so why shouldn't we take every opportunity to use it as He intended and thank Him for that chance?

Lord Jesus: Thank you for choosing to speak to me.

September 3

Send your light and fidelity, that they may be my guide, and bring me to your holy mountain, to the place of your dwelling. Psalm 43:3

Along life's way, we always run into people that 'light up' our life. Sometimes that light is real, reflecting God and His holy truth. And sometimes that light is just an artificial bulb that is bound to burn out, eventually leaving us in the dark with a person we really don't care for. It's difficult, when you're young, to know which is which. That's why it is so important to teach your kids how to recognize the holy light from the fakers. If you don't go to church, at least send your kids with someone so that they can learn the things they will need to know later when they are ready to make a choice between a life with Christ or without.

Jesus said, "I am the light of the world. Whoever follows me will never walk in darkness, but will have the light of life." (John 8:12) And the psalmist wrote, "Your word is a lamp for my feet, a light on my path." (119:105) If you can't see the light with your eyes or your heart, read his word. There you will find His light with your soul.

Lord Jesus: Thank you for lighting my way.

September 4

I have the same hope in God as they themselves have that there will be a resurrection of the righteous and the unrighteous. Because of this, I always strive to keep my conscience clear before God and man. Acts 24:15, 16

Paul was a Pharisee, a teacher of the law; he knew everything there was to know about the law. One of the things that the Pharisees believed was that there would be a resurrection of the dead one day. The Sadducees, on the other hand, thought that when you're gone, you're just gone: no afterlife, no eternal life, and no judgment. (If you're interested in learning more about the Jewish sects, history, or their life in general, visit the Jewish Virtual Library.[13])

Because Paul believed in a judgment day, it colored everything he did and said. Any failings would have been handled right away and not allowed to fester, either for himself or toward someone he might have hurt or offended. But the only offense he would not apologize for was if someone was offended by his preaching of the gospel.

I think we need more people like Paul today, people who aren't afraid to offend someone when they talk about their faith. More people like this in the 1900's might have prevented many of the problems that we face in our world today. Maybe we would still have prayer in schools instead of guns.

Lord Jesus: Help me keep a clear conscience yet still speak the truth in love.

September 5

Hear this, O priests, pay attention, O house of Israel, O household of the king, give ear! It is you who are called to judgment. For you have become a snare at Mizpah and a net spread upon Tabor. Hosea 5:1

The Lord has a tender spot in His heart for the oppressed, and He warned the leaders of ancient Israel, both the priests and the king, that He was going to judge them for leading the people astray and not teaching them properly. He still feels this way today. He is unhappy with the leaders of this country (and the world) who are oppressing their people and not allowing them to be taught Biblical principles. He is really unhappy about priests and pastors who have taken advantage of their congregants, and is equally displeased with persons who lead His preachers and teachers into sinful relationships.

I believe that those who have positions of responsibility in teaching the people will be held to a much higher standard of righteousness and care on judgment day. More than once God chastised the priests for their self-centeredness and lack of diligence in teaching and helping the Israelites and Judeans to be faithful to Him. But then it's hard to teach someone good habits when you don't have them yourself.

If you have accepted a position of teaching in your church, please refrain from sinful behaviors and take care to teach only Biblical truth.

Lord Jesus: Help me to teach others in a proper way.

September 6

Make no mistake: God is not mocked, for a person will reap
only what he sows, because the one who sows for his flesh will
reap corruption from the flesh, but the one who sows for the
spirit will reap eternal life from the spirit. Galatians 6:7, 8

We've already talked about reaping and sowing – quantitatively. Here is the discussion of quality. One of the Galatians was evidently caught in some sinful behavior, and the congregation wanted to know what to do with him. For Paul, it was like, 'DUH! Tell him to clean up his act!'

Too often today, we are unwilling to confront people who are engaging in sinful lifestyles. And oftentimes when we do, we lose friends. Those whom we are trying to correct should be grateful that they have friends who care. Instead, they drop us and continue with their lifestyle choices without heeding the warnings which have come from the Lord through us. Or sometimes they may continue to be friendly, but deny that they are living in sin.

Regardless of the nature of the sins, if you are appealing to your flesh, then the end result is the destruction slated for those who refuse to deny their flesh – hell. In times of temptation, we need to turn to the holy Spirit and ask for help. That's what He's there for. And Paul writes in his first letter to the Corinthians that God will provide a way out of temptation; you simply need to seek it. Ask the holy Spirit to show you the way out, and take it! Even if it means running away from the source of temptation, it's better to live to fight another day and be safe from falling.

Lord Jesus: Show me the way to holiness.

September 7

Nebuchadnezzar exclaimed, "Blessed be the God of Shadrach, Meshach and Abednego, who sent his angel to deliver the servants that trusted in him; they disobeyed the royal command and yielded their bodies rather than serve or worship any god except their own God." Daniel 3:95

When I was young and went to Bible School in the summer, they taught us a song: "Shadrach, Meshach and Abednego worshiped the Lord though the king said, 'No.' Into the fiery furnace they were cast, but the Lord delivered from its awful blast!"

It took a huge leap of faith for those three to refuse to worship the golden statue of the king and accept that they would die for their faithfulness to the Lord. The king was so enraged at them that he ordered the furnace to be heated to seven times its usual level, and the servants that threw them in were consumed by the fire for getting so close. Once inside, the Lord released their bonds and enveloped them in a cocoon of sorts where they sang his praise.

A similar thing will happen when the antichrist takes over the world. He, too, will have a statue that all will have to worship or else die. Revelation doesn't speak of him having a furnace, though. It says that the faithful will lose their heads for their 'testimony about Jesus and for the word of God.' ISIS likes to behead their victims. Is that significant? How strong is your faith, and how much do you love your life?

King Nebuchadnezzar praised the God of Shadrach, Meshach and Abednego, but he still failed to convert and serve Him. Later on in his reign, he was banished by God for his pride and arrogance and was made to live like a wild beast for seven years. He learned the lesson in the short-term, but failed to write it on his heart.

Lord Jesus: Fill my heart with faithful trust in you.

September 8

If we discerned ourselves, we would not be under judgment;
but since we are judged by the Lord, we are being disciplined
so that we may not be condemned along with the world.
1 Corinthians 11:31, 32

If there were no God, then we would not have to worry about condemnation and eternal judgment. But because there is and we are subject to His final judgment, we are constantly under His scrutiny for correction and improvement. Proverbs 3:12 says, "For whom the LORD loves he reproves, and he chastises the son he favors." Children without discipline will always go astray.

The Catholic Church believes in Purgatory, a place in the afterlife where someone is sent for punishment for unresolved sins and lessons they failed to learn while alive, before moving on into heaven with Jesus. Some say this is bunk. All I can say is that even before I became Catholic I believed in an idea that I called 'spiritual rehab' where people would go for a review of the lessons they failed to learn while alive. This is one of those things that we can't really know for sure until we get there. But in light of that possibility, I like to keep up on my lessons and repentance – just in case. I prefer to prepare as if it is true in the event that I could be wrong rather than think that it's bunk and then find out that I'm definitely wrong.

Lord Jesus: Grant me the grace to accept correction here and take care of my sins before I die.

September 9

If your enemy is hungry, give him food to eat; if he is
thirsty, give him water drink. In doing this, you will heap
live coals on his head, and the LORD will reward you.
Proverbs 25:21, 22 (NIV)

Yesterday I talked about torment on the other side. Today, it's torment on this side — not for us, but rather our enemies. And at our hands! This is a big step, one that many of us would have trouble taking. You know you want to smack them upside the head or speak nasty things to them, but Solomon says that if you can exercise self-control and not only be nice to them but also provide for their needs, you will cause their head to burn from shame. You get street cred from the Lord for exercising restraint and also rewards for another day. It's like rubbing their nose in their own animosity. It also shows them that you've moved on to a better place.

Who are you harboring hard feelings toward? Is it possible that you can find a way to be nice to them? I still want to give my second ex a black eye, so I know that I still have some work to do. I don't know what would happen if I ran into him somewhere, and frankly, I don't really want to know. I'm afraid I'd fail.

Lord Jesus: Give me the grace to let go of animosity and grow in kindness.

September 10

"How can you say to your brother, 'Brother, let me remove
that splinter in your eye,' when you do not even notice the
wooden beam in your own eye? You hypocrite! Remove the
wooden beam from your eye first; then you will see clearly
to remove the splinter in your brother's eye." Luke 6:42

Before I gave up my notion that I was in control of my life and Jesus
was along for the ride, I couldn't understand this verse. Once I let go
and gave him the lead, He opened my eyes and my heart to understand
things in the Bible that I had had trouble with before. I couldn't read
the book of Hebrews – it just didn't make any sense to me. Now, it's one
of my favorite books.

The splinters and the beams are sins. Jesus says here that it's easy for
us to see the sins of others and overlook our own, and that we have no
business telling someone to clean up their act until we have taken care
of our own business. It's like the old saying, "That's the pot calling
the kettle black." Only after we are cleansed of our own iniquities
can we help others understand their own and encourage them to seek
repentance.

Lord Jesus: Open my eyes to see.

September 11

As you do not know the path of the wind, or how the body is
formed in a mother's womb, so you cannot understand the work
of God, the Maker of all things. Ecclesiastes 11:5 (NIV)

Just once I'd like to get a peek at the big picture or the playbook that
God is using. I don't know what your quest is in your life, but mine is
'understanding.' The most often-asked question out of my mouth or in
my mind is, "Why?" And I think that having an insider peek would
go a long way toward fulfilling my quest. On the other hand, I might

also find that I'd be so horrified by what I see there that I might lose my mind. I can't imagine what seeing all of the sins of the world every moment of every day is like. I think just seeing one second's worth might be enough to scare me to death – literally.

There is no way that we can ever comprehend the big picture with our itty-bitty pea-brains other than to know that 1) Man is fallen; 2) God sent his Son to create a path of reconciliation; 3) Jesus fulfilled that mission; and 4) When we believe in the One whom God sent and follow Him, we are saved. We can't see the wind to know from where it comes or to where it's going; we don't yet understand all about how babies are formed; and we won't understand all of the intricacies of the plan of salvation until we stand in the eternal presence of Christ. And once we're there, it won't matter.

Lord Jesus: Help me to understand what I need to know and let the rest go.

September 12
My God will fully supply whatever you need, in accord with his glorious riches in Christ Jesus. Philippians 4:19

I used to think that I knew what I needed: then I found myself with two ex-husbands. It was at that time that I realized how really ignorant I am about what I need, so there's no way I could ever begin to guide someone else to the answers that they might be seeking. The only thing I can tell someone else is the same thing I tell myself: Only God knows what it is that each one of us needs. And what He has in store for me is infinitely more glorious than anything I could ever imagine for myself.

After my second divorce, I was asked out by some older men and also had friends that tried to set me up with dates. I told them all, "No thanks. I'm not looking for a companion, friend, or replacement partner." I needed time to heal, first of all. And second, I didn't want to be forced to try to feel things that they might expect and I could not offer. I'm really glad I said no to all of those offers. What I told God was, "If you want me to have someone, you send him to me, because I sure don't know how to pick one." He hasn't sent anyone yet, and I am quite fine with that. I like teaching the kids, doing the work that I have, taking care of my mom, and having an occasional lunch with a girl-friend. My life is full, and I am finally satisfied with what He has given me. I could ask for more, but I honestly wouldn't know what to do with it!

Lord Jesus: Thank you for supplying what I need, not what I think I want.

September 13

Along both banks of the river, fruit trees of every kind shall
grow; their leaves shall not fade, nor their fruit fail. Every
month they shall bear fresh fruit, for they shall be watered
by the flow from the sanctuary. Their fruit shall serve for
food, and their leaves for medicine. Ezekiel 47:12

I wonder if these are trees of life like the one the Lord had in the Garden of Eden that Adam and Eve weren't supposed to eat from. That act of disobedience was one of the reasons that they were kicked out of the garden. The other was because God didn't want them to eat from the tree of life and live eternally with their knowledge and ability to sin. They would have been like Satan then – alive forever and prone to selfish disobedience.

These are the trees that grow along the banks of the River of Life which flows from the throne of God. I'm still not sure if this reference is to the eternal kingdom or if it's the millennial reign of Christ here on earth before the final judgment. Not that it matters. If we get to see it, it means we're in! It will, however, be a very cool thing to see. I saw a man on TV recently that told of how he died, went to heaven, and came back. He said he saw fruit trees there in heaven. When he walked up to a pear tree and picked a piece of fruit, another blossomed out the branch in the same place right away. That's the way I have always pictured the bread and fish doing when Jesus fed the huge crowds with a tiny amount of food. Maybe I'm onto something there....

Lord Jesus: Feed me from your trees.

September 14

For the mystery of lawlessness is already at work. But the one who restrains is to do so only for the present, until he is removed from the scene. And then the lawless one will be revealed, whom the Lord will kill with the breath of his mouth and render powerless by the manifestation of his coming.
2 Thessalonians 2:7, 8

Just when you thought the world couldn't get any worse, you find out that there is a divine being holding back the spirit of lawlessness from being full-blown. However, the day will eventually come when the Lord will stop him from fighting against them and allow the devil to hold full sway on earth. That is very frightening to me. I wonder if there will be any police, or if all of the security will be martial law under the National Guard.

These lawless ones will even have their own leader – the antichrist. It's terrifying to think of the devil being the supreme leader of all the earth, but that's what he will be; the antichrist will be the devil incarnate. You may ask how he will be able to rise to power – won't people be able to stop him? The answer is that he won't appear evil initially. It is likely that there will be a global collapse of the monetary system. This man will have all the answers to get the world back in operation and will step in to solve the world's problems.

Luke tells us in the book of Acts that King Herod spoke to some people who said, "This is the voice of a god, not of a man." Immediately, because Herod did not give the glory to God, an angel of the Lord struck him down, and he was eaten by worms and died. (Acts 12:22, 23) But this will not happen with the antichrist. God will allow him free reign until the moment that He has decided that the end will come. If we survive the great earthquakes that are to come during that time, this is what we will be looking forward to. Do you understand now why it is so important to get right with God? Only with His wisdom will we be able to discern these things and know what to do and when.

Lord Jesus: Open my heart to see the true evil in our world.

September 15

Welcome is his mercy in time of distress as rain
clouds in time of drought. Sirach 35:24

There are times in our lives when it seems that nothing goes right – you can't speak the right words, you can't get things done in a timely fashion, it feels like God doesn't hear your prayers, and you feel like you don't have any friends left that understand you. You feel isolated, unmotivated, maybe even lost. It may seem like God is far away, but He is still right next to you. St John of the Cross calls these times 'the dark night of the soul.' And God isn't gone, He's just checking to see if we really care whether He pays attention or not. Once this time has passed, you will find that you are closer to Him than before.

The hard part is patiently waiting for the end to this time of spiritual drought. And yes, I have been through this trial. I couldn't speak to you properly if I hadn't. It's not something you can adequately prepare for or explain. It has to be experienced. And if you truly desire to grow closer to God, this will be part of your journey. Mine lasted for over a year, and I never gave up on Him. I thought it was me – that I wasn't doing something right – that I had made Him angry somehow. Then the director of the youth program that I serve with gave me a book about St John and the dark night of the soul. It was around the time I was coming out of my testing, and it helped me to understand the dryness that I had experienced. In the end, His mercy came flooding back and what a welcome relief it was! Like rain in a time of drought....

Lord Jesus: Thank you for not letting go of me.

September 16

And whatever you do, in word or in deed, do everything
in the name of the Lord Jesus, giving thanks to God
the Father through him. Colossians 3:17

Think about everything you did today, or maybe yesterday. Can you honestly say that you would NOT be ashamed to claim every deed in the name of Jesus? If not, perhaps you might want to reconsider doing some of those things in the future. This verse is one that got to me some time back in my early stages of Christian growth. It was what caused me to walk away from people who were telling crude jokes, rethink flippant remarks before I let them fly, and stopped me from engaging in a host of activities.

But I have to confess that there were times when I shouldn't have done or said things, and yet I did. They usually happened when I was unhappy. So when you know that you aren't up to par on the happy scale, maybe it's best to stay at home if you can and stay out of trouble. Jesus would prefer that you handle it that way. Ask him to uplift you to get you back on track more quickly. And remember, whether you do it in His name or not, He's still there with you.

Lord Jesus: Help me to do only those things that give you glory.

September 17

Those whose steps are guided by the LORD, whose ways
God approves, may stumble, but they will never fall,
for the LORD holds their hand. Psalm 37:23, 24

Something I have never been able to understand is a person who has lived their whole life professing faith in God who then walked away from him during or after a crisis when the end result was not the outcome that the person desired. If Job had had that kind of faith, there would be no book about him. And the writer of Ecclesiastes says this: "When times are good, be happy; but when times are bad, consider this: God has made the one as well as the other. Therefore, no one can discover anything about their future." (7:14)

So God didn't save your spouse from a dreadful disease? Consider this: maybe He missed that person and wanted them home with Him. Also, it is a common idea in the Church that everyone has a set time to die. Perhaps your special someone's time was up. That time isn't stamped on our foot or our forehead, so when it comes it is most often a surprise. And sometimes things just happen, and God simply lets them with no explanation as to why.

Anyone can claim faith when times are good, but it takes true faith to stand with God through hard times knowing that He can fix the problem and yet chooses not to. Disease most often doesn't come from God – it comes from our unhealthy choices in life. Stay with him, no matter what comes, because He not only holds your hand, He also holds you in his hand. And He's trying to lead you through that tough time, so let Him. After all, He never promised it would be easy – only that it would be worth it.

Lord Jesus: Open my heart to feel your hands around me.

September 18

To satisfy the one who recruited him, a soldier does not become
entangled in the business affairs of life. 2 Timothy 2:4

Where does Jesus rate on your list of priorities? Is He an acquaintance?
A friend? Sibling? Spouse? Boss? How many times a day so you think
of Him or consider what He would want you to do in any given situation?
How you view Him should tell me how much you do for Him. If He is
an acquaintance, you don't think of Him often or have much concern
for His wishes. If He is a friend, you probably talk to Him a couple
of times a week and ask if there's anything He needs or wants to talk
about. If He is your sibling, you care about what happens to Him and
look out for His interests. If He is your spouse, you do everything you
can to please Him. And if He is your boss, you strive to complete the
tasks assigned to you to the best of your ability. You want to be the first
one considered for that next big promotion, after all.

Paul uses the analogy of a soldier here in his directives to Timothy. When
you are in the military, you obey orders – regardless – or suffer the
consequences for insubordination. Your entire life and focus is following
your leader through thick and thin to achieve the end goal. Depending
on your commitment to Jesus, this may be what your life's work should
look like – a soldier in the service of the King – setting aside all of your
own interests to achieve the will of the Commander-in-Chief. And once
in a while you get shore leave to recharge your batteries and come back
refreshed to go at it again. Bear in mind the words of Jesus himself to the
disciples and those following Him: "Whoever wants to be my disciple
must deny themselves and take up their cross and follow me." (Mark 8:34)

So what kind of relationship do you have with Jesus? Do you need to
review what you promised Him or what He has asked you to do? Is
He pressing you for more of your time? Maybe He wants to be closer
with you than you are right now – perhaps He would like to give you a
promotion and take you into battle with Him.

Lord Jesus: Show me how I perceive you.

September 19

In his hand is the soul of every living thing, and
the life breath of all mankind. Job 12:10

At the Last Supper when Jesus was talking about what was going to happen later that night, He told Peter that Satan had asked to sift the disciples. (Luke 22:31) We also know that God gave Satan permission to undo all of the blessings that God had given to Job. (Job 1:12) Each of us should ask ourselves if we could ever warrant such a sifting or trial, and if the answer is yes, how do we plan to survive and thrive afterwards?

God holds everything in His hands; there is nothing that is beyond His reach. Nothing happens on this earth without His knowledge or permission. We should take comfort in this knowledge. If something is to happen to one of us, it is for His purposes. And even if it comes at the hand of the evil one, there is some good that will come from it. The hard part in this is accepting that our life can be sacrificed for the greater good, letting go of our selfish desire to remain here with our family and friends, and allowing God to get on with His work.

Our next breath is never promised, and we must live every moment as if it could be our last. Viewing life in this context, what do you need to do today to correct errors from your past, heal old wounds, and allow yourself to look forward with great expectations?

Lord Jesus: My next and every breath is for you.

September 20

Whoever obeys and teaches these commandments will be
called greatest in the kingdom of heaven. Matthew 5:19b

Jesus told his disciples, "Whoever exalts himself will be humbled, and whoever humbles himself will be exalted." (Luke 18:14) Humility is a basic requirement for any who would consider themselves disciples of Christ. Some people try to teach with an ego the size of Cleveland or an attitude that says, "I'm holier than you." And while you may get away with that in the world of academia, it doesn't fly with Jesus. He wants people who know that they need His mercy in order to continue through every day; that they can't complete any task without His blessing.

Today's verse comes from the Sermon on the Mount, and closely follows the Beatitudes, the teaching on salt and light, and Jesus' statement that He did not come to abolish the law but to fulfill it. He made this statement to stress His desire that people share life's instructions with others around them.

One of the first things that God told the Hebrews to do after He gave them the law was to teach it to their children, to bind it on their hands and their foreheads, to contemplate it day and night, and to write it on their doorposts. (Deuteronomy 6:6-9) Do you think He was serious about them learning it? Teaching it?

I believe that one of the reasons that the world is in the rotten shape it's in today is because people haven't taught their children the precepts of God, and every generation just falls further and further away from him and His plans. It happened in ancient Israel with disastrous results, and it is happening today all over the world.

Lord Jesus: Remind me to contemplate and teach your love and laws at every opportunity.

September 21

While from behind, a voice shall sound in your
ears: "This is the way; walk in it," when you would
turn to the right or to the left. Isaiah 30:21

I've taken a lot of wrong turns in my life; more than once I have failed to
ask of Jesus, "What should I do?" And I think this has been the hardest
thing for me to learn: to know that I have someone who is always there
to turn to and ask for directions.

Whom have you sought counsel from in your life? Has anyone ever
given you bad advice or led you in the wrong direction? Jesus never will.
But as I said, the hard part is remembering to ask. And it's especially
hard when you can't see Him sitting right next to you, or hear Him as
He whispers in your ear while the whole world is screaming around you.
Try starting a new habit: Before you head out into the world each day,
take a moment to ask Jesus to show you the path for the day and each
step along the way.

*Lord Jesus: Please enable me to hear your voice guiding me in
the right direction.*

September 22

For such people are false apostles, deceitful workers who
masquerade as apostles of Christ. And no wonder, for even Satan
masquerades as an angel of light. 2 Corinthians 11:13, 14

It seems unfair that the adversary gets to pretend that he is the One
we follow. Our limited brains aren't fully capable of comprehending
the ins and outs of the spiritual realm, so we frequently fall for his
ploys. I remember one time when I thought that I had received a gift
from God, but I was wrong. It came packaged as the perfect gift, but
it required compromise on my part to accept it. The really sad part is

that I recognized this fact but chose to ignore it. In the end, it caused me nothing but heartache and nearly ruined my life.

When that perfect gift comes along, the one you've always dreamed of, whether it's a car, a person, or a job, make sure you know the heart of the source of the gift. And if you can't identify the source, maybe you shouldn't accept it. "Test everything. Retain what is good. Avoid all evil." (1 Thessalonians 5:21, 22)

Lord Jesus: Show me your light in your gifts and protect me from the evil one.

September 23
Do not my words promise good to him who
walks uprightly? Micah 2:7b

'Good' isn't always money. Sometimes good is simply the absence of trails for a time. But there's a lot of preaching about prosperity going on in the world these days. "Think and grow rich!" they say. The problem I see with this is that we aren't supposed to pursue money. We're supposed to pursue righteousness and the Lord. And as a reward for our faithfulness He will provide security in whatever form He chooses. Many times it is in the form of money when He knows that the people He gives it to will give it back because they understand the source of their favor.

I prayed and asked to win the lottery one time so that I could pay off my bills and some family members' as well. I also had plans to share it with several not-for-profits that I support. He told me No and gave me to understand that if He graced me in that way, I would forget about Him. I was sad that I wasn't going to win, but I was more saddened to know that I wouldn't be the person I had thought I would be after winning. I guess this is why I always have just enough and not too much.

Lord Jesus: Thank you for showing me my own heart.

September 24

Do not quench the Spirit. Do not despise prophetic
utterances. Test everything, retain what is good. Refrain
from every kind of evil. 1 Thessalonians 5:19-22

In the time in which we live, I think the Lord is letting a lot of people get away with a lot of stuff. I don't mean that He is excusing their behavior, but rather that He is withholding grave punishment until a day that is yet to come. In looking at the world, He shows what hour we live in and allows each one to recognize or ignore the signs to their own peril.

I hear many people in the world saying that the end is near. Jesus said to the people of his day, "Repent! For the kingdom of heaven is at hand for you!" Notice He ended that statement with the words 'for you.' I believe that everyone is given the opportunity to see and comprehend the time in which they live and adjust their life according to what they see. Some prefer to let others tell them what time it is, supposing that they know more about it.

I prefer to read the word of God and make my own determinations. I don't trust anyone to tell me what time it is for me. As for the world, it's a scary place today. And I confess that I have trouble seeing any change for the better coming. I don't doubt that God could change it if He wanted to, but He would rather we do it ourselves while praying for His intercession.

So in your view of the current times, where do you see the world in 5 years? 10 years? 20 years? Do you have hope for a peaceful world? Are you listening to the holy Spirit or some other spirit that is keeping you in ignorance? We have a priest that says there is no evidence that we are in the end times; I guess it depends on what you consider the end times. The last seven years? No, I don't think we're there. The beginnings of the birth pains? (Matt 24) I definitely think we're experiencing those. But don't take my word for it – read it for yourself. Start with Matthew 24; then read 2 Peter 3, Romans 1 & 2, and 2 Timothy 4. Follow up with Revelation. Make your own determination. And test everything I say and everything you hear.

Lord Jesus: Grant me an extra share of your Spirit that I may judge the times for myself with understanding.

September 25

The LORD's fire came down and consumed the holocaust, wood, stones, and dust, and it lapped up the water in the trench. Seeing this, all the people fell prostrate and said, "The LORD is God! The LORD is God!" 1 Kings 18:38, 39

This is one of my favorite events in the Old Testament. There is widespread pagan worship going on in Israel, and Elijah challenges all 450 of the priests of Baal to a duel of the deities. The pagan priests set up their altar and call upon their god to light the fire and burn up their offering. For hours and hours they cut themselves and cried out to no avail. When they finally gave up, Elijah went to work.

Elijah built up the altar of the Lord that had fallen down from disuse. Then he had a trench built around it and had 4 very large jars of water dumped over the meat, wood, and altar three separate times. The water covered everything and filled the trench. Then Elijah called to the Lord God Almighty and asked him to send down fire from heaven to light his sacrificial offering. The Lord obliged. The fire was so hot that it burned up not only the holocaust, but also the stones and the water in the trench. The people then recognized how powerful God was, but even then they didn't remain faithful to him. Elijah slaughtered all of the priests of Baal that day, and then he ran off in fear of Queen Jezebel who had murdered all of the priests and prophets of God that she could find.

With a God in his corner that could perform what He did that day, there should have been no one on this earth for Elijah to fear. We have that same God in our corner, and so we should never run either – but we do. We run and run and run. Usually it's from Him that we're running, because we're unwilling to step out in faith to make the changes in our lives that He desires or do the tasks that He requests. We're like Jonah, buying a ticket to Tarshish and running away from responsibility.

Lord Jesus: Give me the courage to step up to your requests and stop running.

September 26
I have been crucified with Christ; yet I live, no longer
I, but Christ lives in me. Galatians 2:19b, 20a

There are a lot of mysteries in the Christian faith – things that we have to accept by faith knowing that we will likely never have true understanding of them here. I feel like this is one of those things. Because we believe that Jesus died for our sins and accept His gift of salvation, we are no longer our own but His possession. He bought us with His blood. The graces we receive through baptism and confirmation are outward signs of inward beliefs that we are children of the Most High – brothers and sisters in Christ – saved by His sacrifice and filled with His Spirit. The mystery is how we can be found in sin and yet still be saved.

The old law showed how sinful man can be. Salvation through Christ shows how good one can become with His help. Christ lives through me. He may not walk this earth physically himself, but He still has hands and feet and tongues to speak; they belong to you and to me. We are His servants if we claim salvation. Under these assumptions then, we should be progressing along a path that shows that we are becoming more like Him and seeking that which is lost.

Lord Jesus: Make yourself known through me.

September 27

Not a single promise that the LORD made to the house of
Israel was broken; every one was fulfilled. Joshua 21:45

How many promises have you broken in your lifetime? I've had a few.
Sometimes they were made because of lack of foresight – I couldn't see
a time when the request would no longer be feasible. Sometimes they
were made in ignorance of information that was not shared that had
significant implications on my ability (or willingness) to keep it. And
let's face it – sometimes it was just plain laziness.

As I have gotten older, I have used these experiences to gauge the
requests that people make of me, and rarely do I make a promise any
more. I'm simply not willing to be tied to someone's request knowing
that there is a good chance that they haven't shared all of the pertinent
information that is tied to the outcome, or that circumstances will
change and make me unable to fulfill that obligation. I try to teach my
kids, "Don't make any promises that you might be unable or unwilling
to keep." Be conscientious of your reputation.

Thankfully, God doesn't have this problem. He knows all of space and
time – everything that has and will happen – every choice we will
make before we make it. And yet He still promises to love and protect
us so long as we remain faithful to Him. That is the only condition for
receiving all of his promises: remain faithful to Him. And for the value
of all of His promises, I think that is a small request, a small price to
pay for eternal security.

Lord Jesus: Thank you for always keeping your promises.

September 28

Then I saw another beast come up out of the earth; it had two
horns like a lamb's but spoke like a dragon. Revelation 13:11

Someday, if I live long enough, I would not be surprised to see the false
prophet come out of the Church. He would be a lying spirit, of course,
but how else do you suppose he will deceive the elect? He has to appear
genuine at the start in order to get people on board his bus. Then, only
after he has seduced them with all the right words, he will show his true
colors. Let us hope that he will slip up at least once so that the elect
who are following him will have a chance to see who he truly is before
they are led to receive the mark that will condemn them to hell. This
man will be the enforcer for the antichrist. He will do amazing things,
according to scripture, and confound those whose faith is weak.

So how will we know him? He will be second in command to someone
who is quickly taking control of the world stage. He will be known for
his miracles for, as scripture says, he will call down fire from heaven.
Who knows what else he will be able to do? Whatever his acts entail, he
will have the power to force all people to worship the antichrist or have
them put to death. True Christians will have two choices at that point:
go into hiding or step forward and be martyred. I suspect that eventually
they will come door-to-door checking to see if you have your household
god in order and that you're saying the proper 'prayers.'

I can't say honestly that I'm looking forward to that day. My only hope
is that, if they come to my door and see that I don't have the mark or
the 'abomination that causes desolation' in my home, I will have the
strength to do as Jesus did and say, "Thy will be done." I'll be praying
for divine protection at that point. My fault. I already am!

***Lord Jesus: When the time comes, help me to see the one who
speaks falsely for who he really is.***

September 29

I will bless you abundantly and make your descendants as countless as the stars of the sky and the sands of the seashore; your descendants shall take possession of the gates of their enemies, and in your descendants all the nations of the earth shall find blessing – all this because you obeyed my command. Genesis 22:17, 18

Abram (meaning 'the father is exalted') wasn't perfect, but he did one thing very right – he believed the Lord God when he said he would do something. He wasn't without fear; he was so afraid of the Egyptians when he and Sarai lived there for a time that he said she was his sister. And when God asked him to sacrifice his only son that he had given to him, Abraham (father of many nations) believed that there would be some sort of miracle to replace that son who was born to him at the age of 100 years after he and Sarah had been barren all their lives.

Just think of it – all of the Christians throughout history have been saved because of one man's trust and faith in God. And that one man was alive because of the trust and faith of another man, Noah. What can the Lord do with one man? Well, Jacob's descendants were in Egypt for 430 years. When they were freed from slavery the number who left were 600,000 men plus women and children; likely over one million persons total from about ninety that arrived during the famine.

There isn't anything that is impossible for God. Do you believe that? He offered salvation through one man – Noah; then one more man – Abraham; and finally one more divine man – Jesus. I am one person – how many will read this book? You are one person – what might He do with you if you allow Him to rule your life?

Lord Jesus: Increase my faith and trust in you.

September 30
She said, "If I but touch his clothes, I shall be cured." Mark 5:28

I used to know a woman who said nearly every week at Sunday school that she had prayed to be healed of her malady, but she wasn't getting any better. I always wondered if it was her lack of faith, but only God can speak to that. I myself have a physical condition that I have prayed to be healed from, along with my allergies. The allergies aren't improved, but I suspect that it has to do with dietary choices. The body isn't designed to process artificial sweeteners like I get in my occasional diet pop nor the gmo's that are in much of our food today. Those and other conditions such as poor air quality have to manifest themselves somehow, and if it's allergies rather than cancer for me, I'm good with it.

The other condition is one that is slowly improving by physical things that I do to correct a curved spine. And those advances are the result of meeting certain people who led me to a variety of apparatuses that have brought those improvements. I don't know why He chose to send healing in this way except to say that, for some, healing is an event that has to be shared. Sometimes it's not in his plan that we get what we want right away and give Him glory for it. Perhaps others need to be involved for their own edification or exposure to the faith that I have to share. Sometimes healing isn't an event – sometimes it's a journey.

Lord Jesus: Thank you for sharing my journey of healing with me.

October

October 1

My foes turn back when I call on you. This I
know: God is on my side. Psalm 56:10

Is this your God? The One who causes people to back down when you
call on Him? It should be. If not, is it because He doesn't recognize
your voice when you call? How many people call you on the phone and
say, "It's me"? Do you always know which 'me' it is? Sometimes when
I send an email to someone from a different address than they're used
to, I identify myself before writing my message even though my name
is at the bottom in an electronic signature. Why? Because some people
don't read all the way to the bottom. There might be a cute post script
there that they've missed out on. How dare they!

This is the world that we live in today. People think they know so much
(me included many times) that they don't think they need to read your
info at the end. We're busy or distracted by our cell phones and text
messages, so we don't pay attention to others when they are standing
right next to us and speaking. We are so busy and tired that we don't
finish our prayers because we lay down to do it and fell asleep without
saying, "I love you, Jesus. Good night."

If this is you, maybe it's time to rethink who or what is important and
needs to be recognized in your life. God and Jesus should be first, even
before a spouse or significant other. How many other voices are ahead
of theirs on your call list?

Lord Jesus: Forgive me for not paying more attention to you.

October 2

This saying is trustworthy and deserves full acceptance:
Christ Jesus came into the world to save sinners.
Of these I am the foremost. 1 Timothy 1:15

I've quoted this verse before, and meant it. But the truth of the matter is that all of our sins are gone forever when we give our life to Christ. Then we step out into the street, just about get run over by a vehicle which causes us to curse or swear at the driver, and then we have to start over.

Micah wrote that God throws all of our sins into the sea. (7:19) Hallelujah! They're gone forever! I speculate that there is a cumulative reckoning for our sins until we give them to God for cleansing. Some people have a few things on the roster, while others have tomes devoted to their 'adventures.' Regardless of how much dirt is in your past, ALL of it is washed away when you repent and seek salvation. My goal is to get to the pearly gates with only a couple of minor things that slipped past my attention, while having covered all of the major *faux pas*'s immediately. You know what I mean – it's the 'Oh, crap!' moment when you realize you just screwed up royally and need to go to Confession right now.

Thankfully, God is always listening for those moments and shaking His head when they come. It's like, "What were you thinking? You know better." And you prove that He's right by coming to Him and confessing your failings. Don't worry – it's nothing He hasn't seen or heard before. Everyone is equally guilty, and He doesn't hold it against you once you give it to Him to wipe away. Just restrain yourself from pulling it back out of the sea of forgetfulness where it's dumped. That's what the devil would have you do – take it back and ruminate in guilt over it. DON'T DO IT!!!!! We are not children of guilt, but of freedom. Give it God, and let it go. He still loves you, no matter what your sins are or used to be. And He will continue to love you no matter your future sins. Just remember to repent of them in a timely fashion, and all will be okay in the end.

Lord Jesus: Thank you for erasing the guilt of my sins.

October 3

If you would hearken to my commandments, your
prosperity would be like a river, and your vindication
like the waves of the sea. Isaiah 48:18

There are people inside and outside the Church who think that just
because they believe that God exists, they should receive His blessings.
James wrote, "You believe God is one. You do well. Even the demons
believe that and tremble." (2:19) Some translations say the demons
shudder. Why do they shudder? They do so because they know that they
were wrong in leaving heaven with Lucifer, and someday they will have to
pay for their arrogance and folly. They understand who God is, what He
expects, and the consequences of their choices. Many people today seem
to have their head in the clouds about what God expects of His children.

So what does He expect? He expects to be loved. And when you love
someone, how does that manifest itself? Think about your boyfriend/
girlfriend/spouse/significant other. What do you do for them as a result
of your love for them? God wants the same thing from you: love notes,
flowers, little gifts hidden in unexpected places, sweet murmurings. You
think you can't do those things for him? Maybe that's why you come up
short in the blessing department. Our love notes and gifts to Him are
our acts of charity and kindness to others.

When you love someone, you do things to make them happy. What have
you done lately to make God happy? He wants more than for you to just
believe He exists. He wants you as His bride – His *spiritual* bride. You
are the love of His life. He gave up His Son for you, so that you could
hear about Him, believe, and be reconciled to Him forever. How would
your spouse feel if you simply believed they existed? Who desires a
relationship like that? That wouldn't be much of a marriage, would it?
Relationships are a two-way exchange, each doing for the other out of love.
If you don't show God love and blessings, why should He do it for you?

Lord God: Help me to grow in love and faithfulness to you.

October 4

For it is impossible in the case of those who have once been
enlightened and tasted the heavenly gift, shared in the holy
Spirit and tasted the good word of God and the powers of
the age to come, and then have fallen away, to bring them to
repentance again, since they are recrucifying the Son of God for
themselves and holding him up to contempt. Hebrews 6:4-6

I'm not sure that I can get on board this bus. I have seen people who are
assuredly saved, get led astray, live in debauchery, and find their way
to repentance once again. That's why we pray for those people – to get
them restored to clemency. Just because someone falls off the program
is not cause enough to let them lay there and die, and I don't think that
Jesus does that. I think He reaches out through people who care about
that person and works to bring them back to the fold.

Maybe I have misunderstood the intent of the writer, or perhaps it's a
mystery that I have been as yet unable to fathom. Nevertheless, it won't
stop me from praying for friends that get lost in life and struggle to find
their way. I think it's my job to try to get them to a place of repentance
and restoration. I think it's what Jesus expects of us.

Lord Jesus: Guide me to your truth and to understanding.

October 5

If you remain quietly in this land I will build you up and
not tear you down; I will plant you, not uproot you; for I
regret the evil I have done to you. Jeremiah 42:10

After the Babylonians destroyed Jerusalem, they led most of the Jews
away as captives. The only people they left behind were the poorest
folk who were to take care of the crop trees and vines. That was their
purpose in being there. But when it was all said and done, the people
went to Jeremiah and asked him to consult with the Lord and ask what

He wanted them to do. They agreed that whatever he told them, they would do. And so Jeremiah consulted the Lord. His response was today's verse. The Lord wanted them to stay in the land. I think He wanted some of the chosen ones to remain there and hold down the fort so-to-speak until the rest were to be released and returned at the end of the seventy years of captivity.

There was actually a bit more to His response. He told them that if they refused to stay in Israel and instead went to Egypt seeking safety, He would destroy them there. Guess what they did. If you guessed they called Jeremiah a liar and went off to Egypt, you'd be correct. In the beginning of the book of Jeremiah when the Lord called him to speak to the Jews, He told Jeremiah that they were a stiff-necked people and that they would not listen, but he was to speak to them anyway, confront them about their sinfulness, and call them to repent. And here they are – proving God correct yet again.

The Lord has given me this same mission: reaching out to people to show them their faults, showing them what a better life in the Lord can look like, demonstrating His great mercy, and calling them to repentance and a closer walk with the Lord. If you are one of my flock, know this: There is no greater feeling than being wrapped in the arms of God and taking His promises for your own. He's calling out ... can you hear Him?

Lord Jesus: Take my will and make it your own.

October 6

For while your obedience is known to all, so that I rejoice
over you, I want you to be wise as to what is good, and
simple as to what is evil; then the God of peace will quickly
crush Satan under your feet. Romans 16:19, 20a

Paul praised the Christian Romans for their obedience to God's law in accord with the teachings of the gospel message, but he had one more distinction that he wanted them to take on that would fully separate them from the pagan Romans: assume responsibilities that were loving and kind, and avoid situations that suggested impropriety. The Romans were known for their gymnasiums and public bath houses where the men walked around naked. I think that might be part of the 'evil' that Paul was referring to along with the usual list of sins.

For us, obedience is most often a struggle, and telling good from evil and right from wrong is not always as clear-cut as it should be. It seems like nearly everyone has some kind of agenda that they are trying to shove down your throat, and you can't always trust that what they say about it is true. How sad that we have to question everything that goes on around us, including some things in our own churches.

Some people would say that Paul is suggesting that people should cloister themselves and not pay attention to the world. On the contrary: We must be well aware of the news so that we can be forewarned about things that are out there in order to protect ourselves and our children. And by being faithful to the Lord and His word, He will also provide protection from many of those evils.

Lord Jesus: Protect me and my family from the evils in this world.

October 7

The voice said to me: Son of man, this is where my throne shall be, this is where I will set the soles of my feet; here I will dwell among the Israelites forever. Ezekiel 43:7

In the big picture of hermeneutics (interpretation of Biblical scripture) there is a principle called near-far. Basically, it questions whether a given passage is to be considered prophecy for the near term, for a distant future time, or both. I think this one is both. The Lord was showing Ezekiel how to rebuild the temple when the Jews came back from their stint in Babylon. Once that was done, He could come back and live there in the temple amongst His people. That would be considered the near-term portion of the prophecy. In addition, He will one day drop the New Jerusalem out of the sky (Rev 21:10) and live amongst us as our Lord and God forever. Obviously that time is yet to come – definitely long-term from the time of Ezekiel around 450 bc.

Have you ever thought about scripture as you're reading it? Who was the person who wrote it? What did they look like? What did they eat? What did their house look like? And what about the people they were writing to – how did they view the prophets? The Bible says that Isaiah and Micah walked around barefoot and naked. Jeremiah was lowered into a muddy cistern to die from starvation by some of the residents of Jerusalem during the Babylonian siege, but the king favored him and had him pulled out. The Lord took the life of Ezekiel's wife and did not allow him to mourn for her as a portent to the Jews.

Who were these people, and what can we learn from their lives? They were obviously faithful and obedient, some to the point of death. And even though the Israelites committed evil and murderous acts against His servants in times past, He still plans to one day be among them forever. By the time that happens, many things will have changed. Many of the Israelites will have accepted Jesus as their long-awaited savior. And the chosen ones will be more than Jewish – they will be from every nation on earth.

Lord Jesus: I look forward to the day when you live among us.

October 8

Everyone in the crowd sought to touch him because power
came forth from him and healed them all. Luke 6:19

Some things I find just too hard for me to imagine. My humanity gets in the way of understanding. I know how it feels when I'm around someone who steals your energy, and that's only one person. I can't help but wonder if Jesus, in His humanity, still had an unlimited supply of energy from His divinity. And while I like to be hugged, I don't know how well I could handle everybody crowding in and wanting to touch me. I don't like crowds – they scare me – all those people shoving you around so that you can't go where you want but only where they lead you. I could never do Mardi-Gras. Concerts and the state fair are bad enough.

On the other hand, if I were one of those people, you bet I'd be working my way in to get some of that! Can you imagine the scene? I bet it wasn't pretty. I don't expect it was one of those 'After you' 'No, after you' kind of scenarios, do you? Whatever it was, He was an amazingly patient person to do it.

We can still lay our hands on Him today. Just close your eyes, reach out to Him and ask for healing. "Only say the word, and my servant shall be healed." (Matthew 8:8)

Lord Jesus: Thank you for your healing and your patience.

October 9
The LORD is my shepherd; there is nothing I lack. Psalm 23:1

What do you know about sheep? Well, if you live in town, probably not much. Most country folk don't know a lot about sheep either. When I was young, we pastured some for a friend. I remember when they brought them over that there were some lambs in the flock. As they came off of the truck, they tied rubber bands around their tails. The goal was to cut off the circulation and allow the tail to rot off for hygienic purposes. That may have been a good idea for the long-term, but the short-term was nothing but nauseating. The rotting flesh was home to maggots – my first experience with them and one that I prefer to not repeat.

Sheep eat differently than the cows with which I was more familiar. Cows bite off the grass which then grows up again. Sheep pull up the grass by the roots causing an area to become barren in pretty short order and necessitating reseeding. Sheep are skittish – they run from anyone who is not the shepherd they are familiar with. I also read somewhere that they are so stupid that they will stand in a stream and drink, and then drown as their wool soaks up so much water that they get carried off in the flow (if it's swift enough).

Being referred to as a sheep is not meant to be flattery. But if you stop and think about it, we are pretty much sheep in light of Jesus' wisdom and abilities. He has to be our shepherd because we do stupid things like stand in streams and drink (metaphorically speaking). Praise God! for His faithfulness in looking after His flock. And when one of us runs off, He never fails to go looking for us. (Luke 15:3-7)

Lord Jesus: Thank you for being my shepherd.

October 10
The message of the cross is foolishness to those who are perishing, but to us who are being saved it is the power of God.
1 Corinthians 1:18

There comes a time in every Christian's life when things just suddenly begin to make sense. For me, it was the day that I realized that I was a total fool and unable to manage my life. I think the reason I couldn't manage it was because I had been saved, but failed to make the necessary course corrections that a profession of faith is supposed to bring about. My life was no longer my own; I had given it to Christ, but I was still trying to drive the bus. It really doesn't work that way. He is the driver, the navigator, and the repairman all at the same time. When I see those license plates on the fronts of cars that say "God is my Co-Pilot", I want to tell them to "Switch seats!" I understand that 'co-' means that the two work together, but He needs to be the primary pilot while we provide support for the mission.

Think of how little each of us knows about how to be saved and be good Christian children to God. Now try to view it from the standpoint of someone who was not raised in church and doesn't know who Jesus really is or what a life of faith is all about. We must seem pretty crazy to that person, don't you think? If you know someone who has never been to church, invite them. It might just be the thing that they really need and have been searching for all of their life.

Lord Jesus: Lead me to those who need to find you.

October 11

But though you are master of might, you judge with
clemency, and with much lenience you govern us; for
power, whenever you will, attends you. Wisdom 12:18

There's nothing God couldn't do to us if He wanted to. We are less than the equivalent of insects in view of His power and might. And yet He still thinks of us as children, pursues us with love, and longs for our company. Once you become His child, He will move mountains to keep you close. It is not possible to comprehend the love that He has for us and which He gives in the form of blessings, especially mercy.

No matter what we do, even if we require discipline, God always tempers His actions with love. That is the prime directive: love. It is what drives His pursuit of us and the one lesson we need to learn above all others while we live. It's how people will know that we are Jesus' followers, because they see that we have love. Even when we seek to correct the behavior of others, we must temper our words with love. No kingdom was ever won and kept with hate, and only the spirit of love will overcome the evil in this world.

Lord Jesus: Teach me to speak the truth in love.

October 12

*Now the Spirit explicitly says that in the last times some will
turn away from the truth by paying attention to deceitful
spirits and demonic instructions through the hypocrisy
of liars with branded consciences. 1 Timothy 4:1, 2*

This is the time when those who call themselves Christians will begin
to support questionable practices. I call them questionable, God calls
them sin. The evil one has infiltrated the Church and twisted the truth
in such a way that people believe that 'hate the sin, love the sinner'
means that we condone their sins by making life easier for them to
commit those sins. Let me be clear: I don't condemn those who have
abortions or live as homosexuals, but I don't condone their actions
either. For me it is the same as someone who lies, cheats, or steals. It's
all sin. I have sin, too, by the way. And I have to take care of my own
condition in the eyes of God.

One problem today is that people won't admit that they have sin. Maybe
they don't read the Bible, or maybe they think it doesn't apply to them.
But the fact remains: anyone who thinks that they will be free from
judgment after living a life of sinfulness (as outlined in the Scriptures)
has been deceived. If they would ask God, He would tell them. And if
He told them, they would have to deal with it. I can't help but wonder
if this is why they don't ask.

The devil has been working on this erosion of morals and the wasting
away of the Church for thousands of years. He's patient because he
knows once it gets too bad, the Lord will step in and put an end to his
evil reign.

Lord Jesus: Help me be free from the influence of lying spirits.

October 13

All the nations you have made shall come to bow before
you, LORD, and give honor to your name. Psalm 86:9

At the end of days there will be a moment when everyone will stand
before God, both the saved and the unsaved, and all will bow before
Him. Those who are saved will be filled with joy. Those who are not
saved will be filled with dread, because they now have to give a reason
for their choice to deny him. There is no excuse that will get them into
heaven. They had an entire lifetime to choose God, and yet they didn't.

Think of all the people you know that aren't saved. When your turn
comes to stand before God, He's going to ask why you didn't try to gather
them in. What are you going to say?

*Lord Jesus: Help me to speak to those around me who are not
saved.*

October 14

If I were still trying to please people, I would not
be a slave of Christ. Galatians 1:10c

You and I both know that you can't please all of the people all of the
time. Most people can't please one person a fraction of the time! So
why try? It is not our responsibility to make other people happy, nor is
it theirs to make us happy. So if you are in a relationship and expect
another person to fulfill you and generate happiness, you are likely
to be disappointed. I see so many people that haven't yet come to the
realization that happiness lies within ourselves. It doesn't come from
outside, but from inside.

Paul recognized that his message was offensive to many of the Jews and
artisans of his day. He was taking away the law of Moses from the Jews
as well as the livelihood from the craftsmen who fashioned the idols of

their day. But God didn't put him (or us) here to please others. Our job is to please the Lord by utilizing the gifts that He has given us to use for His kingdom and His glory.

It wasn't until I stopped thinking of me and how I could please others that I finally learned how to be me – the official me that God created me to be. And guess what – I'm happier alone with God than I ever was as a married person.

Lord Jesus: Teach me how to be happy.

October 15

Then he returned to his disciples and said to them, "Are you
still sleeping and taking your rest? Behold, the hour is at hand
when the Son of Man is to be handed over to sinners."
Matthew 26:45

I can only imagine the condition of Jesus while He was in the garden at Gethsemane praying that the Father would take away the need for Him to suffer the horrific trials and pain that were coming upon Him. While He's miserable and crying out in agony, the disciples are sleeping nearby. Every time I read this verse, I hear Jesus' voice resounding with a hint of sarcasm and disappointment in it, and I see myself being the one He is speaking to.

No matter how many works I do, how many souls I save, or how many seeds I plant, it can never be enough to take away that feeling that I still haven't done enough. Many of the Saints slept on boards, rocks, or hard ground and scourged or flagellated themselves, and yet they still felt inadequate. I, myself, haven't come to that point of self-mortification. It's hard enough for me to keep being a saint with a small s, much less try to be a Saint with a capital s. And yet 11 of the 12 original disciples have been made Saints by the Church despite the fact that they all turned and ran when the soldiers came to arrest Jesus. But then, 10 of them were martyred now that I come to think of it.

Lord Jesus: I am unworthy; help me to rise above my inadequacy.

October 16

But mark this: There will be terrible times in the last days. People will be lovers of themselves, lovers of money, boastful, proud, abusive, disobedient to their parents, ungrateful, unholy, without love, unforgiving, slanderous, without self-control, brutal, not lovers of the good, treacherous, rash, conceited, lovers of pleasure rather than lovers of God – having a form of godliness but denying its power. Have nothing to do with such people. 2 Timothy 3:1-5 (NIV)

I know I've talked about the nature of people repeatedly already, so I will not spend time on that again. I simply wish to point out that there is a pattern that is developing, not just in the United States but all over the world, that closely follows the deterioration of the Hebrews before the Lord destroyed both Judah and Israel. If there is anything that you can do in your little corner of the world to combat this frightening decline in morality, please do it! You could start a Bible study in your home; but if you do, please be aware of any local legislation that prohibits such activities – unless, of course, you're willing to go to jail, and then you can have a prison ministry. Work in a local youth program that teaches kids to have respect and morality. Be a mentor or a Boys & Girls Club sponsor. And if you're really patient and brave, you can be a foster parent.

Please, just keep an eye out for those who don't believe in the principles of propriety. It's for you and your children's safety.

Lord Jesus: Keep me aware the true nature of those around me.

October 17

For just as from the heavens the rain and snow come down and
do not return there until they have watered the earth, making
it fertile and fruitful, giving seed to him who sows and bread
to him who eats, so shall my word be that goes forth from my
mouth; it shall not return to me void, but shall do my will,
achieving the end for which I sent it. Isaiah 55:10, 11

I like to think of the Lord as a gardener. He plants seeds, waters them,
grows plants and vines that produce fruit, and harvests those fruits.
He manipulates people and situations (in a positive way) to get specific
persons together to maximize the benefits of His efforts. Everything he
does has a purpose which will benefit His children and His kingdom
in some way, and everything requires fertilization for growth. His word,
the Bible, is the food that nourishes our spirit and gives us hope and
correction. His Word, Jesus, brings us salvation and a model to imitate.

It takes more than just reading God's word to make it come alive in a
soul – contemplation and application are also required. And the great
thing about the growth that transpires in you is that it flows out like
a stream or fountain that waters the world around you. How strong a
stream are you putting out? Could it be more like a river with just a bit
more work?

*Lord Jesus: Make your word in me a river that flows out over
the earth and waters everyone around me.*

October 18

Not that of ourselves we are qualified to take credit for
anything as coming from us; rather, our qualification comes
from God who has indeed qualified us as ministers of a
new covenant, not of letter but of spirit; for the letter brings
death, but the spirit gives life. 2 Corinthians 3:5, 6

Paul spent a lot of time separating the new covenant from the old, grace versus the law. His teaching was that the law brought death because it pointed out sinfulness. Grace, on the other hand, qualifies one for absolution from sins and requires only the law of love as put forth by Jesus and recorded in the book of John for us: "This I command you: Love one another." (John 15:17)

Love can only come from the Spirit of God, as do all of our gifts. There is nothing I take credit for that is good in my life – all of the good comes from God. Me, as myself, is a sinful one, born of the flesh, and needing deliverance through Christ Jesus. Nevertheless, He still uses me to spread His wishes and word, and I do this because of my love for Him. What has God qualified you for that you haven't yet done?

Lord Jesus: Make me a minister of your covenant.

October 19

I will go back to my place until they pay for their
guilt and seek my presence. Hosea 5:15

Playing hard-to-get is a dangerous game at any time, but especially if you're talking about your salvation. Everyone has their limits – even God. And if you drive Him to the point of excessive frustration, He may withdraw His pursuit of you and wait for you to come to Him. What if you run out of time here before you go to Him for reconciliation? That's a scary prospect. And then you'll *have* to go to him, but it will be too late. What will you say to Him then?

Lord Jesus: I'm sorry for making you wait.

October 20

"Do to others as you would have them do to you. For if you love those who love you, what credit is that to you? Even sinners love those who love them. And if you do good to those who do good to you, what credit is that to you? Even sinners do the same." Luke 6:31-33

Jesus always wants to know how we set ourselves apart from the crowd. Not how we appear to be different, but how we actually think, feel, and act differently than those who are not His followers. We are called to be working in the world but also spiritually apart from the world. In essence, He's asking each of us what we do to be more righteous in his eyes than the next person. And while we should never compare ourselves to others, it does sometimes help to view someone else's works to see if there is a better way of doing things – some way that we can improve our performance.

Once we are saved, we are to perform at a higher level than we did before. And then we can be those persons whom others look to in order to find those better ways of doing things. Step up and lead by example, for you never know who may be watching.

Lord Jesus: Help me to be a better example to others of your righteousness.

October 21

And I detested all the fruits of my labor under the sun, because I must leave them to a man who is to come after me. Ecclesiastes 2:18

This verse makes me think of the man whose harvest was so big that he had to tear down his old barns and build bigger ones to hold it all. He was then planning to kick back and relax. (Luke 12:17-19) It took me a long time to get that parable, but the gist of it is that we are not to rely on our previous spiritual works to keep us in God's good graces. We have to keep working.

The writer in Ecclesiastes keeps working for literal things, but he's mad because he can't spend it all himself. His complaint is that the fruits of his labor will go to someone else when he dies. There's nothing spiritual here for me. This is materialism pure and simple from my point of view. And it's a horrible thing to express. If you have so much that you can't spend it all, you should be sharing it with widows, orphans, and the homeless – you know, Matthew 25: what you did for these least of my brothers, you did for me.

Mother Teresa said she saw Jesus in every face she served – Matthew 25 at its finest. So if you have too much and don't know what to do with it all, just walk the streets. I'm sure you'll have no trouble finding places to distribute your money or goods. Food pantries and missions all over our country are begging for assistance. Won't you help them serve those who are in need?

Lord Jesus: Help me find good organizations that can utilize my surplus properly.

October 22

There is no fear in love, but perfect love drives out fear because
fear has to do with punishment, and so one who fears is not
yet perfect in love. We love because he first loved us.
1 John 4:18, 19

Fear does not come from God. Love comes from God. Those who fear do not truly know God or His power. Fear comes from the evil one to stop us from trusting God and fulfilling our mission. Love comes from God so that we can be good examples of Him and lead others to Him.

God doesn't want us to be scared or weak. He wants us to trust in His love for us and be filled with that love so that it spills over to everyone we come into contact with.

Lord Jesus: Fill me with your love; drive out my fears.

October 23

Does any other nation change its gods? – yet they are
not gods at all! But my people have changed their
glory for useless things. Jeremiah 2:11

I'm horrible. I sit in church and try not to judge people based on what they are wearing (or not wearing as the case may be). I see women with huge stones on their hands, the newest designer fashions, perfectly coiffed hair and nails, and kids that reek of coddling and comfort, and I wonder: how much do they give to the church? In the parking lot there are Audis, Beamers, and Cadillacs, and I wonder if they ever pick up anyone who needs a lift to church or a Bible study group. When I get involved with programs, I keep seeing the same people over and over, and I wonder: how many people give no time at all to a program here?

I didn't grow up with much money, but we never did without. And a check always went into the plate on Sunday. When I was married and working in a factory, I worked 70 hours per week and brought home $1000 paychecks. 10% went to the church every week. I kept wondering how long it would be until my husband (who did not go to church) would say something about it. Eventually, he did ask if I thought I might be giving too much to the church. My response was, "The Lord gave me this job even though I wasn't looking for it, and he keeps me healthy and going to work every day. How am I not going to repay him for his goodness to me?" He had no answer. End of discussion.

Sometimes it's easy to see what or who is someone's God (or god), while other times you can never tell. What is important is for each of us to keep our hearts pure and focused on the one true God who provides for our needs and avoid useless things that steal our attention from Him. Who or what is your god?

Lord Jesus: You are the True God.

October 24
Draw near to God, and he will draw near to you. James 4:8a

Have you ever wanted to really know God? Have you ever tried to fathom His mind or His Spirit? Do you think, as I do, that there are no words big enough to ever fully describe Him or the way He makes you feel? If not, maybe you need to try to 'draw near' to Him more often. I like to view myself in my mind kneeling in His presence in prayer, thanking Him for all of His blessings. I also do this when I pray the Rosary. I don't offer those prayers to Mary herself, but to the Lord, and she kneels next to me and prays with me for the intentions that I have offered that day.

There are lots of verses in the Psalms that are praises to the Lord. There are also many that speak of His goodness and mercy and His hatred of sin and evil. Start at the beginning of the book, and as you come across a verse that speaks of His character, stop and contemplate. (*Selah*) Close your eyes and seek His presence; ask for understanding and wisdom.

As you do this more and more often, I believe you will find that you will be changed forever in your relationship with Him. At least I hope that you will. The hard part, as always, is getting started. Don't put it off. Go do it right now before you find something else to distract you.

Lord Jesus: Draw me near to your heart.

October 25
With your counsel you guide me, and at the end
receive me with honor. Psalm 73:24

For those who seek to be faithful followers of Jesus, He provides a guide in the form of the holy Spirit. This Spirit gives counsel when asked, leads us in the guise of our conscience, and provides knowledge of things or situations when necessary. He grants us the ability to discern the decisions we should make that will lead us away from evil and danger, and teaches us how to use our gifts and talents for the glory of the kingdom. He also gives us strength when we are physically, mentally, emotionally or spiritually weak.

When we listen to the leading of the holy Spirit, we can't go wrong. At the end of the day, shouldn't we be sure to thank him? He is the One leading us home, after all.

Lord Jesus: Thank you for the gift of the holy Spirit.

October 26
Every day they devoted themselves to meeting together in the
temple area and to breaking bread in their homes. They ate
their meals with exultation and sincerity of heart, praising
God and enjoying favor with all the people. And every day the
Lord added to their number those who were being saved.
Acts 2:46, 47

How fortunate the early disciples were – they don't seem to have had to work. There are some preachers around today that make a good enough salary that they can devote nearly 100% of their time to their ministry. As a side note, I'd like to point out that vacations and regular days off are *always* a necessity for pastoral staff. One can only handle everyone else's problems for so long without a break, so please respect their time off.

It's really important to show to the world the joy that comes from the holy Spirit as well as a unified front. It makes people on the outside want to get some of it. And that's what we're after anyway – leading souls to Christ. Luke wrote that the early Church was joyful, sharing their study time and meals together, and 'enjoying favor with all the people' – that's all the people outside the ruling class. Herod had James beheaded, and Peter was in jail awaiting a similar fate until the angel of the Lord came and set him free. (Acts 12:1-19) And of course the disciples were constantly performing miracles that kept drawing the people in.

Wouldn't it be great if we could spend all of our time studying the word of God and sharing meals with other joyful people? I bet it would be more appealing to the outside world. Who wouldn't want to hang out with positive, upbeat people? And after so long, they wouldn't be able to help themselves from getting saved.

Lord Jesus: Grant us the grace to build a more joyful community of believers.

October 27

After purifying the temple, they made a new altar. Then, with fire struck from flint, they offered sacrifice for the first time in two years, burned incense, and lighted lamps. 2 Maccabees 10:3

Have you ever heard of **Chanukah**? You might better recognize it spelled Hanukkah – the Jewish festival of lights or also called the Feast of Dedication. Jesus was in Jerusalem during this festival as is mentioned in John 10:22. If you don't have a Catholic Bible, you might not be aware of the nature of this festival (unless you're Jewish). In the books of 1 and 2 Maccabees, the story is told of how the land of Israel is once again being overrun by outsiders – this time the Greeks. The Greeks abolished the Hebrew laws including the honoring of the Sabbath. But the worst thing of all was the desecration of the temple by the Gentiles through the performance of debaucheries in the courts and sacrificing unclean animals on the altar.

The family Maccabeus retreated to the wilderness to avoid the genocide going on in the city of Jerusalem and the uncleanness taking place in the temple. Others came out to join up with them, and eventually they challenged the Hellenists and defeated them. They purified the temple as was proscribed in the law, and re-dedicated the lighting of the menorah. And while there was not enough sacred oil to keep the lamp burning for even one day, the oil miraculously burned for eight days while a new supply could be prepared.

Lord Jesus: Keep my lamp burning.

October 28
In the same way, the Lord ordered that those who preach
the gospel should live by the gospel. 1 Corinthians 9:14

Practice what you preach. We've all said it to someone in our lifetime. It's the opposite of 'Do as I say, not as I do', which is justification for absolutely nothing. It sounds neat when it rolls out, but it's saying straight up that you're a two-faced autocrat. I've been on both sides of this statement, I'm not proud to say. But I can say with absolute certainty that while there is no justification for hypocrisy, it happens much of the time. And until the day when we all reach heaven and are freed from the flesh of our bodies, it will continue to be an issue.

When it happens to your pastor, ask him (or her) to repent, and then give them another chance. Everyone has a weak moment sometime. But if it keeps happening, they need to go. If they can't properly administer their office with honor, it's time to search for someone who can. Remember what Jesus said about the Pharisees: If the blind lead the blind, they will both fall into the pit. (Matthew 15:14) Don't be a Pharisee!

Lord Jesus: Keep me honest in my service.

October 29

Shall I acquit criminal balances, bags of false weights?
Micah 6:11

One thing that the Lord has always been critical of in his people is their tendency to fall into less then desirable business practices. One of the reasons that Jesus was so angry with the money-changers and the vendors selling animals in the temple was the fact that they were gouging the people who came there to sacrifice and worship. It was a sticking spot in the Hebrews' history and was one of the things that the prophets Isaiah, Ezekiel, Hosea, Amos, and Micah all challenged the people about. You can see from the number of prophets speaking about this matter that the Lord had an ax to grind with the people who were evidently not getting the message.

This verse speaks to me as well. I work in a business where products have to be measured out for sale, and the amount of product should be as represented on the package. And it really annoys me when I buy a bag of chips, open it up, and there's less than half a bag. I get that it's weight and not volume and that settling that takes place, but it still aggravates me that there's so much air in that bag. It's still a misrepresentation in my mind.

Lord Jesus: May I never misrepresent what I offer in business or faith.

October 30

"Lord, do not trouble yourself, I am not worthy that you should enter
under my roof. Therefore, I did not consider myself worthy to come to
you; but say the word and let my servant be healed." Luke 7:6b, 7

And this from a Roman soldier. Jesus couldn't get many of His own
people to believe in his abilities, but here was a Gentile from a pagan
country, a soldier from the occupying force in Israel coming to Him
and believing so strongly that He says Jesus doesn't even have to come
to the house. The soldier realizes that Jesus' power is so great that He
has only to say the words, and the servant, not present but home in
bed, will be healed. So great was the faith of this man that he took a
healing, not for himself, but for someone else – an act of mercy for a
friend and co-worker.

Jesus can still do this today. I think that people ask for healing, but
for some reason they don't believe that they deserve to be healed. Let
me just say that if he healed Mary Magdalene who is rumored to be a
prostitute, and a Roman soldier that he'd never even met, there is no
reason for any of us to despair. Healing comes in proportion to your
faith. When in doubt, follow James' directions: Call the presbyters,
be anointed with oil, and have them lay their hands on you and pray.
(Jas 5:14, 15)

Lord Jesus: Grant me healing through your grace.

October 31

"Even if you now remain silent, relief and deliverance will
come to the Jews from another source; but you and your father's
house will perish. Who knows but that it was for a time like
this that you obtained the royal dignity?" Esther 4:14

There are two things in this passage that speak to me. First is the fact
that, if the Lord offers an opportunity to someone and they decline, He

goes to someone else and makes the offer to them. I know this to be true. Back in 2003, He asked me to write a book – not this kind of book but rather a book about the end times. I started to work on it but got down on myself for not having any publishing knowledge, connections, or credentials. I was a simple person studying my little heart out trying to gain understanding about the purported rapture that had been made popular by the <u>Left Behind</u> series of books. I quit. So someone else wrote the book. There are actually several books out there now that I have read whose authors came to the same conclusions that I did, but they were several years behind me. Oops.

The second thing I see here is the idea of Divine intervention and predestination. Jeremiah was told that he was chosen for his job as prophet from before the time he was born. Here we see the possibility that Esther was born to fulfill this opportunity to save the Jews from extinction because of her favor from the king as the most desired of his wives.

For some reason I have nearly always believed in these three things: predestination, divine intervention, and limited time opportunities. I can only presume that the holy Spirit must have taught me at some time for some good reason; maybe to get me to follow His directions.

Lord Jesus: Lead me to fulfill my entire mission for this life.

November

November 1

Whoever does not provide for relatives and especially family
members has denied the faith and is worse than an unbeliever.
1 Timothy 5:8

I have a friend who has a husband with advanced MS. She takes care of him
at home because every time he goes to a facility for her to have a break, he
gets sick and ends up in the hospital. Her family has nothing at all to do
with them, and his family only has enough contact to cause her problems.

I've known them for several years now, and just in this last year his
parents have finally begun to help her out a bit. She has had workers come
to her home to help care for him, but nearly every one that comes is either
passive-aggressive, wacky in the head, or steals from them. It's a horrible
situation. Did I mention that all of the estranged family members go to
church every Sunday? (Except for the one atheist, of course.)

Paul says that these kinds of people are worse than unbelievers. I
wonder what they would say to that. I wonder what Jesus will say when
they show up at the throne. Remember Matthew 25? I think these might
end up going to the goat side if they don't have a change of heart.

UPDATE: At the time of revision, her parents have started visiting her
and treating her kindly, although they don't help her with caring for her
husband. One level of prayer answered! Hallelujah!

*Lord Jesus: Open the eyes of our family members to see the needs
of their own.*

November 2

If a man again touches a corpse after he has bathed, what did
he gain by the purification? So with a man who fasts for his
sins, but then goes and commits them again: Who will hear
his prayer, and what has he gained by his mortification?
Sirach 34:25, 26

One of the most prevalent statements in the wisdom literature writings
is, "The fear of the Lord is the beginning of wisdom." Those who
fail to repent and attempt to put aside their sins are not following the
Lord's directive and should expect Him to continue to poke at their
conscience. These people are the seed that fell on rocky places and
withered because they had no root. (Matthew 13:5)

But those who are more likely to receive a blast of the Lord's wrath are
those who confess their sins yet have no plans to stop their activities.
Why? Because they readily acknowledge by confession that they have
these sins, and yet they have no intention to quit them. They failed to
repent. Confession is for accidental sins – things we fall into and then
recognize as a mistake. Willful sins are those for which no remorse is
felt and which will bring us even greater condemnation for our failure
to relent to his commandments.

Lord Jesus: Teach me remorse.

November 3

No creature is concealed from him, but everything
is naked and exposed to the eyes of him to whom
we must render an account. Hebrews 4:13

Once upon a time, I was stupid and ignorant. I thought I was getting
away with things. It didn't occur to me back in those days to think about
the fact that God sees everything I do. Someday we'll all have to stand
in front of Him and explain our actions, see the grief that our actions

caused, and feel the pain that we have caused others. Do you think you might have done things differently in the past if you had been aware of this information? I know I would have.

Thank God for His mercies! All of those things are forgiven. It's amazing how many things I don't want to do any more now that I understand better the consequences of my actions. I want my review to show smiles and saved souls, not tears and heartaches.

Lord Jesus: Thank you for opening my eyes to the effects of my actions.

November 4

But God is merciful and forgave their sin; he did not utterly destroy them. Time and again he turned back his anger, unwilling to unleash all his rage. He was mindful that they were flesh, a breath that passes and does not return. Psalm 78:38, 39

This is the old way of God. Yes, I know, he is the same yesterday, today and forever. But the day will come when he will not take into account the flesh of anyone. The day will come when mercy will end – the day of the final judgment.

Whenever I hear the word mercy I think of the movie "Absolute Power." Clint Eastwood plays a thief that witnesses a murder by the president of the United States. The CIA comes after him but can't catch him, so they go after his daughter instead. One agent shows up at the hospital with a syringe of lethal material, but Clint's character catches him before he can use it. The deadly syringe is then seen sticking out of the agent's neck who requests mercy. The thief tells him, "Sorry. I'm fresh out."

Ecclesiastes 3:1 says that there is an appointed time for everything, and a time for every affair under the heavens. Eventually everything will come to an end – whether it's your time to die or to be judged.

Are you ready for that day today? "Behold, I am coming soon. I bring with me the recompense I will give to each according to his deeds." (Revelation 22:12)

Come, Lord Jesus.

November 5
I know your tribulation and poverty, but you are rich.
Revelation 2:9a

The Christians at Smyrna were not wealthy when it came to earthly things, and yet the Lord said that they were rich. He said they were living with poverty and afflictions, so what kind of wealth did they have? It was an intangible, something that many people don't understand: faith.

I have long wondered about what comprises faith, and I still can't put my finger on it. It is certainly belief in God and trust in His providence, but I think there's more. If I say I have faith and yet don't pray, am I a liar? If I say I trust God but don't consult Him when I make a decision, am I exercising faith? Doesn't being faithful to someone entail involving them in everything you do?

In Smyrna, there was a group of people who were persecuting the Christians for their beliefs, as was common in the early days of the Church. The Lord warned these Christians that some would go to jail and suffer several days. He also suggested that some might perish: "Be faithful, even to the point of death, and I will give you the crown of life." (v. 10c) It is hard for many of us to imagine that people went through this type of persecution then or even recognize that there are still people in the world who suffer this ordeal today. But it is happening. Whether or not we will experience these things in our lifetime is known only to God.

For those who overcome the persecution and remain faithful to God, He will grant a place in His eternal kingdom. I've often wondered if I could be so faithful as to not deny Him should I be faced with death for my beliefs, and I have come to the conclusion that I, myself, am not capable of such boldness and bravery. But with the spirit in me, giving me strength and wisdom, I believe I could make it. I hope that I never have to find out, but nothing in this life is guaranteed.

Lord Jesus: Thank you for your warnings and your sustaining grace.

November 6

Who is there like you, the God who removes guilt and pardons sin for the remnant of his inheritance; who does not persist in anger forever, but delights rather in clemency. Micah 7:18

Micah was a contemporary of Isaiah, a prophet who also spoke of destruction to Israel and Judah for their many sins and failure to cling to the precepts of God. Most of us today don't actively worship idols of gold and silver, but I have noticed that I do sometimes give too much time and energy to things or pastimes that have little or no value.

Idols today have a different context than they did in the days of Micah. The one that I struggle with the most is what I call my brain breaks: spider solitaire and mah-jongg. Either one on its own for a short period is not a big issue – I sometimes need a break from some form of work that is causing me frustration. The problem comes when I sit down at the computer at home and play for two hours when I have other things I should be doing, for the kingdom or not. I'm not saying that people can't have a vacation. Everyone needs time away from the stresses of life for a bit. The difference is that a vacation is time that is set apart for relaxation and an extended brain break, while mine is just self-indulgence and laziness.

My point in this is that sometimes we get off track – maybe for a couple of hours, a couple of days, or as much as a couple of years. God is always there, nudging us back onto the path, waiting patiently for us to return. And once we recognize our sinfulness and turn from it and ask for mercy, God is faithful to forgive and to throw our sins 'into the sea.' As I've heard some evangelist say, "It's covered by the blood!" God remembers my past iniquities no more. Too bad our friends and family aren't always so kind.

Lord Jesus: Thank you for shedding your blood that my blood can be made clean.

November 7

For you were called for freedom, brothers. But do not
use this freedom as an opportunity for the flesh; rather,
serve one another through love. Galatians 5:13

The heading of this section in my Bible is 'Freedom in Christ.' Paul is still berating the Galatians for falling prey to some misguided teachings about observances from the old law which he calls 'a yoke of slavery.' He also states that if you take up that yoke again after having cast it aside, that you are in a fallen state – alienated from Christ.

Much of the written law was for personal matters: cleanliness, foods to eat or not eat, and household observances. When Jesus came, the focus changed. The new law is love. That's it – just love. And it seems to be the one thing that many people can't seem to do. We are called to love God and our neighbors, not our self.

I don't have to tell you how many folks there are out there who only seem to love themselves. When it comes to any decision, it's always the one that does the most for their position. They don't take into consideration the feelings or beliefs of anyone else. It's all about their convenience. Paul speaks of a little yeast working through the whole dough. It only takes one person with the wrong focus to screw up a whole group of people. Their influence can spread like a contagious disease until someone stands up and puts an end to their nonsense.

When Jesus came and set up the new covenant, He promised the gift of the holy Spirit. The Spirit focuses on the inside of a person, convicting our souls of the things that need changed which are then manifested on the outside. It also prompts us to change the things of the world to better reflect the things of Christ – in short, to show and to share love with the world.

Paul says we are called to be free: free from the old law, free from temple sacrifices, free to serve with love – not a physical love, but rather a spiritual and emotional love; a love driven by the prompting of the Spirit of God, not the spirit of self. The people who were teaching the old law with the new were not showing love, they were thinking of themselves. They had not given up the yoke of slavery and were trying to force it onto others who were not already so burdened. So if someone brings their yoke to you, don't take it. Rather, help them to remove it from their own shoulders and cast it away. Then you will be showing the proper focus.

Lord Jesus: Teach me to take the focus off of myself and place it on you.

November 8
God makes the earth yield healing herbs which the
prudent man should not neglect. Sirach 38:4

I've never been a big one to go to a doctor; I have little or no faith in them. But then I've never been terribly sick, either. I like to take herbal supplements to fill in the gaps in my dietary intake, because a healthy body is less likely to fall ill.

When the body becomes sedentary and the diet too rich in all the wrong things, that's when problems begin. We weren't meant to be stationary when we work or to eat processed foods, gmo's, and loads of sugar. Everything that you put into your body that isn't in the form that God created turns into fat or gets collected in the organs and intestines as toxins. And when the body loads up on toxins is when the breakdown begins. Is it any wonder that the average American human body is overweight and pre- or full-blown diabetic?

There are herbs and plants that will cleanse these toxins out of the body. Look online for information, but don't look at medical sites – they want to treat your symptoms rather than cure the problem. Try sites such as http://www.realfarmacy.com/ that offer current info and articles about how to improve your health holistically. And if you grow your own food, check out http://www.gardenvigor.com/ for products that will boost the nutrient content of your produce and herbs.

Since they want us dead, the radical Islamists could just leave us alone to self-destruct; looks like most of the nation will be dead in twenty years or less from cancer and diabetic heart attacks anyway.

Lord Jesus: Lead me to the herbs that will make me healthier.

November 9

Do you not know that the unjust will not inherit the kingdom of God? Do not be deceived; neither fornicators nor idolaters nor adulterers nor boy prostitutes nor sodomites nor thieves nor the greedy nor drunkards nor slanderers nor robbers will inherit the kingdom of God. 1 Corinthians 6:9, 10

Take a look around. Check out the news. Do you see anyone out there that is doing any of these things? Oh – nearly everyone in the news is doing at least one of these things. Occasionally there is a token feel-good story where these might not apply, but as a general rule, the human race has fallen deep into the pit of sinfulness as governed by this list. And you might say that those people on the news aren't Christians, so they wouldn't be written in the book of life anyway.

You might be surprised to find out how many of them actually ***do*** go to church. Did you know that there are churches just for gays and lesbians?

Or that there is now a Bible called the Queen James translation? It has all of the homosexual references removed. I've noticed that there seems to be a lot of excessive drinking among Catholics. Idolatry is everywhere – most people just don't recognize that they have fallen into subjugation. And greed isn't just the lust for money, but for power, control, food, and drink as well. It is my personal opinion that if we could remove greed from the world, there would be no other sins.

The Lord said through the prophet Jeremiah, "I will judge you on that word of yours, 'I have not sinned.'" (Jer 2:35) Those who claim to be without sin will be punished worse than those who admit their sin and yet can't seem to quit. It's a matter of the heart, and only each individual and the Lord can see in there. Many people refuse to look into their own hearts, and I suspect that those are ones who need to most, yet they might be terrified by what they find there.

Lord Jesus: Show me the sins of my heart.

November 10

Offer praise as your sacrifice to God; fulfill your vows to
the Most High. Then call on me in time of distress; I will
rescue you, and you shall honor me. Psalm 50:14, 15

There are a lot of people these days who have little or nothing materially, but that should not stop them from praising God with whatever they have – even if it's only their voice. It saddens me that there are not more people being helped in the world and that so many are homeless.

I've mentioned to you that my parish is pretty wealthy. We have an organization that serves those in need. The average amount of funds spent in the summer is obviously less than the winter, but it is still a substantial amount. They help people with utility bills, medications, rent, and food supplies. Once a month they put out special collection bins to take up funds for the program, and once a year they pass the plate a second time as a dedicated offering. Everyone who receives assistance gets a visit from a pair of representatives to assess the need onsite and pray with the prospective recipients.

All of the people involved in this program have made a vow to serve the less fortunate of our community. It is their goal to enable those served to praise the Lord in their time of distress because he provided a rescue for them.

Lord Jesus: Thank you for those who enable others to give you praise.

November 11
Blessed are the peacemakers, for they will be
called children of God. Matthew 5:9

What is it about 'peace' that is so elusive? It's what nearly everyone says they want, but so few have it. And no one seems to be serious about working to create it, personally or globally.

The very first time I read this verse, it spoke to me. There are some of us who absolutely abhor confrontations. We will always try to smooth over waves in the relationships of people around us because it makes us miserable to see them in such a state. I think everyone knows someone who is constantly 'stirring the pot' and trying to 'steal' peace from others. They seem to thrive on conflict. Stay away from these people, for they are not from God. They may have received salvation at some time, but they have strayed from the path. Pray for them, for they are not at peace.

Evangelization is like that sometimes. You try to give someone peace through the Gospel, but they see you as trying to take what peace they have. They don't recognize that their peace is false. Many people will refuse to grow or accept that they don't have all the answers. They're absolutely convinced that they've got it all figured out, but they're really living in blissful ignorance.

Paul wrote of the 'peace that passes understanding,' the peace that comes from God. You can't create it; you have to ask for it and be led into it. You also have to be willing to accept that you don't have all the answers and never will – that some things are simply out of your hands and beyond earthly knowledge. Get over it and move on.

Lord Jesus: Please help me find the peace that passes understanding.

November 12

Thus says the LORD: Observe what is right, do what is just; for
my salvation is about to come, my justice about to be revealed.
Isaiah 56:1

In every life there is a day of reckoning. I'm not talking about the judgment day, although that will come as well. I'm talking about the day when all your actions will catch up with you. You and I both know someone who has been creating anguish and distress in people's lives for ages. And no matter how many times you read them the riot act, they just shrug you off and go on.

One of the things that I have had to learn and that I share with others is that you have to rise above their level of iniquity and say, "They will get theirs, and I won't have to lift a finger to make it happen." I learned this from King David who wrote in one of his psalms, "For he who avenges blood remembers; he does not ignore the cries of the afflicted." (Psalm 9:12) He's talking about God.

Some people that I share this observation with don't want to wait; they want those who create their distress to get it from God now. But that isn't how He works. He chooses the time and place. Some may actually get away with their misbehaving their entire life on this side, but I think that will only make their reckoning worse on the other side. At least if they get knocked down here, there is a chance, no matter how small, that they could repent. And it isn't right for us to burn with the desire to see their downfall. That is evil on our part.

Lord Jesus: Help me to rise above the evils around me and wait for your justice.

November 13
Save others by snatching them out of the fire; on
others have mercy with fear.... Jude 23

Sometimes when we see a person struggling in their life, we want to try to help that person resolve their issues. Remember when I talked about having a prayer or accountability partner? Here's a good reason for making that person the same gender as you.

Here is a scenario I have witnessed more than once: One of two parties suggests getting together for a coffee or something at either's home to talk about problems. The two parties are of opposing genders, and find that they get along very well. They agree to meet again and talk some more. Did I mention that one or both are married? Before long they're engaged in an extramarital affair, and there are even more problems than when they started out. What began as a desire to help someone out of marital troubles has turned into streams of tears, packs of lies, and possibly a divorce or two.

Second scenario: A lady has problems at home and wants to talk to the pastor about them. She comes to the office and they close the door for privacy. Before long, they are engaged in inappropriate behavior. He has failed to take the proper precautions to protect his honor as a pastor and hers as a congregant. In both cases, they failed to show fear with their mercy as they attempted to snatch someone out of the flames.

Each of these situations grew out of a desire to do good, but the devil got into the mix and twisted their desire for healing into a desire for self-gratification. Please use caution when trying to assist a fellow believer who is struggling with life issues. If someone of the opposite gender asks you for help, suggest that someone else be involved in order to create a barrier between you.

Lord Jesus: Remind me to not be alone with someone of the opposite gender unless absolutely necessary.

November 14
Better is one day in your courts than a thousand elsewhere;
Better the threshold of the house of my God than a
home in the tents of the wicked. Psalm 84:10

Every day presents a challenge to remain holy. At nearly every turn there is an opportunity to slip off the righteousness wagon and fall into a pile of sin. Most advertising campaigns are designed to appeal to the basic instincts and generate an emotional response. More and more, shock is being used to sell along with the sex that has been used for years. It takes a conscious effort to set ourselves apart from the wickedness that closes in on us every day.

The way I fight my battles is to envision myself in the throne room of God, appealing for his mercy to keep me from willful sins and ask for help in avoiding the propensity to become fixated on some of these shocking ads that I see. I eliminated the nasty music and crude dj problem by only listening to Christian music on the radio or playing my own cd's.

This psalm was written by the sons of Korah. Assuming that this is the way they truly felt, I am in total agreement that there is no better place to be than in the courts of God. And even if I had to be like a homeless person in a doorway in order to stay with God, I would still be happy.

Lord Jesus: Allow me to sit at the door of your house!

November 15

If anyone thinks he is religious and does not bridle his tongue but deceives his heart, his religion is vain. Religion that is pure and undefiled before God is this: to care for orphans and widows in their affliction and to keep oneself unstained by the world. James 1:26, 27

When a heart is hardened due to self-interest there can be little impact on it. I remember when the Lord was convicting me for the things that I needed to change in my life in my early days of faith. Every Sunday at church I would hear the sermon, and it was for me, telling me how I was grieving the Spirit. I then had two choices that I could make in my life: I could stop going to church and remove the source of grief, or I could listen to the Spirit and do something about what I was feeling. I chose to continue to go to church and make changes in my life. Some of my choices were not totally supported at home, but I did them anyway — they were the right things for me to do.

James says that we need to refrain from being polluted by the world, and it would seem an obvious thing that would not need to be said. But unless I am intentional about keeping myself pure, I can easily fall back into those things that I did before. It's doing what is right versus doing what is easy. Unwholesome is easy: it's looking in the mirror and seeing nothing that impacts. When you look in the mirror and see things that you don't like and want to change, it's then that life begins to be interesting. And exercising restraint is the harder thing to do.

James also talks about religion that is worthless. I like to say that I don't have a religion — I have a way of life that is based on faith in God. Some people would call it religion, but not me.

Lord Jesus: Thank you for convicting me, leading me, and giving me strength to do the right thing.

November 16

Take heed, therefore, lest, forgetting the covenant which the LORD, your God, has made with you, you fashion for yourselves against his command an idol in any form whatsoever. For the LORD, your God, is a consuming fire, a jealous God. Deuteronomy 4:23, 24

Have you ever wondered, seriously, about whether or not you have some form of idol in your life? I've been in the homes of collectors that are stuffed to the gills with every conceivable form of their special collectible: rabbits, turtles, frogs, cats, dogs, angels, (fill in the blank). I used to collect pewter figurines, but I decided that they were becoming too special to me, so I sold them in a garage sale. By contrast, I have never been in a home that was full and overflowing with figurines or paintings of Jesus, crucifixes, Nativities, or one that contained all inspirational prints on the walls. That's not even my own house.

How do you spend your extra cash? Is it on sporting events, collectibles, or cars? Homeless shelters, food pantries, or family members who aren't as well-off as you? Jesus says, 'Where your heart is, there your treasure will be also.' (Luke 12:34) What do you treasure?

Lord Jesus: Be my treasure!

November 17

The last enemy to be destroyed is death. 1 Corinthians 15:26

David says in Psalm 110:1, The LORD said to my Lord: "Sit at my right hand until I make your enemies a footstool for your feet." In this instance, the 'Lord' who will have all his enemies placed under his feet is Jesus. And whether it is spelled with a capital or a small case "L", the word lord always denotes one who is in a position of authority. It was widely known from the prophecies that the Messiah would be a son of David, and Jesus Himself used that passage to stump the Pharisees when He asked, "If David calls him Lord, how can he be his son?"

The spiritual vision of many people is very limited. They simply can't fathom the things of the spiritual realm nor see beyond what is at the end of their nose. And because of the invisible nature of the entities that reside in the spiritual realm and the activities that take place there, it is often difficult to understand their nature. Which brings us to the verse for today.

You might think that the only enemies that Jesus would have are the unclean spirits that roam around wreaking havoc and destruction among His children, but there is more to it than that. Everything that came to man as a result of the fall – pain, toil, sadness, disease, and death – these must all be defeated in order for the everlasting kingdom to commence. Jesus defeated death by being resurrected by God. And at the end of all things, death will be thrown into the lake of fire along with the devil.

Lord Jesus: Thank you for rescuing me from eternal death.

November 18

They have not cried to me from their hearts when they
wailed upon their beds; For wheat and wine they lacerated
themselves, while they rebelled against me. Hosea 7:14

One of the signs of zeal in the Middle East in the days of the prophets was the practice of cutting oneself. It was a form of self-mortification that was supposed to demonstrate the depth of emotion and faithfulness of a worshiper. The Israelites were not following the precepts of the Lord, but were instead worshiping pagan gods. They did these things to themselves, and they were not receiving any blessings from either the gods they worshiped (which weren't really gods anyway) or the Lord God. And instead of asking why things weren't getting better when they cried out (not to God), they instead chose to continue to cut themselves more and seek rescue from inanimate statues.

Cutting oneself today is most often associated with depression and anger,[14] which are destructive pastimes and require some form of assistance. When I feel out of sorts I always pray for release from unclean spirits first (just in case), then seek herbs or medications to re-establish healthy endocrine levels. If you suspect that someone you love or know is suffering from depression or anger issues, watch for this sign; it could indicate an escalation of intensity. The person who engages in this type of activity requires help from someone who cares about them.

Lord Jesus: May my worship always be for you only.

November 19

Warn a divisive person once, and then warn them a second time.
After that, have nothing to do with them. You may be sure that
such people are warped and sinful; they are self-condemned.
Titus 3:10, 11 (NIV)

I don't know how many times in this book I've said that we should try to get others to give up their sins. Feels like too many, but it's the one thing we're really supposed to do. It is the greatest manifestation of loving our neighbor. Here, Paul says that we should warn someone about their tendency to cause divisions only twice, and then walk away and leave them alone.

Divisiveness cannot be part of the Christian's lifestyle: it shows love to no one, lifts up no one, and causes bad feelings. Divisiveness comes from an inner urge to destroy peace and comfort, and you know that can't be from God. If you find yourself wanting to destroy someone's peace, Paul would call you warped, sinful, and self-condemned. Maybe you'd like to rethink those desires.

Lord Jesus: Protect me from divisive people.

November 20
For your imperishable spirit is in all things. Wisdom 12:1

I've often wondered if everyone is born with the holy Spirit in them, and somewhere along the line we either get saved and activate His gifts, or else we become so evil that He refuses to live there and leaves. I suppose it's possible that He is still in the evil people in the world, but I don't know how He could stand to live there.

I know that before I was saved I still had a conscience, but perhaps that was because they had raised me in the church. I know without any doubt that God created me to teach, to write, and to share the gospel with anyone who will listen. A lot of people don't like my messages, but I wasn't put here to please people. (Glad I finally figured that one out!) So even in the days of my sinfulness, I have no doubt that the holy Spirit was still in me and trying to push me back onto the path that I was meant to follow. I believe the same is true for you. If He has been pushing you, maybe you need to pay more attention to where He's trying to lead you.

Lord Jesus: Lead me.

November 21
Then Jesus said, "I came into this world for judgment,
so that those who do not see might see, and those
who do see will become blind." John 9:39

Jesus did not come into the world to judge its inhabitants. (John 12:47) What he came to do was present the kingdom of God to us in a form that was understandable, teach us a better way of loving God and serving our neighbors, and give us the opportunity to receive salvation. In so doing, He would then allow people who were truly seeking God to find Him. Their blindness from the veil would be lifted, and they would then be able to see who Jesus truly was – the Son of God. Alternatively, those who believed that they already knew God from their studies and teaching of his law (those who thought they could 'see') would be blinded by the truth that they were unwilling to accept because of the hardness of their hearts.

When you look to Jesus, what do you see? Do you see someone who judges you, or someone who tries to lead you out of the darkness? Do you see someone who condemns, or someone who loves and encourages? If you see a distant God who judges and condemns, you aren't seeing Jesus. He loves us so much that He left heaven and lived and died as a man to rescue us from our fallen state so that we could be with Him and our Father eternally in heaven. This is who you should see – a loving, caring friend who thirsts for your company; one who can't wait for you to come to salvation and eventually return to His side to stay forever.

Lord Jesus: May I thirst for you as you thirst for me.

November 22

Go, my people, enter your rooms and shut the doors behind you; hide yourselves for a little while until his wrath has passed by. See, the LORD is coming out of his dwelling to punish the people of the earth for their sins. The earth will disclose the blood shed on it; the earth will conceal its slain no longer.
Isaiah 26:20, 21 (NIV)

The Day of the Lord will not be one of glory. Perhaps you are thinking that I did not say that correctly, but I assure you, I did. The Day of the Lord is not the day of Jesus' return. This day is the one that God has set aside for the destruction of the evil and unclean persons left at the end of days and is mentioned several times in the Old Testament.

I may not think like many modern Bible scholars, but I believe that all of the seven final judgments will be poured out within a very short period of time, perhaps less than a week. The fifth bowl is the one that throws the kingdom of the beast into darkness. In the annals of the Catholic Church there is a prophecy that has been revealed to several people throughout history – the prophecy of the three days of darkness, delivered by the Blessed Virgin Mary.

Most of the people who received this prophecy were made Saints after their death, including Padre Pio. It is not known for certain if any one of those who received this message knew of the others who reported it. There is one man who also received it in 1987 on a pilgrimage to the town of Medjugorje, Bosnia where Mary has been appearing to a small group of people daily since 1983.[15] He was unaware of this prophecy and resisted sharing it with the world.[16]

I think that this passage from Isaiah is a reference to that time – the same time that will be the darkness mentioned in Revelation near the time of the battle of Armageddon, the fifth bowl of judgment. The prophecy says that only the holy (blessed) candles will give light during this time in the homes of the righteous (if there are any left), and that the evil people of this world will be destroyed at that time.

This will be the final Passover to be made upon this earth. When the angel of the Lord passes over on these three days, no one should look outside to see the results of his passing nor open the door for any reason.

Lord Jesus: Protect me from the darkness.

November 23

It is a fearful thing to fall into the hands of the living God.
Hebrews 10:31

Some people don't want to change their life. They are happy living in disregard of the commitments that set us apart as Christians. Living a life of sin after being saved is an affront to Jesus, and the writer of this letter says, "How much more severely do you think a [person] deserves

Donna Noble

to be punished who has trampled the Son of God under foot, who has treated as an unholy thing the blood of the covenant that sanctified him, and has insulted the spirit of grace?"

Once we are saved we are typically baptized, washing away the sins of the old life. We come up from the water washed clean, made new, momentarily without sin. And then we open our eyes. The sins of this new life are cleared away as we constantly ask for forgiveness. I believe this forgiveness is based in part on our intentions. When we know we are supposed to be growing in holiness and we use our salvation as a backup plan, we are out of line.

The Scriptures say, "Repent, and be baptized." To repent is to have remorse for sin and stop doing it. At least, try to stop doing it. There is always a battle for one type of sin that is hard to let go of. If you are fighting such a battle, wanting to stop, and are asking forgiveness, I think you're okay. It's when you don't want to stop and keep on doing it that you get into trouble.

If you were baptized, you owe your life to Jesus. How do you think He will act when you cross over and have to explain why you trampled on His cross?

Lord Jesus: Change my heart toward repentance.

November 24
Therefore the prudent man is silent at this
time, for it is an evil time. Amos 5:13

This verse really speaks to me, especially since we've found out that the government has access to every conversation, text, and email. Of course, those of us who watched the Bourne movies already knew what they were up to.

I have rarely been one to hold my tongue when I had something to say. I have even been accused of being too honest – that is to say that some folks thought that I should keep my mouth shut instead of always speaking my mind. So now I'm a little less vocal on occasion, but not if it comes down to the right thing to do. And I also try to bear in mind Jesus' words, "Whoever acknowledges me before others, I will also acknowledge before my Father in heaven." (Matthew 10:32)

So in this time of political upheaval and social unrest, how do we determine when it is appropriate to speak up and when to keep our mouth closed? There's only one way: you have to listen to the holy Spirit's guidance. He will tell you the right time to speak, when to be silent, and what to say. Just remember that Big Brother is watching and listening to everything. Be careful of what you say in a phone call, text, or email. The day will come when it just might get you arrested or even killed.

Lord Jesus: Guide me when I speak.

November 25
Some people's sins are public, preceding them to judgment;
but other people are followed by their sins. 1 Timothy 5:24

Some folks can't seem to keep their business to themselves, but are always telling everything they have going on – much to the embarrassment of those around them sometimes. Their sins are also frequently on display for everyone to view, for many have no shame any more. These are the ones that are easily avoided (relatively speaking). You always know where you stand with them, and where they are standing is where you don't want to be. And since they can't keep their activities private, it is easy to recognize their shortcomings and bad influence on younger minds and point them out. (Not that they care about being a bad influence.)

Other people are so good at hiding their sins and their reputation is so squeaky clean that you would think that many of them walked on water (pun intended). This group is harder to know how to avoid since they don't share their sins up front. Some hide them so well that you may not see them for years even after you've married one of these people. The only way to know for sure if you should avoid someone is to pray and listen to holy Spirit leading you through that gut feeling, or ask their friends (if you can find some).

Lord Jesus: Keep me safe from the secret sinners.

November 26

Son of man, these men have the memory of their idols fresh in
their hearts, and they keep the occasion of their sin before them.
Ezekiel 14:3

Here in Ezekiel, the Lord had taken the prophet to Jerusalem in the spirit and shown him the priests and elders worshiping graven images in the temple. The Lord then ordered their slaughter. One of the objections that the Lord had toward them was that, when they came to Him, they brought the memories of their idols with them. It would be like you or I sitting in church on Sunday morning and reliving our trip to the bar and the lust we felt for someone the night before. Can you think of anything that might be more offensive to God? Reliving and enjoying your sins in His presence? Even when we confess our sins we should not feel enjoyment but rather remorse that we allowed something to happen. And we should not relive it but rather remember that it happened only long enough to ask forgiveness for it and then let it go.

In the Catholic Church you aren't supposed to take Communion if you have unconfessed mortal sin. It goes back to what Paul said in his first letter to the Corinthians regarding bringing judgment upon yourself if you partake in an unworthy manner. (1 Corinthians 11:27-29) Let us not be sinful or unworthy when we go to seek him.

Lord Jesus: Have mercy on me, a sinner!

November 27

Let us not grow tired of doing good, for in due time we shall
reap our harvest if we do not give up. Galatians 6:9

Do you ever feel like you're always giving and never getting? Does it make you tired and want to give up serving? Take heart, dear one, you are not alone. It's ok to feel this way, but not ok to stay that way. Occasionally we hit a wall that marks a position of growth for us. When we get there, we find that we have to push extra hard to keep moving forward. (PUSH: **P**ray **U**ntil **S**omething **H**appens)

This may be the time when you want to take a spiritual vacation. DON'T! Some people go off on sabbatical from service and never come back. Paul told the Galatians to not give up. And I'm telling you "Don't give up!" Keep your faith and take a short break maybe, but please come back to Jesus when you're done. The harvest time is coming; don't miss out on your share!

Lord Jesus: Grant me the grace to continue to serve, even when I'm tired of giving to others and being nice.

November 28

Bring the whole tithe into the storehouse that there may be
food in my house, and try me in this, says the LORD of hosts:
Shall I not open for you the floodgates of heaven to pour
down blessing upon you without measure? Malachi 3:10

We've already talked about giving, tithing, and blessings, so why have I given you this verse? Because the Lord wants more than anything for us to trust Him in everything. By tithing, you not only show your trust in His providence, but you also supply funds for programs that allow others to hear the gospel through missionary trips and other programs. Don't you want everyone to be able to hear the good news and make up their own mind about salvation? Wouldn't you like to get some points in your heavenly account for those who are saved through a donation that you gave?

I've tithed for a long time, and through all of those years I have never wanted for anything. I didn't always have a lot or extra, but I was always warm, dry, fed, and my car never ran out of gas. Everything ebbs and swells, including our faith. May your faith never ebb so much that you decide to stop giving back to the Lord for His generosity. You know you can't out-give the Lord.

Lord Jesus: Grant me the grace to keep giving to you as I should.

November 29

Not only that, but we even boast of our afflictions, knowing that affliction produces endurance, and endurance, proven character, and proven character, hope, and hope does not disappoint, because the love of God has been poured out into our hearts through the holy Spirit that has been given to us. Romans 5:3-5

Paul had a unique perspective on things. He had a life-changing encounter with the risen Christ on the road to Damascus and became the most avid speaker for Jesus in all of history (my opinion). Most people don't want to be riddled with afflictions, but Paul says here that, without troubles and trials you'll never grow. If you never grow, you'll not accumulate treasures in heaven. If you have no treasure in heaven, you shouldn't cry when we get to the eternal kingdom and you get shoved out to the edge of the crowd when Jesus is in the middle.

It seems to me that many humans have a tendency to want more of most things except God. I can't help but think that maybe some believe that they have salvation and that's good enough. Maybe for some people, it is. Not for me. I want to be as close as I can get to Jesus when the time comes to be with Him for all eternity. This is my hope. And let's not forget that James said that faith without works is dead.

In order to have this position in heaven, I have to overcome these afflictions that Paul talks about: everyday trials, sufferings, and temptations allowed for my growth. Verse 8 says, "God proves his love for us in that while we were still sinners Christ died for us." I started out as a sinner, and I will die a sinner. The important thing is that I recognize my sins and work to overcome them with the strength that Christ gives me.

Lord Jesus: Strengthen me to overcome my sins and grow in my salvation.

November 30
Is it time for you to dwell in your own paneled houses
while this house lies in ruins? Haggai 1:4

This verse is from the time frame when the Jews had returned to Jerusalem from bondage in Babylon. The first thing they did was rebuild the wall and their homes. This is understandable since they needed to be safe from the outlying settlements that were trying to prevent them from restoring the city. The problem was that they kept on living in the city in their finished homes, and the temple wasn't completed. They had started the work, but were stopped by an edict from the ruler who followed Cyrus that was unaware of the plans. The Lord finally had to step in and get the Jews back to work – with or without the government's permission.

I don't think God is cynical or sarcastic, but I always hear a bit of an edge to His voice when I read this. It's like the voice I hear when I read about Jesus in the garden asking the disciples if they are still sleeping and resting while He's pouring His heart out to God to try to stop the crucifixion. (Mark 14:41)

How many things are you trying to complete these days? Is there anything on your list that God has asked you to do that you keep shoving to the bottom of the list or that you're ignoring altogether? Maybe you should consider taking care of the temple and then getting back to your own paneled home.

Lord Jesus: Forgive me for being selfish and ignoring your requests.

December

December 1

"The person who is trustworthy in very small matters is also trustworthy in great ones; and the person who is dishonest in very small matters is also dishonest in great ones." Luke 16:10

Sometimes when I read things that Jesus said, I have to really think about it and try to find a way to apply it before I can truly understand His intent. This is one of those verses. It really didn't sink into my brain until one day when I was coming home from church. I had gone to early Mass on Sunday, and there were very few vehicles on the road. One of the intersections that I pass through has an arrow to turn left that has to be green for you to turn. The vehicle in front of me rolled up in the left turn lane and ran the arrow without even slowing down. I hadn't been paying much attention to it, but as it was driving away I could read the print on the side – it was a church van.

I pulled up to the light and thought, there's no traffic, no reason to sit here and wait for the cycle to come around again. I could just do like the church van driver. That's when the holy Spirit taught me about this verse. I was not in a hurry to get anywhere, and it's illegal to run red lights. These may seem like very small matters to some, but they're everything to God. Our actions when no one else is looking show what is truly in our hearts. If that church van driver runs red lights with no consideration of legality, where else is he or she cutting corners? I just hope that there were no kids in that van. That's not a very good role model for kids, especially from a person who represents a church. Where are you cutting corners?

Lord Jesus: Remind me to be faithful in small matters.

December 2

Cast your bread upon the waters; after a long time
you may find it again. Ecclesiastes 11:1

This is me. It seems like He's always asking me to cast my bread onto
the river and watch it float away, never knowing if we will meet up again
downstream. He challenges my faith pretty regularly, asking me to
invest in Him and His kingdom. Sometimes He asks for time – there's
always someone who needs a trustworthy ear that will listen and a
shoulder to lean on. Sometimes He asks for talent – there's always some
project at the church that requires my 'special abilities'. Sometimes He
asks for treasure – there is a never-ending supply of people in our city
that need provisions. And sometimes, as in the case of this book, He
asks me to provide all three.

I perceived a couple of years ago that He wanted me to do this, and
as was the case with the end-times book, I had started it but never
finished it. In the fall of 2012, He asked me one day, "Where is that
book I asked you to write?" So here it is. This is me casting my bread
upon the waters and stepping out in faith. This is me not making the
same mistake this time that I made the last. This is not my book – it
is His. And I hope that I have heard Him correctly in the things He
wished me to say and the questions He wanted asked. The bulk of the
funds that come in from the sales will go to projects and organizations
that provide service and assistance for people in need. I have all that
I need – a comfortable home, reliable transportation, and food in my
pantry. It would be remiss for me to keep the funds and not share them
with those in need, especially when I don't consider them as belonging
to me. They are His, and they will go to the programs that He tells me
to support with them.

Lord Jesus: Increase my faith.

December 3

"For the one who is least among all of you is the
one who is the greatest." Luke 9:48b

How many people do you know who voluntarily go last, take the hardest
or dirtiest jobs, and rarely (if ever) ask for anything. They don't want
glory; they don't want money; they don't want a promotion. They just
want to get the job done to the best of their ability. They want to be sure
that everyone else is taken care of before they take care of their own
needs. (Sounds like a US Marine to me.)

This verse is Jesus putting the disciples in their place. They wanted to
argue over who was the greatest; I want to know how they gauged their
accomplishments. Was it by the number of people that were healed at
their hands? Number of unclean spirits cast out? Who had known him
the longest? It's obvious that they didn't know him very well – if they
had, that discussion would never have taken place. Or maybe the devil
decided to puff up all of their egos at once.

When God sent Samuel to Jesse to anoint one of his sons as king,
Samuel didn't know which son it would be. Because of the heritage of
the people, they started with the obvious human heir – the eldest son.
When Samuel saw him, he was impressed. Tall, handsome, and well-
built, this was surely the one. But God told him No, this was not the one.
"Do not judge from his appearance or from his lofty stature, because I
have rejected him. Not as man sees does God see, because man sees
the appearance but God sees into the heart." (1 Samuel 16:7) Samuel
went through seven of Jesse's sons, all of whom were rejected by the
Lord. Finally they brought in the youngest, David, from the pasture. It
was likely an affront to all of the brothers that the youngest was made
king, but God chose the one with the heart most like His own – the
heart of the shepherd, the heart of the servant, the heart filled with love.

Lord Jesus: Teach me to have a heart like yours.

Donna Noble

December 4

For the people or kingdom shall perish that does not serve
you; those nations shall be utterly destroyed. Isaiah 60:12

The number of people in the world who claimed to be Christian in 2011
was almost 2.2 billion or about 32% of the earth's total population,
down from 35% a century earlier. It is the largest group claiming a
'religion' followed by Islam at roughly 25% of the population.[17] The
largest areas of concentration of Christians in the past were in Europe
and North America. However, in the past century, the percentages in
those areas have dropped while the numbers in Africa and Southeast
Asia have increased. The numbers would suggest that areas that were
considered heathen 100 years ago have been brought to salvation, while
the numbers of saved in the modern nations are returning to a non-
Christian condition. The tables are turning. Perhaps the missionaries
should be working here as well as across the seas.

Despite the fact that 80% of Americans in 2013 claim to be Christian[18],
there is an alarming rate of decline in the freedoms pertaining to the
exercise of religion, primarily focused on the restriction of the Christian
faith: bans on Nativity scenes in public places, no public prayer in
schools, and legislation to the detriment of the Christians' freedom of
speech and evangelism. 20% of non-Christian Americans and 80%
of the world's population say they don't personally know a Christian.
Globally, that means that 5.6 billion of the world's 7 billion people don't
know a Christian. If 32% are Christian, how can 80% not know one?
Unless, of course, the percentage has dropped from 32% to less than
20% in the past two years.

One thing I know from reading the Bible is that when God is fed up with
the hedonistic and heathen way of life that permeates society, hHe will
step in and act. And that is never a good way to end a society.

Lord Jesus: Awaken those who claim you to action.

December 5

"Give, and gifts will be given to you; a good measure, packed
together, shaken down and overflowing will be poured
into your lap. For the measure with which you measure
will in return be measured out to you." Luke 6:38

When I was in grade school, I remember someone telling me that you
should never wish something bad on someone else. If you did, whatever
you wished on them would come back on you. Alternatively, whatever
you prayed for someone else to receive in the form of a blessing, you
would receive that as well. So I try not to think evil thoughts about
anyone, even the mass murderers I see on the news. Instead, I pray
for them to be set free from the evil that has controlled them and that
caused them to commit such a heinous crime. I pray that their eyes will
be opened to see the horror of the acts they committed and drive them
to repentance. I pray that somehow the Lord can break into their cold,
hardened heart and change it into a penitent one.

When I pray for my family and friends, I ask for them to be blessed with
health, wealth, and happiness. And whenever I hear of an organization
in town that needs supplies for the needy, I try to be a generous giver
just in case I myself need that service one day. There was a time when
I would hear of a need and think to myself that I needed to go get some
stuff to help them out, but then I would never get it done. Or I would buy
some items but then fail to deliver them in a timely manner. God told
me one day that my all of my good intentions were absolutely worthless;
they helped no one at all. Do it or don't, but get off the fence of apathy.
Your guideline for helping others should be, 'as much as you can give
and be joyful about doing it.' And when you meet God face-to-face one
day, may He then say to you (and me), "Well done, good and faithful
servant."

Lord Jesus: Make me generous and cheerful giver.

December 6

Better to take refuge in the LORD than to put
one's trust in mortals. Psalm 118:8

I have loved many people in my life, and I'm sure many have loved me. Unfortunately, none of us has ever been 100% dependable to those who count on us. There is only one who is always dependable, one whom we can always turn to for comfort. But I think a lot of us don't always think to turn to Him first because we can't see Him or call Him on the phone. Many use Him as a last resort instead of a first line of defense.

Other human beings will always let you down some time, that's just the way it is. God never will. He may not give you what you want, but that's because He's got something better coming down the line. Perhaps He hasn't blessed a relationship of yours because He knows that the person you desire isn't going to stand for you or with you down the way. Turning away now is easier than if you marry and find out five years from now that they were never faithful to you.

"Seek first the kingdom and his righteousness, and all these things will be given you besides." –Jesus, as quoted in Matthew 6:33

Lord Jesus: Teach me to trust you first rather than people around me.

December 7

"Stand up in the presence of the aged, and show
respect for the old." Leviticus 19:32a

It isn't just the elderly who get disrespected these days – it seems like it's everyone. There's always someone out there that has something nasty to say about someone else, and doesn't hesitate to say it out loud. My grandma always said, "If you can't say something nice, don't say anything at all." I guess not everybody's grandma did so.

I don't know how it is in the rest of the country, but in my state, there has been an increase the past few years of young men breaking into the residences of elderly women and raping, robbing, and murdering them. I just don't get it. If you have an elderly someone in your family that lives alone, please check on them often, and make certain that they have some way to contact police. Remember: they raised you and took care of you when you were growing up. Now it's your turn to take care of them. Love on them while there's still time.

Lord Jesus: Please protect the elderly who have no one to look after them.

December 8

"God has overlooked the times of ignorance, but now he demands that all people everywhere repent because he has established a day on which he will 'judge the world with justice' through a man he has appointed, and he has provided confirmation for all by raising him from the dead."
Acts 17:30, 31

I don't know if you've noticed, but there are more people on TV giving glory to God for the successes in their lives than in recent years, and it's coming from sports figures, musicians, and actors. I also perceive that there is a growing movement to stop God from even being mentioned in regulated public forums. I'm surprised that they haven't removed the Christian images from the courthouses and exteriors of government buildings all over the country. But maybe since the ones trying to drive God out aren't Christians, they don't recognize Moses, Michael, and the other figures in the murals and carvings.

Things are coming to a head, and I expect that there will be even more ugly things to come. I don't know if you watch NASCAR racing but, in case you were unaware, they always have a prayer before their races. I wonder how long before someone forces that to stop. And I love that they have their own ministry team that travels to all of the tracks and holds a church service every Sunday before a race.

I perceive that lines are being drawn with Christians on one side and non-believers on the other. People who believe in God but are not active Christians (including many in the Church) are standing by and watching their freedom to choose a life in Christ be swept away. They don't realize that they will lose even more than that at a later date. Jesus said that He will spit out the ones who are neither hot nor cold in their faith. (Revelation 3:16) Apathy will be an eternal undoing for many, but they just haven't yet realized it yet. Your future is in your own hands. Where do you want to spend it? The day is coming – like a thief. Don't get caught by surprise.

Lord Jesus: Awaken me to the time that remains.

December 9
As they walked on conversing, a flaming chariot and flaming horses came between them, and Elijah went up to heaven in a whirlwind. 2 Kings 2:11

I wish we could see things like this today. There wouldn't be all this discussion of whether or not there's a God. Or would there? With the technology that we have today, many would probably not believe it even if they witnessed it first-hand. They'd think it was a hologram or some other kind of computer trick.

There were only two persons recorded in the Bible as going up to heaven without dying: Enoch and Elijah. I would have liked to have known Elijah. Those were the days when the Lord still did really awesome things to be witnessed like calling down fire from heaven as I talked about before. Elijah was fed by ravens (1 Kings 17:2-6) and restored a dead boy to life. (1 Kings 17:18-23) But this is by far the neatest thing that happened around him, in my opinion. He was with Elisha, his protégé. Elisha asked Elijah to be his replacement when he was gone and to receive a double portion of the Lord's Spirit. Elijah told Elisha that if he was able to witness him leaving the earth, he would get his wish. And so Elisha did see this event, and received that which he had asked for.

There is no note of why the Lord took Elijah up without requiring him to die as everyone else is required to do. And the only thing said about Enoch was that he walked faithfully with God, had sons and daughters, lived 365 years, and 'then he was no more, because God took him away.' (Genesis 5:24)

Lord Jesus: Enable us to see your heavenly servants working here on earth.

December 10

So then you are no longer strangers and sojourners, but you are
fellow citizens with the holy ones and members of the household
of God, built upon the foundation of the apostles and prophets,
with Christ Jesus as the capstone. Ephesians 2:19, 20

Once upon a time in the world, there were Jews and there was everybody else – the Gentiles. God had told the Jews to stay away from the Gentiles because they were pagans who worshiped inanimate idols. God wanted them to be separate to keep the Jews from falling away from Him, but that didn't happen. They went out and married them, and brought their pagan practices back to the community which then spread. This was the cause of the fall of King Solomon and the split of the kingdom into Israel and Judah. Before the split they were all Israelites, but afterward, the Judahites became simply Jews. And today, all Hebrews are referred to as Jews.

There was still a lot of animosity between the Jews and Gentiles when Jesus first left and the Church was beginning to grow. And as the Jews had been persecuted by the pagans before Christ, so now the Jews turned the tables and persecuted the Church. The Jews had the history of the chosen people, and now we claim that history as our own history of the Church. We claim the prophets and apostles as our guides and Jesus as our leader. We are no longer strangers in the world, but rather the chosen people and members of the holy family of God.

Lord Jesus: Thank you for adopting me!

December 11

"I prayed for this child, and the LORD granted my request.
Now I, in turn, give him to the LORD; as long as he lives,
he shall be dedicated to the LORD." 1 Samuel 1:27, 28

One of my favorite women in the Bible is Hannah, a woman who had the misfortune of being infertile. She was married to a man who preferred her to his second wife who was not infertile and rubbed Hannah's nose in that fact on a regular basis. Hannah went to the tabernacle and spent many hours in tearful prayer, requesting the Lord's intervention to remove her shame and give her a son. Her promise to Him was that if He granted her request, she would give Him that son to be His servant. The Lord granted her request, and after she had weaned young Samuel, she gave him to the priest to raise as a servant in the tabernacle of the Lord.

People today still make bargains with the Lord to get what they want or to be rescued from a hazardous situation. If you make one of those requests with a condition or promise, be sure to keep it without changing the conditions after the fact. I don't think God tolerates liars or cheaters very well.

Lord Jesus: Hold me to the promises I've made to you.

December 12

"Behold, I stand at the door and knock. If anyone hears
my voice and opens the door, I will enter his house and
dine with him, and he with me." Revelation 3:20

Luke writes in 11:9 that Jesus said that we should knock, and the door
will be opened to us. But the hour grows late, and He is not waiting for
us to come to Him. He is roaming the earth and knocking on the doors
of hearts and asking admittance. I have been praying, at the Lord's
command, for a celebrity that is not saved. He is not hearing the voice
of the Lord calling and knocking. I perceive that this person is not any
closer to salvation now than when I started praying for him three years
ago. I have written a few letters to this person, but have as yet to receive
a response. I will keep praying.

I suspect that you know someone who is also in need of this intercessory
prayer that will break open the stone surrounding their heart that is
preventing Jesus from entering. Don't put off those prayers. Begin
praying for that person right now. They will thank you on the day that we
all receive our rewards for our offerings. And while you're at it, please
pray for our nation and leaders.

*Lord Jesus: Please soften the stone that surrounds the hearts of
our friends and leaders. They need you – please send someone
to them to show them just how much they need you.*

December 13

A tester among my people I have appointed you, to
search and test their way. Jeremiah 6:27

This is me – the tester. This is why I had to write this book. There are
a lot of people in this nation today who also share this mission with
me. You'll find many of them on the Jim Bakker Show on the TCT and
Daystar networks. If there were only me saying this, as I believed back

in 2003, I would think twice or even three times that I was off kilter. But there are too many people coming up with the same message without any form of collusion. And as I have been writing this book, I see the pastors on television also saying the same things that I have written.

Many pastors, however, are not saying these things; they are in denial. If your pastor is preaching that peace and prosperity will come again to this country, find a new church! That one is the false prophet. And remember the words of Paul when he spoke of the times of the end: While people are saying, "Peace and safety," destruction will come on them suddenly, as labor pains on a pregnant woman, and they will not escape. (1 Thessalonians 5:3)

Search your heart and pray for wisdom. You will find, if you are meant for eternal salvation, that what we are saying is true. And be careful of the pastors you watch – even on Christian television. Not all of them are faithful to the gospel.

Lord Jesus: Lead me to the truth of your gospel and the time I am living in.

December 14

To the clean all things are clean, but to those who are defiled
and unbelieving nothing is clean; in fact, both their minds and
their consciences are tainted. They claim to know God, but
by their deeds they deny him. They are vile and disobedient
and unqualified for any good deed. Titus 1:15, 16

Jesus told a parable about seed scattered and how it grows, or doesn't grow as the case may be. The people who hear the word and receive it but don't water or nurture it end up losing their salvation because they fail to recognize that it isn't a momentary thing to receive Jesus. It should be a way of life that sets you apart from the heathen lifestyle you had before. You can't have it both ways – though some do try. Think of it this way: they met Him and believed His message of redemption, but they neglected to listen long enough to hear the part where they progress to sanctification.

Remove that veil, and see the unclean things that need removed from your heart.

Lord Jesus: Direct us to you and to our sanctification.

December 15
For the just man falls seven times and rises again,
but the wicked stumble to ruin. Proverbs 24:16

Many times in our lives we make the wrong decision. It doesn't matter what causes us to do so; the important thing to recognize is that we cannot stay in that place of regret and guilt. Take your brokenness and repentance to your Savior and lay it at the foot of the cross. Allow the blood from His hands and feet to wash it away. Get the poison out of your heart and mind, and let it go. There is no sin that He will not forgive if you but ask for His mercy, and there will be rejoicing by the angels in heaven for your penitence and wisdom. (Luke 15:10)

When you let go of your sins they are no longer a stumbling block for you. The wicked, however, will continue to stumble over their old failures as well as their new ones so long as they fail to come to Jesus for forgiveness, salvation, and release. Don't continue to stumble. Go to Jesus, and be set free.

Lord Jesus: Thank you for your mercy and loving-kindness.

December 16

If anyone builds on this foundation with gold, silver, precious
stones, wood, hay, or straw, the work of each will come to
light, for the Day will disclose it. It will be revealed with
fire, and the fire will test the quality of each one's work.
1 Corinthians 3:12, 13

Some day we will all have our works examined for quality. They will
be thrown into the refiner's fire of the Lord, and those things that have
no value will be burned up. The works that will gain us rewards will
have the dross burned away to reveal the true quality of our actions and
intentions just as precious metals are refined in fire.

Every day the Lord sends some fire our way to test our actions; call it
'trial by fire.' Sometimes we get burned, and other times we send that
fire shooting out to others to test them as well. My hope is that someday,
when I go for my 'examination', my works will be great enough to make
a crown from the gold and jewels left behind in the fire. If that's going to
happen, I think I need some more opportunities to get my actions in gear!

"Surely the day is coming; it will burn like a furnace. All the arrogant
and every evildoer will be stubble, and the day that is coming will set
them on fire," says the LORD Almighty. (Malachi 4:1a)

Lord Jesus: Help me to see my works as you do.

December 17

May he grant you joy of heart and may peace
abide among you. Sirach 50:23

The early believers in Jerusalem were said to be joyful and at peace with
one another while living in community and sharing all things amongst
themselves. (Acts 2:45-47) That peace and joy could be ours today if
we would only give up our notions of self and wealth accumulation. We

aren't meant to be hoarders of the Lord's blessings but rather willing to share all good things that he gives us. It is truly surprising how good it makes me feel to be able to share with people who are in need. If you haven't been doing this yourself, give it a try.

I guess you could just wait around and see if He feels like giving you some joy, but why not generate a bit of it on your own while you're waiting. The looks of gratitude and heartfelt thanks will melt even the hardest of hearts.

Lord Jesus: Show me the way to joy and peace.

December 18

After the master of the house has risen and locked the door,
then will you stand outside knocking and saying, 'Lord, open
the door for us.' He will say to you in reply, 'I do not know where
you are from.' And you will say, 'We ate and drank in your
company and you taught in our streets.'" Luke 13:25, 26

There are people who have been in the presence of the holy ones for much of their lives yet have failed to receive salvation or make Jesus Lord of their lives. This message is for them: you came to church, but you never took the messages to heart; you worked on projects for the church, but you never went where I tried to send you; you took all the glory for yourself and never gave any of it to me; you spent your money on what you wanted to buy, but gave none to the organizations that I had contact you; I gave up my life for you, and you gave me nothing in return. And yet you expect me to give you the keys to the kingdom? Sorry. No dice. Off you go to the place where the selfish, conceited, and unsaved go, where 'the worms that eat them do not die, and the fire is not quenched.' (Mark 4:48) There will be many sad people on that day that treated the Church of God as a social club.

Lord Jesus: Am I truly saved?

December 19

In your observance of the commandments of the LORD, your
God, which I enjoin upon you, you shall not add to what I
command you nor subtract from it. Deuteronomy 4:2

I wonder what the Pharisees, Sadducees and scribes were confronted
with when they got to the other side. The Sadducees would have been
shocked to be there since they didn't believe in an afterlife. The
Pharisees and scribes were likely none too happy either since they
basically re-wrote the entire law to give it more 'flesh' so-to-speak. They
fine-tuned the law down to specifics of what you could and couldn't do,
how to do it, and how to get around it. They didn't just give it more flesh
in content, but they made 'the flesh' its focus.

There were Jews who tried to make the newly-saved Gentiles subject to the
whole law of Moses. Paul and the apostles made it known that they did not
support this practice. They only had a few rules that they thought the new
converts should abide by, and they pertained to dietary practices outlined
in the law that were designed to keep the people safe from disease.

There are still people today who want to try to tell you how to live and
how to worship. Don't listen to them. Just read the Bible and do what it
says. Abide by the Ten Commandments, love the Lord, your God, and
love your neighbor. That will cover everything you need to know.

Lord Jesus: Write your laws on my heart.

December 20

As proof that you are children, God sent the spirit of his Son into our
hearts, crying out, "Abba, Father!" So you are no longer a slave but a
child, and if a child then also an heir, through God. Galatians 4:6, 7

I received the right to call on Him when He invited me to join His
family. I ran from Him for a long time, but I finally got tired of fighting.

Chances are good that you know someone who is running as well. Pray that the Lord will give you the words that will stop their flight and bring them home.

Paul says that the Spirit we received when we joined the family cries out to God for us. It doesn't call Him Lord or God or Father, all rather formal names or terms. Rather, the Spirit cries out *'Abba!'* a term meaning Daddy – one which is much more intimate, familiar, and child-like. That's how we should think of Him: Daddy – the Provider of all things which are good; the Protector from all harm; the Rescuer from dangerous waters; the One who loves us unconditionally and never wants us to leave home.

This is my God. Is He yours? I used to pass a church on my way to work every day. There was usually a pithy saying on the yard sign. One day it read 'Feel far from God? Which one of you moved?' It was just what I needed to hear at that time. It awakened me to the Spirit inside me and started a string of events that would change the whole course of my life, landing me here today with you. God bless you all.

Lord Jesus: Thank you for hearing me and coming to me when I call.

December 21

Tell this to Zerubbabel, the governor of Judah: I will shake
the heavens and the earth; I will overthrow the thrones of
kingdoms, destroy the power of the kingdoms of the nations.
Haggai 2:21, 22a

God is on the throne. He is in control. A lot of crazy dictators think they are, but they're delusional. The Lord is simply letting them trample on the people so that they will be ready to rise up on the day that He has chosen. Take a look at our own nation: Congress makes laws that don't apply to them and cause hardship for their own constituents; the president bypasses the Constitution and uses his executive power to enact unjust laws; there are drones flying over our own nation which spy on us in conjunction with the satellites in orbit. Nothing you say over any phone or internet line is private. The people are becoming polarized in their political views and economic positions: the haves get more, and the have-nots are losing the little they have, whether you're referring to the economy or to freedoms. No place is safe. I catch myself locking my car doors as soon as I get in.

The powers in place will continue to do what they are doing until the Lord puts a stop to it. We will continue to lose freedoms until there are none: no free speech, no right to bear arms, no freedom of religion. Everything will be in favor of those who have money and authority, and that's not me. Yet Hallelujah! I serve the greatest power in the universe! I may suffer here, but when He comes, I will trample His (and my) enemies under my feet. (Isaiah 26:5, 6)

The shakings have started. Which side have you chosen: win now and suffer later? Or suffer now and win later?

Lord Jesus: Shake the heavens and come down.

December 22
Therefore, a Sabbath rest still remains for the people of
God. And whoever enters into God's rest, rests from his
own works as God did from his. Hebrews 4:9-10

Life is a struggle. It seems like every day has more and more personal, business, and mental battles. But I think the true source of these battles is mostly spiritual. Everything that happens over there bleeds through to over here. When you try to serve the Lord in a faithful manner, the devil recognizes your efforts and generates more hostility and agitation in your proximity. Even if you prevent him from getting to you directly, he will stir up those around you so that you get spillage from their disturbances.

He doesn't want the faithful to get off easy and serve without 'consequence.' I find myself saying to friends (and to myself), "No good deed goes unpunished." You get rewards from Jesus, but you also get thumped by the evil one as often as he can get to you. This is why I look forward to the day when the battles are done – the day when I can rest at the side of the Lord. It takes a lot of energy to fight these battles, even when you understand the source.

"By the seventh day God had finished the work he had been doing; so on the seventh day he rested from all his work. Then God blessed the seventh day and made it holy, because on it he rested from all the work of creating that he had done." Genesis 2:2, 3

Lord Jesus: I look forward to resting with you.

December 23
Let everything that has breath give praise to
the Lord! Hallelujah! Psalm 150:6

Every day the animals, rocks, trees, and waters give glory to the God of heaven that created them. Should His children be any different? He is with us every moment of our entire life watching over us, warning us to not go some places and encouraging us to go to others. He doesn't want to be apart from us at any moment, but desires to be in our every thought – just as we are in His. We are created in His image and for His glory – should we not give Him praise for His great providence and majesty? Jesus told the Pharisees when they tried to stop the people from shouting Hosanna! that if they were silent, the rocks would cry out. (Luke 19:39, 40) May our voices be lifted high with the stones and all of creation as we give praise to the King every day of our lives.

Hosanna to the King!

December 24

For to us a child is born, to us a son is given, and the government
will be on his shoulders. And he will be called Wonderful Counselor,
Mighty God, Everlasting Father, Prince of Peace. Isaiah 9:6

When Jesus was born, He wasn't delivered in a palace, or an inn or
even a home as would have been the custom. He was born in the dirtiest
place in town, a stable. He wasn't surrounded by fawning relatives and
helpful midwives, but rather animals – quiet creatures of God. And the
first group of guests called to His side was not the priests and scribes,
but shepherds – the lowest social caste in the society. St John wrote, 'He
came to that which was his own, but his own did not receive him.' (John
1:11) The ultimate priest and king was heralded by angels, worshiped
by shepherds, and ignored by everyone else.

I like the fact that God called the shepherds to the stable since that was
what Jesus would become – our Shepherd – leading His flock home to
the kingdom of God; taking the social outcasts and turning them into
a great nation of royalty through adoption into the family of the King of
kings. David was a shepherd who became a king. Jesus was a king who
became a shepherd. I love the way God works!

May your day be blessed with great joy and peace! Merry Christmas,
my friends....

Thank You, Lord, for the event we call Christmas.

December 25

The angel said to them, "Do not be afraid; for behold, I
proclaim to you good news of great joy that will be for all
the people. For today in the city of David a savior has been
born for you who is Messiah and Lord." Luke 2:10, 11

Shepherds: the lowest social wrung on the Jewish population ladder.
They were rough, tough, and smelly. Their job was keeping the flock
together, making sure none got lost, and protecting them from wild
animals as well as from themselves. They're not the brightest of animals
after all. Why did the angels only go to the shepherds? They could have
called to the whole city, the whole country, but we're told that they only
approached the shepherds.

My question is, who watched the flocks while the shepherds went to
the stable? Somebody had to get delegated to stay behind, or else they
had to go in shifts. You know I'd want to be first to go check it out. And
I would be wondering as I traveled, Who else will I see when I arrive
there? How long of a line will there be? Will I be allowed in since I'm
not nobility? Imagine my surprise when I arrive and there is no one
else there; only Mary, Joseph, and a brand new baby boy. (I think there
might have been some other people in that stable since the inn was full,
and they might have helped when Jesus was born. You know God always
has the proper people in place for the big events.)

So here I am, a simple shepherd, kneeling in awe at this beautiful child.
He's quiet, sleeping. I ask the mother if I may hold her Son – she allows
me to do so. As I take the child in my arms, I am filled a great sense
of peace, joy, and wonder. Someday, this will be the man who saves the
world from sin and shame – the Son of God; Emmanuel – God with us;
Yeshua – Jesus; Almighty God in human form. My heart and my mind
are changed forever. Someday He will be a shepherd like me, only He
will tend the flock of God. Amen. Alleluia!

Lord Jesus: Thank you. I love you.

December 26

Have no anxiety at all, but in everything, by prayer and petition, with
thanksgiving, make your requests known to God. Philippians 4:6

This is one of my favorite chapters in the Bible. It was very foundational
for creating the person that I am today. When I was first trying to read
the Bible all the way through, I really didn't know much about the
stories in it. I had some vague recollections from Sunday school when
I was about 8 or 9 years old, but that was pretty much it. I had no idea
who Paul was or that he did so much and suffered so much. So when I
read his epistles I was fascinated by the things he was saying: how to
live, how not to live, forgiveness, and focus.

I especially treasured these passages that talk about how to relate to
Jesus: "The Lord is near," is a simple but very powerful statement
reminding me that He is at my right hand at all times; He sees
everything I do (and don't do) and understands my struggles. I also
took to heart immediately Paul's directive to not be anxious about
anything, but to hand my troubles over to God and let Him take care
of them. I understand that I am not typical in doing this. Most people
can't simply let go of anxiety and say to God, "Here you go – take care
of this for me. Let me know when it's done." But I can most of the time.

As a result of my trust, I have trouble with the Scripture where Jesus
says to keep asking for something. To me, that shows impatience and
a lack of trust in God's willingness to help. I know He hears me the
first time I ask for something, and I trust that He will take care of it
in whatever way fits into His plan, at whatever time everyone else gets
their ducks into line. That's the hard part – waiting for everybody else
to get with the program and take care of their business before I can
get my issues taken care of. Maybe it's because they're too busy asking
and asking and not listening for an answer and a new direction. Maybe
not – I've been wrong before. Maybe I've got more of that child-like
trust than I realize.

I assume that this ability of mine to let go is what gives me the peace that I have – the peace that passes understanding. It seems that no matter how bad things get, I can usually maintain a cool head and know what to do to get through a rough patch. It's matter of being in fairly constant touch with him. I don't just pray in the morning and at night – it's an all-day event. It's being thankful for little things like a narrow miss by a rude driver, rescuing the lives of little creatures that run in front of my car, people who call me when I'm tired and need a lift, flashes of his beautiful creation, and requests throughout the day for strength and wisdom to get through whatever is on the plate for the day, which has been piled pretty high lately. Do you need some trust and peace? You know where to find it. Go get some!

Lord Jesus: Teach me to trust in you and have peace.

December 27

Though the fig tree does not bud and there are no grapes
on the vines, though the olive crop fails and the fields
produce no food, though there are no sheep in the pen
and no cattle in the stalls, yet I will rejoice in the Lord, I
will be joyful in God my Savior. Habakkuk 3:17, 18

There aren't many people who could see things as this prophet does. Even when there was no food and no livestock, he still had God – therefore, he had hope. How many times have you been without food or shelter? Have you thanked God for the privilege of receiving his providence? What about hope? Have you ever been without hope? I don't think I ever have. I've been close a few times, but I don't think I've ever lost it completely.

When a person does lose all hope is the time that they begin to contemplate suicide. If you had the power to stop even one person from killing themself due to a lack of hope, would you? By giving to shelters, missions, and food pantries, you can help boost hope in the lives of those who have fallen on hard times. Just because you don't know anyone who is lost or without hope doesn't mean they aren't out there. Love your neighbor….

Lord Jesus: Show me how to give hope to others.

December 28

May the God of peace, who brought up from the dead the great
shepherd of the sheep by the blood of the eternal covenant,
Jesus our Lord, furnish you with all that is good, that you may
do his will. May he carry out in you what is pleasing to him
through Jesus Christ, to whom be glory forever. Amen.
Hebrews 13:20, 21

The gospel is full of mysteries: bodies are healed and demons cast out by 'the word'; the dead are restored to life with no ill effects; that which is divine takes on the form and nature of fallen humanity and keeps itself pure; the blood of one innocent person is shed, and the whole world can then receive salvation by faith in the covenant of this blood; the Resurrection of the One creates a new pathway for those who will believe to find their way to the side of the Father in heaven; and the veil in the temple is torn from the top down showing that the Father Himself is now allowing all people to come to Him personally (no temple or animal sacrifice required); and blessings are bestowed on the faithful who believe and trust in the Divine Son of God, the firstborn from the dead, the great Shepherd of the flock, our Lord and Savior, Jesus Christ. Anything there you'd like to claim?

Lord Jesus: Rain down your glory and blessings upon your flock!

December 29

Give ear, listen humbly, for the LORD speaks. Give glory to the
LORD, your God, before it grows dark; before your feet stumble
on darkening mountains; before the light you look for turns
to darkness, changes into black clouds. If you do not listen to
this in your pride, I will weep in secret many tears; my eyes
will run with tears for the LORD's flock, led away to exile.
Jeremiah 13:15-17

I feel sorry for Jeremiah. I don't know how old he was when the Lord
called to him to begin his mission work, but he lived most of his life
bucking the system, living with death threats, and mourning for the
people of Judah who would not listen to the word of the Lord that was
delivered through him. He is commonly known as the weeping prophet.
There is no record that any of the people changed their hearts as a result
of his preaching and prophecies.

I understand some of what he went through. There are a lot of people
today who think that I'm a crack-pot trying to stir up fear. They are the
same as the Judeans, and unfortunately, their fate may be the same
unless they finally relent and repent. There will be many more shakings
to come before the final seven years commence. It concerns me that
they are missing out on blessings in the meantime. Trial by fire will be
close for them, and they may get a little singed.

Better a little singed and accepted than no salvation at all. The Lord
keeps telling me that the harvest time is here. Can you feel it?

*Lord Jesus: Awaken the spirits that are living in denial to your
presence and plans.*

December 30

The Spirit and the bride say, "Come." Let the hearer say, "Come."
Let the one who thirsts come forward, and the one who wants
it receive the gift of life-giving water. Revelation 22:17

The most basic belief in the Catholic Church is that the bread and wine are transformed into the body and blood of Jesus during the liturgy, a process called Transubstantiation. When I was a pastor several years ago, it was my responsibility to set up the host and juice that we used for Communion. I had been praying for the Lord to teach me His truth, and one thing that He taught me, long before I became Catholic, was that the bread and juice (or wine) were much more than a symbol: they truly become His body and blood when blessed by the pastor. (See John 6) Catholics call it 'Eucharist' which means 'thanksgiving.' Needless to say, when I began to attend Mass, I wasn't really surprised to find that this is a core belief for Catholics.

After I receive the Eucharist at Mass I go back to my pew, kneel down, and thank Jesus for my salvation. I thank him for sharing His sacrifice with me. And I ask Him to make His presence in me a fountain welling up to eternal life, not just for me, but all those whom I come into contact with. I pray this prayer for you today – that you have been watered by the fountain that He has created in me that now spills over into your life; may your faith be increased beyond your imagining; may His thirst for you and your love never be quenched; and may you find it in yourself to love Him in return with a burning passion that never fails. May you and I meet one day in the eternal kingdom and worship together.

Lord Jesus, Come!

December 31

The last word when all is heard: Fear God and keep
his commandments, for this is man's all; because God
will bring to judgment every work, with all its hidden
qualities, whether good or bad. Ecclesiastes 12:13, 14

Here we are at the end of another year, another New Year's Eve, another
Auld Lang Syne. I hope that I've been able to teach you a thing or two,
and that you have opened your mind to all of the possibilities that are
yours in the Lord. Remember: "No good thing does he withhold from
those whose walk is blameless." (Psalm 84:11)

This I recommend to you: Fear God and keep his commandments, and
may you be blameless when at last we all appear before him.

And now:
> "The Lord bless you
>   and keep you;
> the Lord make his face shine on you
>   and be gracious to you;
> the Lord turn his face toward you
>   and give you peace."
>   -Numbers 6:24-26

God bless you, my friend.

Epilogue

LORD, Father and Master of my life,
permit me not to fall by [my words]!
Who will apply the lash to my thoughts,
to my mind the rod of discipline,
that my failings may not be spared,
nor the sins of my heart overlooked;
Lest my failings increase,
and my sins be multiplied;
Lest I succumb to my foes,
and my enemy rejoice over me?
LORD, Father and God of my life,
abandon me not into their control!
A brazen look allow me not;
Ward off passion from my heart,
let not the lustful cravings of the flesh master me,
surrender me not to shameless desires.

-Sirach 23:1-6 (NASV)

Appendix A
List of Scriptures Used by Day

Jan 1 Matthew 6:24
Jan 2 Psalm 86:11
Jan 3 1 Corinthians 5:8
Jan 4 Zechariah 4:6
Jan 5 2 Timothy 2:3
Jan 6 Isaiah 30:1
Jan 7 Matthew 5:6
Jan 8 1 Kings 9:6, 7
Jan 9 Ephesians 4:30, 31
Jan 10 Judges 6:15
Jan 11 Philippians 2:1, 2
Jan 12 Psalm 37:12, 13
Jan 13 John 21:15
Jan 14 Hosea 8:3
Jan 15 Daniel 9:13b, 14
Jan 16 Numbers 20:8a, 11
Jan 17 Revelation 12:7, 8
Jan 18 2 Samuel 22:2b, 3
Jan 19 Matthew 6:14, 15
Jan 20 Psalm 4:9
Jan 21 Matthew 10:28
Jan 22 Zephaniah 3:17, 18
Jan 23 Colossians 3:23
Jan 24 Sirach 11:7
Jan 25 Luke 12:15
Jan 26 Jeremiah 5:31
Jan 27 Revelation 12:17
Jan 28 1 Samuel 15:22
Jan 29 Mark 4:24, 25
Jan 30 Wisdom 19:13
Jan 31 Romans 11:21, 22

Feb 1 Isaiah 31:1
Feb 2 2 Timothy 4:3, 4
Feb 3 Ecclesiastes 10:20
Feb 4 Luke 14:11
Feb 5 Isaiah 48:17
Feb 6 Mark 13:6
Feb 7 Isaiah 58:6, 7
Feb 8 Ephesians 4:17, 19
Feb 9 Wisdom 5:15
Feb 10 1 John 4:20
Feb 11 Hebrews 12:11
Feb 12 Sirach 37:17, 18
Feb 13 Mark 5:36
Feb 14 Ezekiel 14:13
Feb 15 Revelation 3:1, 2
Feb 16 Zechariah 9:16
Feb 17 1 Peter 5:10
Feb 18 Jude 5, 6
Feb 19 1 Kings 18:21
Feb 20 1 Corinthians 4:20
Feb 21 Ecclesiastes 12:1
Feb 22 Luke 5:13
Feb 23 Hebrews 5:13, 14
Feb 24 Daniel 9:18b
Feb 25 2 Corinthians 13:5
Feb 26 Proverbs 11:2
Feb 27 Ephesians 4:27
Feb 28 Sirach 4:12, 13
Feb 29 Luke 14:13, 14

March 1 Wisdom 1:1, 2

March 2 1 Corinthians 15:33

March 3 Ezekiel 3:18

March 4 Luke 6:12

March 5 Hosea 12:7

March 6 Philippians 3:18, 19

March 7 Isaiah 42:1-3

March 8 Hebrews 10:24

March 9 Jeremiah 1:5-7

March 10 Revelation 13:15

March 11 2 Maccabees 8:18

March 12 Hebrews 6:7, 8

March 13 Psalm 84:12b

March 14 Galatians 2:16

March 15 Sirach 34:21

March 16 Matthew 10:26b

March 17 Proverbs 11:4

March 18 Jude 9

March 19 Lament 3:22, 23

March 20 Titus 3:8

March 21 Daniel 3:16-18

March 22 Revelation 3:10, 11

March 23 Wisdom 12:17

March 24 Hebrews 9:22

March 25 Hosea 10:10

March 26 Luke 17:10b

March 27 Micah 7:9

March 28 John 8:34

March 29 Proverbs 17:15

March 30 Ephesians 4:26

March 31 Job 42:1-3

April 1 2 Timothy 4:18

April 2 Hosea 3:4, 5

April 3 John 3:34

April 4 Sirach 39:19

April 5 1 Corinthians 8:13

April 6 Jeremiah 45:4

April 7 Titus 2:7, 8

April 8 Ezekiel 9:9, 10

April 9 John 1:5

April 10 Isaiah 43:1

April 11 Revelation 13:1, 2

April 12 Proverbs 8:35, 36

April 13 Hebrews 7:1, 3

April 14 Amos 9:10

April 15 1 Cor 3:7, 8

April 16 Obadiah 3a

April 17 1 Corinthians 5:11

April 18 Jeremiah 2:35

April 19 Mark 15:17

April 20 Psalm 94:18, 19

April 21 1 John 4:1

April 22 Ecclesiastes 5:3

April 23 Romans 13:11

April 24 Sirach 34:16, 17

April 25 1 Timothy 1:19b

April 26 Daniel 7:21, 22

April 27 Acts 14:22

April 28 Ezekiel 31:10, 11

April 29 John 1:16

April 30 Hosea 11:2a

May 1 Psalm 66:17, 18
May 2 John 15:18, 19
May 3 Isaiah 29:23
May 4 2 Peter 3:3, 4
May 5 Jeremiah 2:7
May 6 Isaiah 61:1, 2
May 7 Galatians 2:21
May 8 2 Corinthians 5:6, 7
May 9 John 14:12
May 10 Isaiah 24:5
May 11 Matthew 16:3b
May 12 Exodus 3:11
May 13 1 Timothy 6:17
May 14 Ezekiel 13:5
May 15 Titus 3:2
May 16 Sirach 35:15
May 17 Matthew 10:34-36
May 18 Psalm 1:1
May 19 Luke 2:19
May 20 1 Kings 19:12
May 21 Mark 14:38
May 22 Isaiah 48:3
May 23 Jude 21
May 24 Hosea 4:14
May 25 1 John 4:10
May 26 Nahum 1:2
May 27 1 Cor 6:19, 20
May 28 Wisdom 14:7
May 29 Ephesians 4:1
May 30 Isaiah 30:15a
May 31 Revelation 13:16, 17

June 1 Ezekiel 28:17
June 2 Corinthians 3:14-16
June 3 Psalm 18:31
June 4 Matthew 10:12, 13
June 5 Proverbs 24:17, 18
June 6 Acts 5:41
June 7 Isaiah 29:13, 14
June 8 1 Corinthians 14:33
June 9 Revelation 13:7
June 10 Ezekiel 17:24a
June 11 Acts 20:30
June 12 Exodus 23:20
June 13 Titus 2:3-5
June 14 Proverbs 20:9
June 15 Matthew 12:36
June 16 Hosea 6:6
June 17 Mark 6:13
June 18 Ecclesiastes 2:26a
June 19 Luke 13:8, 9
June 20 2 Chronicles 15:2
June 21 1 Corinthians 8:6
June 22 Job 22:21
June 23 Matthew 5:41
June 24 Jonah 3:4, 5
June 25 Mark 7:21-23
June 26 Ezekiel 18:32
June 27 Philippians 1:9, 10
June 28 Jude 22
June 29 Hosea 5:4
June 30 Matthew 3:1-3

July 1 Daniel 7:7, 8
July 2 Matthew 23:23
July 3 Zechariah 8:16, 17
July 4 Romans 11:16b
July 5 Psalm 9:10
July 6 3 John 11
July 7 Amos 6:1
July 8 2 Timothy 1:7
July 9 Ezekiel 13:19
July 10 1 Corinthians 3:19
July 11 Ezekiel 18:20
July 12 John12:24
July 13 Ezekiel 13:14
July 14 Luke 23:35
July 15 Hosea 9:6b
July 16 Mark 7:8
July 17 Psalm 37:3-5
July 18 Philippians 2:3
July 19 1 Kings 8:57, 58
July 20 Matthew 27:54
July 21 Proverbs 7:2-4
July 22 Romans 1:29-32
July 23 Jeremiah 35:17b
July 24 2 Corinthians 9:6
July 25 Psalm 106:23
July 26 Matthew 18:8
July 27 Ecclesiastes 1:9
July 28 Matthew 20:14, 15
July 29 Wisdom 11:24
July 30 1 John 1:9
July 31 Zechariah 7:13

Aug 1 Ephesians 3:8
Aug 2 Ezekiel 16:14
Aug 3 Revelation 3:15, 16
Aug 4 Lamentations 4:17
Aug 5 Matthew 13:56-58
Aug 6 Malachi 3:16
Aug 7 1 Thess 5:16-18
Aug 8 Psalm 42:3
Aug 9 2 Timothy 2:22
Aug 10 Amos 5:14
Aug 11 1 Timothy 1:5
Aug 12 Song of Songs 2:15
Aug 13 Hebrews 12:14
Aug 14 Isaiah 7:9b
Aug 15 Revelation 13:10
Aug 16 Ezekiel 33:13
Aug 17 1 Timothy 2:1, 2
Aug 18 Sirach 49:3
Aug 19 1 Corinthians 14:1
Aug 20 Daniel 9:11
Aug 21 Galatians 1:3, 4
Aug 22 Habakkuk 2:3
Aug 23 1 Thess 5:2, 3
Aug 24 Proverbs 6:10, 11
Aug 25 John 12:26
Aug 26 Psalm 73:26
Aug 27 1 John 4:8
Aug 28 Wisdom 11:15, 16
Aug 29 Revelation 10:7
Aug 30 Micah 6:8
Aug 31 Romans 16:17, 18

Sept 1 Sirach 35:16

Sept 2 Mark 9:7

Sept 3 Psalm 43:3

Sept 4 Acts 24:15, 16

Sept 5 Hosea 5:1

Sept 6 Galatians 6:7, 8

Sept 7 Daniel 3:95

Sept 8 1 Cor 11:31, 32

Sept 9 Proverbs 25:21, 22

Sept 10 Luke 6:42

Sept 11 Ecclesiastes 11:5

Sept 12 Philippians 4:19

Sept 13 Ezekiel 47:12

Sept 14 2 Thes 2:7, 8

Sept 15 Sirach 35:24

Sept 16 Colossians 3:17

Sept 17 Psalm 37:23, 24

Sept 18 2 Timothy 2:4

Sept 19 Job 12:10

Sept 20 Matthew 5:19b

Sept 21 Isaiah 30:21

Sept 22 2 Cor 11:13, 14

Sept 23 Micah 2:7b

Sept 24 1 Thess 5:19-22

Sept 25 1 Kings 18:38, 39

Sept 26 Gal 2:19b, 20a

Sept 27 Joshua 21:45

Sept 28 Revelation 13:11

Sept 29 Genesis 22:17, 18

Sept 30 Mark 5:28

Oct 1 Psalm 56:10

Oct 2 1 Timothy 1:15

Oct 3 Isaiah 48:18

Oct 4 Hebrews 6:4-6

Oct 5 Jeremiah 42:10

Oct 6 Romans 16:19-20a

Oct 7 Ezekiel 43:7

Oct 8 Luke 6:19

Oct 9 Psalm 23:1

Oct 10 1 Corinthians 1:18

Oct 11 Wisdom 12:18

Oct 12 1 Timothy 4:1, 2

Oct 13 Psalm 86:9

Oct 14 Galatians 1:10c

Oct 15 Matthew 26:45

Oct 16 2 Timothy 3:1-5

Oct 17 Isaiah 55:10, 11

Oct 18 2 Cor 3:5, 6

Oct 19 Hosea 5:15

Oct 20 Luke 6:31-33

Oct 21 Ecclesiastes 2:18

Oct 22 1 John 4:18, 19

Oct 23 Jeremiah 2:11

Oct 24 James 4:8

Oct 25 Psalm 73:24

Oct 26 Acts 2:46, 47

Oct 27 2 Maccabees 10:3

Oct 28 1 Corinthians 9:14

Oct 29 Micah 6:11

Oct 30 Luke 7:6b, 7

Oct 31 Esther 4:14

Nov 1 1 Timothy 5:8
Nov 2 Sirach 34:25, 26
Nov 3 Hebrews 4:13
Nov 4 Psalm 78:38, 39
Nov 5 Revelation 2:9a
Nov 6 Micah 7:18
Nov 7 Galatians 5:13
Nov 8 Sirach 38:4
Nov 9 1 Cor 6:9, 10
Nov 10 Psalm 50:14, 15
Nov 11 Matthew 5:9
Nov 12 Isaiah 56:1
Nov 13 Jude 23
Nov 14 Psalm 84:10
Nov 15 James 1:26, 27
Nov 16 Deut 4:23, 24
Nov 17 1 Corinthians 15:26
Nov 18 Hosea 7:14
Nov 19 Titus 3:10, 11
Nov 20 Wisdom 12:1
Nov 21 John 9:39
Nov 22 Isaiah 26:20, 21
Nov 23 Hebrews 10:31
Nov 24 Amos 5:13
Nov 25 1 Timothy 5:24
Nov 26 Ezekiel 14:3
Nov 27 Galatians 6:9
Nov 28 Malachi 3:10
Nov 29 Romans 5:3-5
Nov 30 Haggai 1:4

Dec 1 Luke 16:10
Dec 2 Ecclesiastes 11:1
Dec 3 Luke 9:48b
Dec 4 Isaiah 60:12
Dec 5 Luke 6:38
Dec 6 Psalm 118:8
Dec 7 Leviticus 19:32a
Dec 8 Acts 17:30, 31
Dec 9 2 Kings 2:11
Dec 10 Ephesians 2:19, 20
Dec 11 1 Samuel 1:27, 28
Dec 12 Revelation 3:20
Dec 13 Jeremiah 6:27
Dec 14 Titus 1:15, 16
Dec 15 Proverbs 24:16
Dec 16 1 Cor 3:12, 13
Dec 17 Sirach 50:23
Dec 18 Luke 13:25, 26
Dec 19 Deuteronomy 4:2
Dec 20 Galatians 4:6,7
Dec 21 Haggai 2:21, 22a
Dec 22 Hebrews 4:9, 10
Dec 23 Psalm 150:6
Dec 24 Isaiah 9:6
Dec 25 Luke 2:10, 11
Dec 26 Philippians 4:6
Dec 27 Habakkuk 3:17, 18
Dec 28 Hebrews 13:20, 21
Dec 29 Jeremiah 13:15-17
Dec 30 Revelation 22:17
Dec 31 Ecclesiastes 12:13, 14

Priestly Blessing: Numbers 6:24-26
Epilogue: Sirach 23:1-6

Appendix B
Alphabetical Listing of Scriptures Used

1 Cor 1:18 Oct 10

1 Cor 3:7, 8 April 15

1 Cor 3:12, 13 Dec 16

1 Cor 3:19 July 10

1 Cor 5:8 Jan 3

1 Cor 5:11 April 17

1 Cor 6:9, 10 Nov 9

1 Cor 6:19, 20 May 27

1 Cor 8:6 June 21

1 Cor 8:13 April 5

1 Cor 9:14 Oct 28

1 Cor 11:31, 32 Sept 8

1 Cor 14:1 Aug 19

1 Cor 14:33 June 8

1 Cor 15:26 Nov 17

1 Cor 15:33 March 2

1 John 1:9 July 30

1 John 4:1 April 21

1 John 4:8 Aug 27

1 John 4:10 May 25

1 John 4:18, 19 Oct 22

1 John 4:20 Feb 10

1 Kings 8:57, 58 July 19

1 Kings 9:6, 7 Jan 8

1 Kings 18:21 Feb 19

1 Kings 18:38, 39 Sept 25

1 Kings 19:12 May 20

1 Kings 24:15, 16 Sept 4

1 Peter 5:10, Feb 17

1 Samuel 1:27, 28 Dec 11

1 Samuel 15:22 Jan 28

1 Thess 5:2, 3 Aug 23

1 Thess 5:16-18 Aug 7

1 Thess 5:19-22 Sept 24

1 Timothy 1:5 Aug 11

1 Timothy 1:15 Oct 2

1 Timothy 1:19b April 25

1 Timothy 2:1, 2 Aug 17

1 Timothy 4:1, 2 Oct 12

1 Timothy 5:24 Nov 25

1 Timothy 5:8 Nov 1

1 Timothy 6:17 May 13

2 Chronicles 15:2 June 20

2 Corinthians 3:5, 6 Oct 18

2 Corinth 3:14-16 June 2

2 Corinthians 5:6, 7 May 8

2 Corinthians 9:6 July 24

2 Corinth 11:13, 14 Sept 22

2 Corinthians 13:5 Feb 25

2 Kings 2:11 Dec 9

2 Maccabees 8:18 March 11

2 Maccabees 10:3 Oct 27

2 Peter 3:3, 4 May 4

2 Samuel 22:2b, 3 Jan 18

2 Thess 2:7,8 Sept 14

2 Timothy 1:7 July 8

2 Timothy 2:3 Jan 5

2 Timothy 2:4 Sept 18

2 Timothy 2:22 Aug 9

2 Timothy 3:1-5 Oct 16

2 Timothy 4:3, 4 Feb 2

2 Timothy 4:18 April 1

3 John 11 July 6
Acts 2:46, 47 Oct 26
Acts 5:41 June 6
Acts 14:22 April 27
Acts 17:30, 31 Dec 8
Acts 20:30 June 11
Amos 5:13 Nov 24
Amos 5:14 Aug 10
Amos 6:1 July 7
Amos 9:10 April 14
Colossians 3:17 Sept 16
Colossians 3:23 Jan 23
Daniel 3:16-18 March 21
Daniel 3:95 Sept 7
Daniel 7:7, 8 July 31
Daniel 7:21, 22 April 26
Daniel 9:11 Aug 20
Daniel 9:13b, 14 Jan 15
Daniel 9:18b Feb 24
Deuteronomy.4:2 Dec 19
Deuteronomy 4:23, 24 Nov 16
Ecclesiastes 1:9 July 27
Ecclesiastes 2:18 Oct 21
Ecclesiastes 2:26a June 18
Ecclesiastes 5:3 April 22
Ecclesiastes 10:20 Feb 3
Ecclesiastes 11:1 Dec 2
Ecclesiastes 11:5 Sept 11
Ecclesiastes 12:1 Feb 21
Ecclesiastes 12:13, 14 Dec 31
Ephesians 2:19, 20 Dec 10

Ephesians 3:8 Aug 1
Ephesians 4:1 May 29
Ephesians 4:17, 19 Feb 8
Ephesians 4:26 March 30
Ephesians 4:27 Feb 27
Ephesians 4:30, 31 Jan 9
Esther 4:14 Oct 31
Exodus 3:11 May 12
Exodus 23:20 June 12
Ezekiel 3:18 March 3
Ezekiel 9:9, 10 April 8
Ezekiel 13:5 May 14
Ezekiel 13:14 July 13
Ezekiel 13:19 July 9
Ezekiel 14:3 Nov 26
Ezekiel 14:13 Feb 14
Ezekiel 16:14 Aug 2
Ezekiel 17:24a June 10
Ezekiel 18:20 July 11
Ezekiel 18:32 June 26
Ezekiel 28:17 June 1
Ezekiel 31:10, 11 April 28
Ezekiel 33:13 Aug 16
Ezekiel 43:7 Oct 7
Ezekiel 47:12 Sept 13
Galatians 1:10c Oct 14
Galatians 2:16 March 14
Galatians 2:19b, 20a Sept 26
Galatians 2:21 May 7
Galatians 4:6, 7 Dec 20
Galatians 5:13 Nov 7

Galatians 6:7, 8 Sept 6
Galatians 6:9 Nov 27
Genesis 22:17, 18 Sept 29
Habakkuk 2:3 Aug 22
Habakkuk 3:17, 18 Dec 27
Haggai 1:4 Nov 30
Haggai 2:21, 22a Dec 21
Hebrews 4:9, 10 Dec 22
Hebrews 4:13 Nov 3
Hebrews 5:13, 14 Feb 23
Hebrews 6:4-6 Oct 4
Hebrews 6:7, 8 March 12
Hebrews 7:1, 3 April 13
Hebrews 9:22 March 24
Hebrews 10:24 March 8
Hebrews 10:31 Nov 23
Hebrews 12:11 Feb 11
Hebrews 12:14 Aug 13
Hebrews 13:20, 21 Dec 28
Hosea 3:4, 5 April 2
Hosea 4:14 May 24
Hosea 5:1 Sept 5
Hosea 5:4 June 29
Hosea 5:15 Oct 19
Hosea 6:6 June 16
Hosea 7:14 Nov 18
Hosea 8:3 Jan 14
Hosea 9:6b July 15
Hosea 10:10 March 25
Hosea 11:2a April 30
Hosea 12:7 March 5

Isaiah 7:9b Aug 14
Isaiah 9:6 Dec 24
Isaiah 24:5 May 10
Isaiah 26:20, 21 Nov 22
Isaiah 29:13, 14 June 7
Isaiah 29:23 May 3
Isaiah 30:1 Jan 6
Isaiah 30:15a May 30
Isaiah 30:21 Sept 21
Isaiah 31:1 Feb 1
Isaiah 42:1-3 March 7
Isaiah 43:1 April 10
Isaiah 48:3 May 22
Isaiah 48:17 Feb 5
Isaiah 48:18 Oct 3
Isaiah 55:10, 11 Oct 17
Isaiah 56:1 Nov 12
Isaiah 58:6, 7 Feb 7
Isaiah 60:12 Dec 4
Isaiah 61:1,2 May 6
James 4:8 Oct 24
Jeremiah 1:5-7 March 9
Jeremiah 2:7 May 5
Jeremiah 2:11 Oct 23
Jeremiah 2:35 April 18
Jeremiah 5:31 Jan 26
Jeremiah 6:27 Dec 13
Jeremiah 13:15-17 Dec 29
Jeremiah 35:17b July 23
Jeremiah 42:10 Oct 5
Jeremiah 45:4 July 1

Job 12:10 Sept 19
Job 22:21 June 22
Job 42:1-3 March 31
John 1:5 April 9
John 1:16 April 29
John 3:34 April 3
John 8:34 March 28
John 9:39 Nov 21
John 12:24 July 12
John 12:26 Aug 25
John 14:12 May 9
John 15:18, 19 May 2
John 21:15 Jan 13
Jonah 3:4, 5 June 24
Joshua 21:45 Sept 27
Jude 5, 6 Feb 18
Jude 9 March 18
Jude 21 May 23
Jude 22 June 28
Jude 23 Nov 13
Judges 6:15 Jan 10
Lamentations 3:22, 23 March 19
Lamentations 4:17 Aug 4
Leviticus 19:32a Dec 7
Luke 2:10, 11 Dec 25
Luke 2:19 May 19
Luke 5:13 Feb 22
Luke 6:12 March 4
Luke 6:19 Oct 8
Luke 6:31-33 Oct 20
Luke 6:38 Dec 5

Luke 6:42 Sept 10
Luke 7:6b, 7 Oct 30
Luke 9:48b Dec 3
Luke 12:15 Jan 25
Luke 13:8, 9 June 19
Luke 13:25, 26 Dec 18
Luke 14:11 Feb 4
Luke 14:13, 14 Feb 29
Luke 17:10b March 26
Luke 16:10 Dec 1
Luke 23:35 July 14
Malachi 3:10 Nov 28
Malachi 3:16 Aug 6
Mark 4:24, 25 Jan 29
Mark 5:28 Sept 30
Mark 5:36 Feb 13
Mark 6:13 June 17
Mark 7:8 July 16
Mark 7:21-23 June 25
Mark 9:7 Sept 2
Mark 13:6 Feb 6
Mark 14:38 May 21
Mark 15:17 April 19
Matthew 3:1-3 June 30
Matthew 5:6 Jan 7
Matthew 5:9 Nov 11
Matthew 5:19b Sept 20
Matthew 5:41 June 23
Matthew 6:14, 15 Jan 19
Matthew 6:24 Jan 1
Matthew 10:12, 13 June 4

Matthew 10:26b March 16
Matthew 10:28 Jan 21
Matthew 10:34-36 May 17
Matthew 12:36 June 15
Matthew 13:56-58 Aug 5
Matthew 18:8 July 26
Matthew 20:14, 15 July 28
Matthew 23:23 July 2
Matthew 26:45 Oct 15
Matthew 27:54 July 20
Micah 2:7b Sept 23
Micah 6:8 Aug 30
Micah 6:11 Oct 29
Micah 7:18 Nov 6
Micah 7:9 March 27
Nahum 1:2 May 26
Numbers 6:24-26 Dec 31
Numbers 29:8a, 11 Jan 16
Obadiah 3a April 16
Philippians 1:9, 10 June 27
Philippians 2:1, 2 Jan 11
Philippians 2:3 July 18
Philippians 3:18, 19 March 6
Philippians 4:6 Dec 26
Philippians 4:19 Sept 12
Proverbs 6:10, 11 Aug 24
Proverbs 7:2-4 July 21
Proverbs 8:35, 36 April 12
Proverbs 11:2 Feb 26
Proverbs 11:4 March 17
Proverbs 17:15 March 29

Proverbs 20:9 June 14
Proverbs 24:16 Dec 15
Proverbs 24:17, 18 June 5
Proverbs 25:21, 22 Sept 9
Psalms 1:1 May 18
Psalms 4:9 Jan 20
Psalms 9:10 July 5
Psalms 18:31 June 3
Psalms 23:1 Oct 9
Psalms 37:3-5 July 17
Psalms 37:12, 13 Jan 12
Psalms 37:23, 24 Sept 17
Psalms 42:3 Aug 8
Psalms 43:3 Sept 3
Psalms 50:14, 15 Nov 10
Psalms 56:10 Oct 1
Psalms 66:17, 18 May 1
Psalms 73:24 Oct 25
Psalms 73:26 Aug 26
Psalms 78:38, 39 Nov 4
Psalms 84:10 Nov 14
Psalms 84:12b March 13
Psalms 86:9 Oct 13
Psalms 86:11 Jan 2
Psalms 94:18, 19 April 20
Psalms106:23 July 25
Psalms 118:8 Dec 6
Psalms 150:6 Dec 23
Revelation 2:9a Nov 5
Revelation 3:1, 2 Feb 15
Revelation 3:10, 11 Mar 22

Appendix C

Donna's Law

1. PRAY! PRAY! PRAY!
2. Forgive others before they ask, because some never will.
3. Respect everyone you meet until they no longer deserve it.
4. Take responsibility for your actions.
5. Be intentional.
6. Be patient with foolish people.
7. Think for yourself.
8. There is always hope.
9. Read Scripture everyday – even if it's only a couple of verses.
10. Surround yourself with positive people. Negativity steals the energy from a relationship or a room.
11. Trust God in everything, with everything, and for everything.
12. Don't be a victim of your past. Forgive yourself, forgive others, and move on.
13. Live life with a purpose.
14. Pick your battles: not everything is worth fighting over - or for.
15. Don't compare yourself to others. Everyone has his or her own gifts, experiences, and path to walk.
16. Leave a trail of smiles behind you.
17. Don't let people beat you down.
18. Be grateful. Thank God for His blessings – especially the ones that you are unaware of.
19. Count your blessings each day.
20. Count each day as a blessing.
21. You can't control people or what happens to you much of the time. You CAN control how you react.
22. Always tell the truth, and you will never have to remember what you told to whom.
23. Be an individual. Be who you were meant to be, not what someone else thinks you ought to be.
24. Every situation is an opportunity: choose wisely.

25. Don't keep score.
26. Only make promises you are willing or able to keep.
27. Honor your word – it may be the only thing you have left one day.
28. Just because you can, doesn't mean you should.
29. Be a cheerful giver as well as a willing recipient.
30. Recognize your accomplishments and your limitations. Be defined by neither.
31. Never assume anything is true.
32. 'I wasn't raised right' is not an acceptable excuse for bad behavior.
33. Never allow yourself to be defined by someone else's goals, ambitions, or limitations.
34. Never use someone else's sin as an excuse for your own.
35. Judge your own righteousness against the one proper example: Jesus.
36. You can't hate other Christians (or anyone else) and be a Christian yourself.
37. Just because it's legal doesn't make it moral.
38. Just let it go.

Appendix D
General Life Lessons

1. For peace of mind, follow the Golden Rule.
2. Every thought is a prayer.
3. Everyone wants to feel special.
4. A request will produce a better response than will a demand.
5. Don't trust anyone with your money or your body.
6. Always be suspicious of others' motivations; everyone has an agenda.
7. The most dangerous woman is the one who doesn't seem to be pursuing you; the one with great patience and a secret agenda.
8. Pursue the career which gives you the most joy.
9. Don't settle for something less than your ideal.
10. It's okay to change your ideal along the way.
11. Make healthy decisions *most* of the time.
12. Take time to be alone each week.
13. Keep paper and pens all over the house and in the car for inspirational note-taking.
14. Keep a daily journal to record lessons learned and understanding gained.
15. Give stuff away.
16. Buy something new occasionally.
17. Surround yourself with people/things that inspire and uplift you.
18. Listen to or play music every day.
19. Speak to someone each day.
20. Look for beauty in everyone; some hide it better than others.
21. Everything (including relationships) is up for revision, so long as you're not married.
22. Honor your marriage vows.
23. To be in love is easy. To have a relationship is a challenge: one worth having is worth working on to keep.
24. If it seems too good to be true, it normally is.
25. Most men can't be trusted to keep it to themselves.

26. A sigh is something left unsaid.
27. Unhappy people do unhappy things.
28. The limitations are all in my mind.
29. Sex is not love; passion is not love. Only God is love; only God can teach true love.
30. There should always be a better target on the road.
31. It's better to be alone than with the wrong person.
32. The poison has to be removed before the healing can begin.
33. Sometimes the greatest punishment is being trapped inside my own skin.
34. The only way that Satan can defeat God is to steal His children.
35. A good servant doesn't work for pay; he/she works for praise from the Master for a job well done.
36. Most people go through life acutely aware of the sins of others and blissfully ignorant of their own.
37. God turned the garbage of my past into the compost in which to plant the seeds of my future.

Endnotes

1   Saint Joseph Edition of The New American Bible. Catholic Book Publishing Company, New York; 1992.

2   www.biblegateway.com

3   Mother Teresa's Secret Fire, Joseph Langford. Our Sunday Visitor; Huntington, 2008. P.80

4   One Second After, William R. Forstchen. Tom Doherty Associates, LLC; New York, 2009.

5   http://demonocracy.info/infographics/usa/federal_reserve-qe3/money_printing-2012-2013.html

6   http://worldnews.nbcnews.com/_news/2012/05/16/11729795-greeks-withdraw-894-million-in-a-day?lite

7   http://www.bibleinfo.com/en/topics/bible-promises

8   http://www.bibleinfo.com/en/questions/how-many-bible-promises-are-there

9   http://www.examiner.com/article/colorado-baker-faces-year-jail-for-refusing-to-make-cake-for-gay-wedding

10 The Harbinger, Jonathan Cahn. Charisma House; Lake Mary. 2011.

11 http://hotair.com/archives/2013/04/08/army-reserve-training-material-evangelicals-catholics-are-extremist-groups/

12 Mother Teresa's Secret Fire, Joseph Langford. Our Sunday Visitor; Huntington, 2008. P.66

13 http://www.jewishvirtuallibrary.org/index.html

14 http://www.urbandictionary.com/define.php?term=cutting%20yourself

15 http://www.medjugorje.org/

16 http://www.grantchronicles.com/three_days_of_darkness.htm

17 http://www.pewresearch.org/daily-number/number-of-christians-rises-but-their-share-of-world-population-stays-stable/

18 http://www.christianitytoday.com/ct/2013/august-web-only/non-christians-who-dont-know-christians.html